Cram101 Textbook Outlines to accompany:

Purchasing and Supply Chain Management

Monczka and Trent and Handfield, 2nd Edition

An Academic Internet Publishers (AIPI) publication (c) 2007.

You have a discounted membership at www.Cram101.com with this book.

Get all of the practice tests for the chapters of this textbook, and access in-depth reference material for writing essays and papers. Here is an example from a Cram101 Biology text:

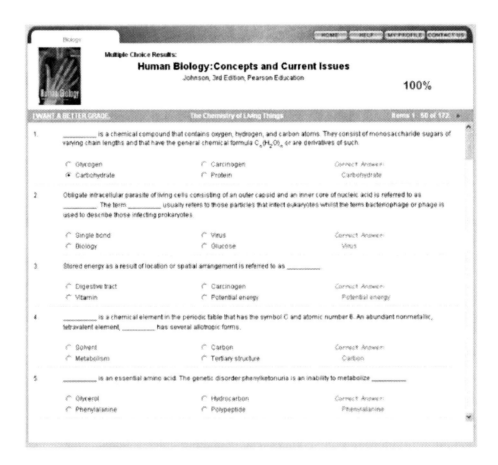

When you need problem solving help with math, stats, and other disciplines, www.Cram101.com will walk through the formulas and solutions step by step.

With Cram101.com online, you also have access to extensive reference material.

You will nail those essays and papers. Here is an example from a Cram101 Biology text:

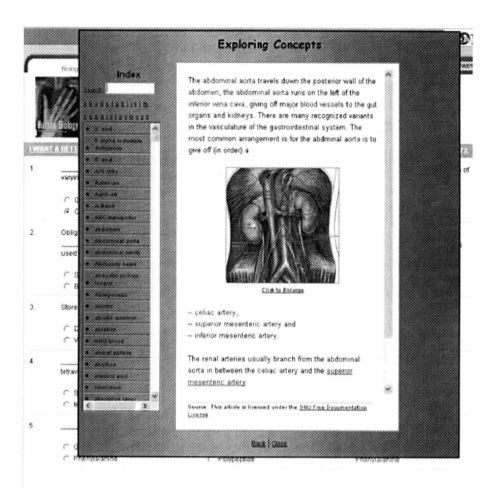

Visit **www.Cram101.com**, click Sign Up at the top of the screen, and enter DK73DW in the promo code box on the registration screen. Access to www.Cram101.com is normally $9.95, but because you have purchased this book, your access fee is only $4.95. Sign up and stop highlighting textbooks forever.

Learning System

Cram101 Textbook Outlines is a learning system. The notes in this book are the highlights of your textbook, you will never have to highlight a book again.

How to use this book. Take this book to class, it is your notebook for the lecture. The notes and highlights on the left hand side of the pages follow the outline and order of the textbook. All you have to do is follow along while your intructor presents the lecture. Circle the items emphasized in class and add other important information on the right side. With Cram101 Textbook Outlines you'll spend less time writing and more time listening. Learning becomes more efficient.

Cram101.com Online

Increase your studying efficiency by using Cram101.com's practice tests and online reference material. It is the perfect complement to Cram101 Textbook Outlines. Use self-teaching matching tests or simulate in-class testing with comprehensive multiple choice tests, or simply use Cram's true and false tests for quick review. Cram101.com even allows you to enter your in-class notes for an integrated studying format combining the textbook notes with your class notes.

Visit **www.Cram101.com**, click Sign Up at the top of the screen, and enter **DK73DW409** in the promo code box on the registration screen. Access to www.Cram101.com is normally $9.95, but because you have purchased this book, your access fee is only $4.95. Sign up and stop highlighting textbooks forever.

Purchasing and Supply Chain Management
Monczka and Trent and Handfield, 2nd

CONTENTS

Purchasing	Purchasing refers to the function in a firm that searches for quality material resources, finds the best suppliers, and negotiates the best price for goods and services.
Management	Management characterizes the process of leading and directing all or part of an organization, often a business, through the deployment and manipulation of resources. Early twentieth-century management writer Mary Parker Follett defined management as "the art of getting things done through people."
Honeywell	Honeywell is a major American multinational corporation that produces electronic control systems and automation equipment. It is a major supplier of engineering services and avionics for NASA, Boeing and the United States Department of Defense.
Supply	Supply is the aggregate amount of any material good that can be called into being at a certain price point; it comprises one half of the equation of supply and demand. In classical economic theory, a curve representing supply is one of the factors that produce price.
Supply chain management	Supply chain management deals with the planning and execution issues involved in managing a supply chain. Supply chain management spans all movement and storage of raw materials, work-in-process inventory, and finished goods from point-of-origin to point-of-consumption.
Materials management	Materials management refers to the activity that controls the transmission of physical materials through the value chain, from procurement through production and into distribution.
Financial crisis	A loss of confidence in a country's currency or other financial assets causing international investors to withdraw their funds from the country is referred to as a financial crisis.
AlliedSignal	AlliedSignal was created through a 1985 merger of Allied Chemical & Dye Corportation and Signal Oil, the company renamed to AlliedSignal on September 19, 1985. The company's involvement in aerospace stems from a previous merger between Signal Oil and the Garrett Corporation in 1968. After that merger, aviation became the company's largest division. In 1999. AlliedSignal acquired Honeywell and took its more-recognizable name.
Supply chain	Supply chain refers to the flow of goods, services, and information from the initial sources of materials and services to the delivery of products to consumers.
Cash outflow	Cash flowing out of the business from all sources over a period of time is cash outflow.
Liquidity	Liquidity refers to the capacity to turn assets into cash, or the amount of assets in a portfolio that have that capacity.
Revenue	Revenue is a U.S. business term for the amount of money that a company receives from its activities, mostly from sales of products and/or services to customers.
Capital	Capital generally refers to financial wealth, especially that used to start or maintain a business. In classical economics, capital is one of four factors of production, the others being land and labor and entrepreneurship.
Inflation	An increase in the overall price level of an economy, usually as measured by the CPI or by the implicit price deflator is called inflation.
Labor	People's physical and mental talents and efforts that are used to help produce goods and services are called labor.
Adjusted for inflation	Adjusted for inflation refers to correcting for price changes to yield an equivalent real rate, or real non-inflationary number. The adjustment divides nominal amounts for different years by price indices for those years -- eg the CPI or the implicit price deflator -- and multiplies by 100. This converts to real values, ie valued at the prices of the base year for the price index.
Productivity	Productivity refers to the total output of goods and services in a given period of time divided by work hours.
Discount	The difference between the face value of a bond and its selling price, when a bond is sold for less

	than its face value it's referred to as a discount.
Commodity	Could refer to any good, but in trade a commodity is usually a raw material or primary product that enters into international trade, such as metals or basic agricultural products.
Manufacturing	Production of goods primarily by the application of labor and capital to raw materials and other intermediate inputs, in contrast to agriculture, mining, forestry, fishing, and services a manufacturing.
Raw material	Raw material refers to a good that has not been transformed by production; a primary product.
Contract	A contract is a "promise" or an "agreement" that is enforced or recognized by the law. In the civil law, a contract is considered to be part of the general law of obligations.
Total quality management	The broad set of management and control processes designed to focus an entire organization and all of its employees on providing products or services that do the best possible job of satisfying the customer is called total quality management.
Product development	In business and engineering, new product development is the complete process of bringing a new product to market. There are two parallel aspects to this process : one involves product engineering ; the other marketing analysis. Marketers see new product development as the first stage in product life cycle management, engineers as part of Product Lifecycle Management.
Quality management	Quality management is a method for ensuring that all the activities necessary to design, develop and implement a product or service are effective and efficient with respect to the system and its performance.
Profit	Profit refers to the return to the resource entrepreneurial ability; total revenue minus total cost.
Realization	Realization is the sale of assets when an entity is being liquidated.
Market	A market is, as defined in economics, a social arrangement that allows buyers and sellers to discover information and carry out a voluntary exchange of goods or services.
Global competition	Global competition exists when competitive conditions across national markets are linked strongly enough to form a true international market and when leading competitors compete head to head in many different countries.
Failure costs	Two sets of costs-internal failure costs and external failure costs are called failure costs. Internal failure costs include those costs that are associated with failure during production, whereas external failure costs are associated with product failure after the production process.
Technology	The body of knowledge and techniques that can be used to combine economic resources to produce goods and services is called technology.
Option	A contract that gives the purchaser the option to buy or sell the underlying financial instrument at a specified price, called the exercise price or strike price, within a specific period of time.
Competitiveness	Competitiveness usually refers to characteristics that permit a firm to compete effectively with other firms due to low cost or superior technology, perhaps internationally.
Deregulation	The lessening or complete removal of government regulations on an industry, especially concerning the price that firms are allowed to charge and leaving price to be determined by market forces a deregulation.
Industry	A group of firms that produce identical or similar products is an industry. It is also used specifically to refer to an area of economic production focused on manufacturing which involves large amounts of capital investment before any profit can be realized, also called "heavy industry".
Niche	In industry, a niche is a situation or an activity perfectly suited to a person. A niche can imply a working position or an area suited to a person who occupies it. Basically, a job where a person is able to succeed and thrive.

Service	Service refers to a "non tangible product" that is not embodied in a physical good and that typically effects some change in another product, person, or institution. Contrasts with good.
Market niche	A market niche or niche market is a focused, targetable portion of a market. By definition, then, a business that focuses on a niche market is addressing a need for a product or service that is not being addressed by mainstream providers.
Product life cycle	Product life cycle refers to a series of phases in a product's sales and cash flows over time; these phases, in order of occurrence, are introductory, growth, maturity, and decline.
Mistake	In contract law a mistake is incorrect understanding by one or more parties to a contract and may be used as grounds to invalidate the agreement. Common law has identified three different types of mistake in contract: unilateral mistake, mutual mistake, and common mistake.
Procurement	Procurement is the acquisition of goods or services at the best possible total cost of ownership, in the right quantity, at the right time, in the right place for the direct benefit or use of the governments, corporations, or individuals generally via, but not limited to a contract.
Competitor	Other organizations in the same industry or type of business that provide a good or service to the same set of customers is referred to as a competitor.
Loyalty	Marketers tend to define customer loyalty as making repeat purchases. Some argue that it should be defined attitudinally as a strongly positive feeling about the brand.
Inputs	The inputs used by a firm or an economy are the labor, raw materials, electricity and other resources it uses to produce its outputs.
Interest	In finance and economics, interest is the price paid by a borrower for the use of a lender's money. In other words, interest is the amount of paid to "rent" money for a period of time.
Logistics	Those activities that focus on getting the right amount of the right products to the right place at the right time at the lowest possible cost is referred to as logistics.
Firm	An organization that employs resources to produce a good or service for profit and owns and operates one or more plants is referred to as a firm.
Information technology	Information technology refers to technology that helps companies change business by allowing them to use new methods.
Production	The creation of finished goods and services using the factors of production: land, labor, capital, entrepreneurship, and knowledge.
Operation	A standardized method or technique that is performed repetitively, often on different materials resulting in different finished goods is called an operation.
Inventory	Tangible property held for sale in the normal course of business or used in producing goods or services for sale is an inventory.
Inventory management	The planning, coordinating, and controlling activities related to the flow of inventory into, through, and out of an organization is referred to as inventory management.
Customer service	The ability of logistics management to satisfy users in terms of time, dependability, communication, and convenience is called the customer service.
End user	End user refers to the ultimate user of a product or service.
Enterprise	Enterprise refers to another name for a business organization. Other similar terms are business firm, sometimes simply business, sometimes simply firm, as well as company, and entity.
Stock	In financial terminology, stock is the capital raized by a corporation, through the issuance and sale of shares.
Intermediaries	Intermediaries specialize in information either to bring together two parties to a transaction or to

Go to **Cram101.com** for the Practice Tests for this Chapter.

	buy in order to sell again.
Market share	That fraction of an industry's output accounted for by an individual firm or group of firms is called market share.
Users	Users refer to people in the organization who actually use the product or service purchased by the buying center.
Warehouse	Warehouse refers to a location, often decentralized, that a firm uses to store, consolidate, age, or mix stock; house product-recall programs; or ease tax burdens.
Distribution	Distribution in economics, the manner in which total output and income is distributed among individuals or factors.
Trust	An arrangement in which shareholders of independent firms agree to give up their stock in exchange for trust certificates that entitle them to a share of the trust's common profits.
Forming	The first stage of team development, where the team is formed and the objectives for the team are set is referred to as forming.
Partnership	In the common law, a partnership is a type of business entity in which partners share with each other the profits or losses of the business undertaking in which they have all invested.
Competitive advantage	A business is said to have a competitive advantage when its unique strengths, often based on cost, quality, time, and innovation, offer consumers a greater percieved value and there by differtiating it from its competitors.
Complexity	The technical sophistication of the product and hence the amount of understanding required to use it is referred to as complexity. It is the opposite of simplicity.
Customer value	Customer value refers to the unique combination of benefits received by targeted buyers that includes quality, price, convenience, on-time delivery, and both before-sale and after-sale service.
Quality improvement	Quality is inversely proportional to variability thus quality Improvement is the reduction of variability in products and processes.
Chrysler	The Chrysler Corporation was an American automobile manufacturer that existed independently from 1925–1998. The company was formed by Walter Percy Chrysler on June 6, 1925, with the remaining assets of Maxwell Motor Company.
Gain	In finance, gain is a profit or an increase in value of an investment such as a stock or bond. Gain is calculated by fair market value or the proceeds from the sale of the investment minus the sum of the purchase price and all costs associated with it.
Payback	A value that indicates the time period required to recoup an initial investment is a payback. The payback does not include the time-value-of-money concept.
Total cost	The sum of fixed cost and variable cost is referred to as total cost.
Frequency	Frequency refers to the speed of the up and down movements of a fluctuating economic variable; that is, the number of times per unit of time that the variable completes a cycle of up and down movement.
Partnership agreement	A document that defines the specific terms of a partnership or business relationship, such as how much work each partner will do and how the profits are divided is a partnership agreement.
Marketing	Promoting and selling products or services to customers, or prospective customers, is referred to as marketing.
Strategic planning	The process of determining the major goals of the organization and the policies and strategies for obtaining and using resources to achieve those goals is called strategic planning.
Accounting	A system that collects and processes financial information about an organization and reports that information to decision makers is referred to as accounting.

Economy	The income, expenditures, and resources that affect the cost of running a business and household are called an economy.
Agent	A person who makes economic decisions for another economic actor. A hired manager operates as an agent for a firm's owner.
Selling agent	Selling agent refers to enterprises or individuals who receive a commission for selling the products of a producer or manufacturer, and they usually do not take ownership of the product.
Purchase order	A form on which items or services needed by a business firm are specified and then communicated to the vendor is a purchase order.
Journal	Book of original entry, in which transactions are recorded in a general ledger system, is referred to as a journal.
Comptroller	A comptroller is an official who supervises expenditures. Comptrollers include both royal-household officials and public comptrollers who audit government accounts and sometimes certify expenditures.
Contribution	In business organization law, the cash or property contributed to a business by its owners is referred to as contribution.
Personnel	A collective term for all of the employees of an organization. Personnel is also commonly used to refer to the personnel management function or the organizational unit responsible for administering personnel programs.
Stipulation	A stipulation is an agreement made between two parties in legal proceedings. A stipulation removes points of contention so that progress can be made during the proceedings.
Brand	A name, symbol, or design that identifies the goods or services of one seller or group of sellers and distinguishes them from the goods and services of competitors is a brand.
Hierarchy	A system of grouping people in an organization according to rank from the top down in which all subordinate managers must report to one person is called a hierarchy.
Ford	Ford is an American company that manufactures and sells automobiles worldwide. Ford introduced methods for large-scale manufacturing of cars, and large-scale management of an industrial workforce, especially elaborately engineered manufacturing sequences typified by the moving assembly lines.
Ford Motor Company	Ford Motor Company introduced methods for large-scale manufacturing of cars, and large-scale management of an industrial workforce, especially elaborately engineered manufacturing sequences typified by the moving assembly lines. Henry Ford's combination of highly efficient factories, highly paid workers, and low prices revolutionized manufacturing and came to be known around the world as Fordism by 1914.
Buyer	A buyer refers to a role in the buying center with formal authority and responsibility to select the supplier and negotiate the terms of the contract.
General Electric	In 1876, Thomas Alva Edison opened a new laboratory in Menlo Park, New Jersey. Out of the laboratory was to come perhaps the most famous invention of all—a successful development of the incandescent electric lamp. By 1890, Edison had organized his various businesses into the Edison General Electric Company.
Value analysis	Value analysis refers to a systematic appraisal of the design, quality, and performance of a product to reduce purchasing costs.
Product cost	Product cost refers to sum of the costs assigned to a product for a specific purpose. A concept used in applying the cost plus approach to product pricing in which only the costs of manufacturing the product are included in the cost amount to which the markup is added.
Evaluation	The consumer's appraisal of the product or brand on important attributes is called evaluation.
Consumer demand	Consumer demand or consumption is also known as personal consumption expenditure. It is the largest part of aggregate demand or effective demand at the macroeconomic level. There are two variants of

	consumption in the aggregate demand model, including induced consumption and autonomous consumption.
Quality control	The measurement of products and services against set standards is referred to as quality control.
Bid	A bid price is a price offered by a buyer when he/she buys a good. In the context of stock trading on a stock exchange, the bid price is the highest price a buyer of a stock is willing to pay for a share of that given stock.
Price competition	Price competition is where a company tries to distinguish its product or service from competing products on the basis of low price.
Recession	A significant decline in economic activity. In the U.S., recession is approximately defined as two successive quarters of falling GDP, as judged by NBER.
Planning horizon	The length of time it takes to conceive, develop, and complete a project and to recover the cost of the project on a discounted cash flow basis is referred to as planning horizon.
Organizational structure	Organizational structure is the way in which the interrelated groups of an organization are constructed. From a managerial point of view the main concerns are ensuring effective communication and coordination.
Innovation	Innovation refers to the first commercially successful introduction of a new product, the use of a new method of production, or the creation of a new form of business organization.
Intranet	Intranet refers to a companywide network, closed to public access, that uses Internet-type technology. A set of communications links within one company that travel over the Internet but are closed to public access.
Cooperative	A business owned and controlled by the people who use it, producers, consumers, or workers with similar needs who pool their resources for mutual gain is called cooperative.
Supplier evaluation	Supplier evaluation refers to a tool used by many firms to differentiate and discriminate among suppliers. A supplier evaluation often involves report cards where potential suppliers are rated based on different criteria such as quality, technical capability, or ability to meet schedule demands.
Cost management	The approaches and activities of managers in short-run and long-run planning and control decisions that increase value for customers and lower costs of products and services are called cost management.
Performance requirement	Performance requirement refers to a requirement that an importer or exporter achieve some level of performance, in terms of exporting, domestic content, etc., in order to obtain an import or export license.
Information system	An information system is a system whether automated or manual, that comprises people, machines, and/or methods organized to collect, process, transmit, and disseminate data that represent user information.
Commerce	Commerce is the exchange of something of value between two entities. It is the central mechanism from which capitalism is derived.
Electronic commerce	Electronic commerce or e-commerce, refers to any activity that uses some form of electronic communication in the inventory, exchange, advertisement, distribution, and payment of goods and services.
Performance measurement	The process by which someone evaluates an employee's work behaviors by measurement and comparison with previously established standards, documents the results, and communicates the results to the employee is called performance measurement.
Operations management	A specialized area in management that converts or transforms resources into goods and services is operations management.
Trend	Trend refers to the long-term movement of an economic variable, such as its average rate of increase or decrease over enough years to encompass several business cycles.

Go to **Cram101.com** for the Practice Tests for this Chapter.

Procurement	Procurement is the acquisition of goods or services at the best possible total cost of ownership, in the right quantity, at the right time, in the right place for the direct benefit or use of the governments, corporations, or individuals generally via, but not limited to a contract.
Purchasing	Purchasing refers to the function in a firm that searches for quality material resources, finds the best suppliers, and negotiates the best price for goods and services.
Management	Management characterizes the process of leading and directing all or part of an organization, often a business, through the deployment and manipulation of resources. Early twentieth-century management writer Mary Parker Follett defined management as "the art of getting things done through people."
Journal	Book of original entry, in which transactions are recorded in a general ledger system, is referred to as a journal.
Materials management	Materials management refers to the activity that controls the transmission of physical materials through the value chain, from procurement through production and into distribution.
Payables	Obligations to make future economic sacrifices, usually cash payments, are referred to as payables. Same as current liabilities.
Service	Service refers to a "non tangible product" that is not embodied in a physical good and that typically effects some change in another product, person, or institution. Contrasts with good.
Transactions cost	Any cost associated with bringing buyers and sellers together is referred to as transactions cost.
Internal customer	An individuals or unit within the firm that receives services from other entities within the organization is an internal customer.
Strategic planning	The process of determining the major goals of the organization and the policies and strategies for obtaining and using resources to achieve those goals is called strategic planning.
Contribution	In business organization law, the cash or property contributed to a business by its owners is referred to as contribution.
Span of control	Span of control refers to the optimum number of subordinates a manager supervises or should supervise.
Buyer	A buyer refers to a role in the buying center with formal authority and responsibility to select the supplier and negotiate the terms of the contract.
Supply	Supply is the aggregate amount of any material good that can be called into being at a certain price point; it comprises one half of the equation of supply and demand. In classical economic theory, a curve representing supply is one of the factors that produce price.
Supply chain	Supply chain refers to the flow of goods, services, and information from the initial sources of materials and services to the delivery of products to consumers.
Capital	Capital generally refers to financial wealth, especially that used to start or maintain a business. In classical economics, capital is one of four factors of production, the others being land and labor and entrepreneurship.
Personnel	A collective term for all of the employees of an organization. Personnel is also commonly used to refer to the personnel management function or the organizational unit responsible for administering personnel programs.
Users	Users refer to people in the organization who actually use the product or service purchased

Go to **Cram101.com** for the Practice Tests for this Chapter.

	by the buying center.
Accounts payable	A written record of all vendors to whom the business firm owes money is referred to as accounts payable.
Customer satisfaction	Customer satisfaction is a business term which is used to capture the idea of measuring how satisfied an enterprise's customers are with the organization's efforts in a marketplace.
Benchmarking	The continuous process of comparing the levels of performance in producing products and services and executing activities against the best levels of performance is benchmarking.
Inventory	Tangible property held for sale in the normal course of business or used in producing goods or services for sale is an inventory.
Invoice	The itemized bill for a transaction, stating the nature of the transaction and its cost. In international trade, the invoice price is often the preferred basis for levying an ad valorem tariff.
Verification	Verification refers to the final stage of the creative process where the validity or truthfulness of the insight is determined. The feedback portion of communication in which the receiver sends a message to the source indicating receipt of the message and the degree to which he or she understood the message.
Audit	An examination of the financial reports to ensure that they represent what they claim and conform with generally accepted accounting principles is referred to as audit.
Contract	A contract is a "promise" or an "agreement" that is enforced or recognized by the law. In the civil law, a contract is considered to be part of the general law of obligations.
Bid	A bid price is a price offered by a buyer when he/she buys a good. In the context of stock trading on a stock exchange, the bid price is the highest price a buyer of a stock is willing to pay for a share of that given stock.
Purchase order	A form on which items or services needed by a business firm are specified and then communicated to the vendor is a purchase order.
Product line	A group of products that are physically similar or are intended for a similar market are called the product line.
Administration	Administration refers to the management and direction of the affairs of governments and institutions; a collective term for all policymaking officials of a government; the execution and implementation of public policy.
Target audience	That group that composes the present and potential prospects for a product or service is called the target audience.
Technology	The body of knowledge and techniques that can be used to combine economic resources to produce goods and services is called technology.
Administrative cost	An administrative cost is all executive, organizational, and clerical costs associated with the general management of an organization rather than with manufacturing, marketing, or selling
Administrator	Administrator refers to the personal representative appointed by a probate court to settle the estate of a deceased person who died.
Continuous improvement	The constant effort to eliminate waste, reduce response time, simplify the design of both products and processes, and improve quality and customer service is referred to as continuous improvement.
Binder	Binder, also called a binding slip, refers to a brief memorandum or agreement issued by an insurer as a temporary policy for the convenience of all the parties, constituting a present

insurance in the amount specified, to continue in force until the execution of a formal policy.

Discount	The difference between the face value of a bond and its selling price, when a bond is sold for less than its face value it's referred to as a discount.
Ordering costs	Costs of preparing, issuing, and paying purchase orders, plus receiving and inspecting the items included in the orders are ordering costs.
Drawback	Drawback refers to rebate of import duties when the imported good is re-exported or used as input to the production of an exported good.
Security	Security refers to a claim on the borrower future income that is sold by the borrower to the lender. A security is a type of transferable interest representing financial value.
Warrant	A warrant is a security that entitles the holder to buy or sell a certain additional quantity of an underlying security at an agreed-upon price, at the holder's discretion.
Ariba	Ariba is a software and information technology services company, headquartered in Sunnyvale, California, USA. The focus of their products and services is cost savings in procurement via electronic commerce, also known as spend management.
Turnkey	A turnkey is a project in which a separate entity is responsible for setting up a plant or equipment (e.g. trains/infrastructure) and putting it into operations.
Exchange	The trade of things of value between buyer and seller so that each is better off after the trade is called the exchange.
Electronic data interchange	Electronic data interchange refers to the direct exchange between organizations of data via a computer-to-computer interface.
Cooperative	A business owned and controlled by the people who use it, producers, consumers, or workers with similar needs who pool their resources for mutual gain is called cooperative.
Commerce	Commerce is the exchange of something of value between two entities. It is the central mechanism from which capitalism is derived.
Foundation	A Foundation is a type of philanthropic organization set up by either individuals or institutions as a legal entity (either as a corporation or trust) with the purpose of distributing grants to support causes in line with the goals of the foundation.
Disney	Disney is one of the largest media and entertainment corporations in the world. Founded on October 16, 1923 by brothers Walt and Roy Disney as a small animation studio, today it is one of the largest Hollywood studios and also owns nine theme parks and several television networks, including the American Broadcasting Company (ABC).
Aid	Assistance provided by countries and by international institutions such as the World Bank to developing countries in the form of monetary grants, loans at low interest rates, in kind, or a combination of these is called aid. Aid can also refer to assistance of any type rendered to benefit some group or individual.
Internal audit	An internal audit is an independent appraisal of operations, conducted under the direction of management, to assess the effectiveness of internal administrative and accounting controls and help ensure conformance with managerial policies.
Gain	In finance, gain is a profit or an increase in value of an investment such as a stock or bond. Gain is calculated by fair market value or the proceeds from the sale of the investment minus the sum of the purchase price and all costs associated with it.
Credit	Credit refers to a recording as positive in the balance of payments, any transaction that gives rise to a payment into the country, such as an export, the sale of an asset, or

Go to **Cram101.com** for the Practice Tests for this Chapter.

	borrowing from abroad.
Budget	Budget refers to an account, usually for a year, of the planned expenditures and the expected receipts of an entity. For a government, the receipts are tax revenues.
Comprehensive	A comprehensive refers to a layout accurate in size, color, scheme, and other necessary details to show how a final ad will look. For presentation only, never for reproduction.
Tariff	A tax imposed by a nation on an imported good is called a tariff.
Interstate commerce commission	A federal regulatory group created by Congress in 1887 to oversee and correct abuses in the railroad industry is an interstate commerce commission.
Outbound	Communications originating inside an organization and destined for customers, prospects, or other people outside the organization are called outbound.
Production	The creation of finished goods and services using the factors of production: land, labor, capital, entrepreneurship, and knowledge.
Logistics	Those activities that focus on getting the right amount of the right products to the right place at the right time at the lowest possible cost is referred to as logistics.
Controlling	A management function that involves determining whether or not an organization is progressing toward its goals and objectives, and taking corrective action if it is not is called controlling.
Industry	A group of firms that produce identical or similar products is an industry. It is also used specifically to refer to an area of economic production focused on manufacturing which involves large amounts of capital investment before any profit can be realized, also called "heavy industry".
Brand	A name, symbol, or design that identifies the goods or services of one seller or group of sellers and distinguishes them from the goods and services of competitors is a brand.
Manufacturing	Production of goods primarily by the application of labor and capital to raw materials and other intermediate inputs, in contrast to agriculture, mining, forestry, fishing, and services a manufacturing.
End user	End user refers to the ultimate user of a product or service.
Purchasing power	The amount of goods that money will buy, usually measured by the CPI is referred to as purchasing power.
Acquisition	A company's purchase of the property and obligations of another company is an acquisition.
Business unit	The lowest level of the company which contains the set of functions that carry a product through its life span from concept through manufacture, distribution, sales and service is a business unit.
Operation	A standardized method or technique that is performed repetitively, often on different materials resulting in different finished goods is called an operation.
Marketing	Promoting and selling products or services to customers, or prospective customers, is referred to as marketing.
Committee	A long-lasting, sometimes permanent team in the organization structure created to deal with tasks that recur regularly is the committee.
Information technology	Information technology refers to technology that helps companies change business by allowing them to use new methods.
Human resources	Human resources refers to the individuals within the firm, and to the portion of the firm's

Go to **Cram101.com** for the Practice Tests for this Chapter.

organization that deals with hiring, firing, training, and other personnel issues.

Advertising	Advertising refers to paid, nonpersonal communication through various media by organizations and individuals who are in some way identified in the advertising message.
Negotiation	Negotiation is the process whereby interested parties resolve disputes, agree upon courses of action, bargain for individual or collective advantage, and/or attempt to craft outcomes which serve their mutual interests.
Evaluation	The consumer's appraisal of the product or brand on important attributes is called evaluation.
Investment	Investment refers to spending for the production and accumulation of capital and additions to inventories. In a financial sense, buying an asset with the expectation of making a return.
Total cost	The sum of fixed cost and variable cost is referred to as total cost.
Appeal	Appeal refers to the act of asking an appellate court to overturn a decision after the trial court's final judgment has been entered.
Inventory investment	Spending by firms on additional holdings of raw materials, parts, and finished goods is called inventory investment.
Market	A market is, as defined in economics, a social arrangement that allows buyers and sellers to discover information and carry out a voluntary exchange of goods or services.
DaimlerChrysler	In 2002, the merged company, DaimlerChrysler, appeared to run two independent product lines, with few signs of corporate integration. In 2003, however, it was alleged by the Detroit News that the "merger of equals" was, in fact, a takeover.
Matching	Matching refers to an accounting concept that establishes when expenses are recognized. Expenses are matched with the revenues they helped to generate and are recognized when those revenues are recognized.
Chrysler	The Chrysler Corporation was an American automobile manufacturer that existed independently from 1925–1998. The company was formed by Walter Percy Chrysler on June 6, 1925, with the remaining assets of Maxwell Motor Company.
Bill of material	A bill of material is a list of all the materials needed to manufacture a product or product component.
Control system	A control system is a device or set of devices that manage the behavior of other devices. Some devices or systems are not controllable. A control system is an interconnection of components connected or related in such a manner as to command, direct, or regulate itself or another system.
Firm	An organization that employs resources to produce a good or service for profit and owns and operates one or more plants is referred to as a firm.
Specialist	A specialist is a trader who makes a market in one or several stocks and holds the limit order book for those stocks.
Consultant	A professional that provides expert advice in a particular field or area in which customers occassionaly require this type of knowledge is a consultant.
Asset	An item of property, such as land, capital, money, a share in ownership, or a claim on others for future payment, such as a bond or a bank deposit is an asset.
General Motors	General Motors is the world's largest automaker. Founded in 1908, today it employs about 327,000 people around the world. With global headquarters in Detroit, it manufactures its cars and trucks in 33 countries.

Revenue	Revenue is a U.S. business term for the amount of money that a company receives from its activities, mostly from sales of products and/or services to customers.
Nuisance	Nuisance refers to that which endangers life or health, gives offense to the senses, violates the laws of decency, or obstructs the reasonable and comfortable use of property.
Interest	In finance and economics, interest is the price paid by a borrower for the use of a lender's money. In other words, interest is the amount of paid to "rent" money for a period of time.
Realization	Realization is the sale of assets when an entity is being liquidated.
Raw material	Raw material refers to a good that has not been transformed by production; a primary product.
Trend	Trend refers to the long-term movement of an economic variable, such as its average rate of increase or decrease over enough years to encompass several business cycles.
Supply and demand	The partial equilibrium supply and demand economic model originally developed by Alfred Marshall attempts to describe, explain, and predict changes in the price and quantity of goods sold in competitive markets.
Outsourcing	Outsourcing refers to a production activity that was previously done inside a firm or plant that is now conducted outside that firm or plant.
Honda	With more than 14 million internal combustion engines built each year, Honda is the largest engine-maker in the world. In 2004, the company began to produce diesel motors, which were both very quiet whilst not requiring particulate filters to pass pollution standards. It is arguable, however, that the foundation of their success is the motorcycle division.
Accounting	A system that collects and processes financial information about an organization and reports that information to decision makers is referred to as accounting.
Production line	A production line is a set of sequential operations established in a factory whereby materials are put through a refining process to produce an end-product that is suitable for onward consumption; or components are assembled to make a finished article.
Bill of lading	Bill of lading refers to the receipt given by a transportation company to an exporter when the former accepts goods for transport. It includes the contract specifying what transport service will be provided and the limits of liability.
Allegation	An allegation is a statement of a fact by a party in a pleading, which the party claims it will prove. Allegations remain assertions without proof, only claims until they are proved.
Damages	The sum of money recoverable by a plaintiff who has received a judgment in a civil case is called damages.
Exempt	Employees who are not covered by the Fair Labor Standards Act are exempt. Exempt employees are not eligible for overtime pay.
Quantity discount	A quantity discount is a price reduction given for a large order.
Quantity discounts	Quantity discounts refer to reductions in unit costs for a larger order.
Regulation	Regulation refers to restrictions state and federal laws place on business with regard to the conduct of its activities.
Covenant	A covenant is a signed written agreement between two or more parties. Also referred to as a contract.
Patent	The legal right to the proceeds from and control over the use of an invented product or process, granted for a fixed period of time, usually 20 years. Patent is one form of

intellectual property that is subject of the TRIPS agreement.

Lien	In its most extensive meaning, it is a charge on property for the payment or discharge of a debt or duty is referred to as lien.
Patent infringement	Patent infringement refers to unauthorized use of another's patent. A patent holder may recover damages and other remedies against a patent infringer.
Merchantable	Merchantable refers to of good quality and salable, but not necessarily the best. As applied to articles sold, the word requires that the article shall be such as is usually sold in the market, of medium quality, and bringing the average price.
Equity	Equity is the name given to the set of legal principles, in countries following the English common law tradition, which supplement strict rules of law where their application would operate harshly, so as to achieve what is sometimes referred to as "natural justice."
Waiver	Waiver refers to an authorized deviation from the terms of a previously negotiated and legally binding agreement. Many countries have sought and obtained waivers from particular obligations of the GATT and WTO.
Uniform Commercial Code	Uniform commercial code refers to a comprehensive commercial law adopted by every state in the United States; it covers sales laws and other commercial laws.
Affirmative action	Policies and programs that establish procedures for increasing employment and promotion for women and minorities are called affirmative action.
Executive order	A legal rule issued by a chief executive usually pursuant to a delegation of power from the legislature is called executive order.
Enterprise	Enterprise refers to another name for a business organization. Other similar terms are business firm, sometimes simply business, sometimes simply firm, as well as company, and entity.
Compliance	A type of influence process where a receiver accepts the position advocated by a source to obtain favorable outcomes or to avoid punishment is the compliance.
Offer and acceptance	Offer and acceptance analysis is a traditional approach in contract law used to determine whether an agreement exists between two parties. An offer is an indication by one person to another of their willingness to contract on certain terms without further negotiations. A contract is then formed if there is express or implied agreement.
Unit cost	Unit cost refers to cost computed by dividing some amount of total costs by the related number of units. Also called average cost.
Attachment	Attachment in general, the process of taking a person's property under an appropriate judicial order by an appropriate officer of the court. Used for a variety of purposes, including the acquisition of jurisdiction over the property seized and the securing of property that may be used to satisfy a debt.
Competitive bidding	A situation where two or more companies submit bids for a product, service, or project to a potential buyer is competitive bidding.
Frequency	Frequency refers to the speed of the up and down movements of a fluctuating economic variable; that is, the number of times per unit of time that the variable completes a cycle of up and down movement.
Performance measurement	The process by which someone evaluates an employee's work behaviors by measurement and comparison with previously established standards, documents the results, and communicates the results to the employee is called performance measurement.
Information	An information system is a system whether automated or manual, that comprises people,

system	machines, and/or methods organized to collect, process, transmit, and disseminate data that represent user information.
Overhead cost	An expenses of operating a business over and above the direct costs of producing a product is an overhead cost. They can include utilities (eg, electricity, telephone), advertizing and marketing, and any other costs not billed directly to the client or included in the price of the product.
Authority	Authority in agency law, refers to an agent's ability to affect his principal's legal relations with third parties. Also used to refer to an actor's legal power or ability to do something. In addition, sometimes used to refer to a statute, case, or other legal source that justifies a particular result.
Open purchase order	Open purchase order refers to a copy of the purchase order sent to the accounts payable department and reviewed prior to payment for the goods ordered. It is intended to eliminate small repetitive requests for expendable supplies, material or services by allowing multiple pickups and billings on one order.
Performance improvement	Performance improvement is the concept of measuring the output of a particular process or procedure then modifying the process or procedure in order to increase the output, increase efficiency, or increase the effectiveness of the process or procedure.
Supplier evaluation	Supplier evaluation refers to a tool used by many firms to differentiate and discriminate among suppliers. A supplier evaluation often involves report cards where potential suppliers are rated based on different criteria such as quality, technical capability, or ability to meet schedule demands.
Variable	A variable is something measured by a number; it is used to analyze what happens to other things when the size of that number changes.
Risk sharing	The distribution of financial risk among parties furnishing a service is called risk sharing.
New product development	New product development is the complete process of bringing a new product to market. There are two parallel aspects to this process : one involves product engineering ; the other marketing analysis.
Product development	In business and engineering, new product development is the complete process of bringing a new product to market. There are two parallel aspects to this process : one involves product engineering ; the other marketing analysis. Marketers see new product development as the first stage in product life cycle management, engineers as part of Product Lifecycle Management.
Product design	Product Design is defined as the idea generation, concept development, testing and manufacturing or implementation of a physical object or service. It is possibly the evolution of former discipline name - Industrial Design.
Product development teams	Combinations of work teams and problem-solving teams that create new designs for products or services that will satisfy customer needs are product development teams.
Material requirements planning	A dependent demand inventory planning and control system that schedules the precise amount of all materials required to support the production of desired end products is referred to as material requirements planning.
Holding	The holding is a court's determination of a matter of law based on the issue presented in the particular case. In other words: under this law, with these facts, this result.
Economic order quantity	Decision model that calculates the optimal quantity of inventory to order under a set of assumptions is called economic order quantity.

Go to **Cram101.com** for the Practice Tests for this Chapter.

Tradeoff	The sacrifice of some or all of one economic goal, good, or service to achieve some other goal, good, or service is a tradeoff.
Distribution center	Designed to facilitate the timely movement of goods and represent a very important part of a supply chain is a distribution center.
Distribution	Distribution in economics, the manner in which total output and income is distributed among individuals or factors.
Stock	In financial terminology, stock is the capital raized by a corporation, through the issuance and sale of shares.
Cycle count	A cycle count is an inventory management procedure where a small subset of inventory is counted on any given day.
Proactive	To be proactive is to act before a situation becomes a source of confrontation or crisis. It is the opposite of "retroactive," which refers to actions taken after an event.
Fund	Independent accounting entity with a self-balancing set of accounts segregated for the purposes of carrying on specific activities is referred to as a fund.
Mutual fund	A mutual fund is a form of collective investment that pools money from many investors and invests the money in stocks, bonds, short-term money market instruments, and/or other securities. In a mutual fund, the fund manager trades the fund's underlying securities, realizing capital gains or loss, and collects the dividend or interest income.
Intranet	Intranet refers to a companywide network, closed to public access, that uses Internet-type technology. A set of communications links within one company that travel over the Internet but are closed to public access.
Average cost	Average cost is equal to total cost divided by the number of goods produced (Quantity-Q). It is also equal to the sum of average variable costs (total variable costs divided by Q) plus average fixed costs (total fixed costs divided by Q).
Efficient communication	Communication that is low cost in its use of resources and effective in the delivery of its message is called efficient communication.
Electronic mail	Electronic mail refers to electronic written communication between individuals using computers connected to the Internet.
Departmental-zation	The dividing of organizational functions into separate units is called departmentalization.
Policy	Similar to a script in that a policy can be a less than completely rational decision-making method. Involves the use of a pre-existing set of decision steps for any problem that presents itself.
Agent	A person who makes economic decisions for another economic actor. A hired manager operates as an agent for a firm's owner.
Competitive advantage	A business is said to have a competitive advantage when its unique strengths, often based on cost, quality, time, and innovation, offer consumers a greater percieved value and there by differtiating it from its competitors.
Organizational goals	Objectives that management seeks to achieve in pursuing the firm's purpose are organizational goals.
Integration	Economic integration refers to reducing barriers among countries to transactions and to movements of goods, capital, and labor, including harmonization of laws, regulations, and standards. Integrated markets theoretically function as a unified market.
Option	A contract that gives the purchaser the option to buy or sell the underlying financial

	instrument at a specified price, called the exercise price or strike price, within a specific period of time.
Product cost	Product cost refers to sum of the costs assigned to a product for a specific purpose. A concept used in applying the cost plus approach to product pricing in which only the costs of manufacturing the product are included in the cost amount to which the markup is added.
Layout	Layout refers to the physical arrangement of the various parts of an advertisement including the headline, subheads, illustrations, body copy, and any identifying marks.
Facility layout	The physical arrangement of resources in the production process is called facility layout.
Vertical integration	Vertical integration refers to production of different stages of processing of a product within the same firm.
Inputs	The inputs used by a firm or an economy are the labor, raw materials, electricity and other resources it uses to produce its outputs.
Long run	In economic models, the long run time frame assumes no fixed factors of production. Firms can enter or leave the marketplace, and the cost (and availability) of land, labor, raw materials, and capital goods can be assumed to vary.
Ford	Ford is an American company that manufactures and sells automobiles worldwide. Ford introduced methods for large-scale manufacturing of cars, and large-scale management of an industrial workforce, especially elaborately engineered manufacturing sequences typified by the moving assembly lines.
Value chain	The sequence of business functions in which usefulness is added to the products or services of a company is a value chain.
Henry Ford	Henry Ford was the founder of the Ford Motor Company. His introduction of the Model T automobile revolutionized transportation and American industry.
Staffing	Staffing refers to a management function that includes hiring, motivating, and retaining the best people available to accomplish the company's objectives.
Productivity	Productivity refers to the total output of goods and services in a given period of time divided by work hours.
Creditor	A person to whom a debt or legal obligation is owed, and who has the right to enforce payment of that debt or obligation is referred to as creditor.
Corporation	A legal entity chartered by a state or the Federal government that is distinct and separate from the individuals who own it is a corporation. This separation gives the corporation unique powers which other legal entities lack.
Bankruptcy	Bankruptcy is a legally declared inability or impairment of ability of an individual or organization to pay their creditors.
Restructuring	Restructuring is the corporate management term for the act of partially dismantling and reorganizing a company for the purpose of making it more efficient and therefore more profitable.
Concession	A concession is a business operated under a contract or license associated with a degree of exclusivity in exploiting a business within a certain geographical area. For example, sports arenas or public parks may have concession stands; and public services such as water supply may be operated as concessions.
Recession	A significant decline in economic activity. In the U.S., recession is approximately defined as two successive quarters of falling GDP, as judged by NBER.
Union	A worker association that bargains with employers over wages and working conditions is called

Go to **Cram101.com** for the Practice Tests for this Chapter.

	a union.
Dealer	People who link buyers with sellers by buying and selling securities at stated prices are referred to as a dealer.
Extended enterprise	Extended Enterprise is a concept typically applied to a networked organization in which a dominant enterprise "extends" its boundaries to all or some of its suppliers. An extended enterprise can be seen as a particular case of a virtual enterprise and therefore a manifestation of a Collaborative Network.
Supply chain management	Supply chain management deals with the planning and execution issues involved in managing a supply chain. Supply chain management spans all movement and storage of raw materials, work-in-process inventory, and finished goods from point-of-origin to point-of-consumption.

Go to **Cram101.com** for the Practice Tests for this Chapter.

Authority	Authority in agency law, refers to an agent's ability to affect his principal's legal relations with third parties. Also used to refer to an actor's legal power or ability to do something. In addition, sometimes used to refer to a statute, case, or other legal source that justifies a particular result.
Purchasing	Purchasing refers to the function in a firm that searches for quality material resources, finds the best suppliers, and negotiates the best price for goods and services.
Management	Management characterizes the process of leading and directing all or part of an organization, often a business, through the deployment and manipulation of resources. Early twentieth-century management writer Mary Parker Follett defined management as "the art of getting things done through people."
Supply	Supply is the aggregate amount of any material good that can be called into being at a certain price point; it comprises one half of the equation of supply and demand. In classical economic theory, a curve representing supply is one of the factors that produce price.
Organizational structure	Organizational structure is the way in which the interrelated groups of an organization are constructed. From a managerial point of view the main concerns are ensuring effective communication and coordination.
Supply chain management	Supply chain management deals with the planning and execution issues involved in managing a supply chain. Supply chain management spans all movement and storage of raw materials, work-in-process inventory, and finished goods from point-of-origin to point-of-consumption.
American Airlines	American Airlines developed from a conglomeration of about 82 small airlines through a series of corporate acquisitions and reorganizations: initially, the name American Airways was used as a common brand by a number of independent air carriers. American Airlines is the largest airline in the world in terms of total passengers transported and fleet size, and the second-largest airline in the world.
Supply chain	Supply chain refers to the flow of goods, services, and information from the initial sources of materials and services to the delivery of products to consumers.
Operation	A standardized method or technique that is performed repetitively, often on different materials resulting in different finished goods is called an operation.
Manufacturing	Production of goods primarily by the application of labor and capital to raw materials and other intermediate inputs, in contrast to agriculture, mining, forestry, fishing, and services a manufacturing.
Service	Service refers to a "non tangible product" that is not embodied in a physical good and that typically effects some change in another product, person, or institution. Contrasts with good.
Customer service	The ability of logistics management to satisfy users in terms of time, dependability, communication, and convenience is called the customer service.
Technology	The body of knowledge and techniques that can be used to combine economic resources to produce goods and services is called technology.
Managing director	Managing director is the term used for the chief executive of many limited companies in the United Kingdom, Commonwealth and some other English speaking countries. The title reflects their role as both a member of the Board of Directors but also as the senior manager.
Personnel	A collective term for all of the employees of an organization. Personnel is also commonly used to refer to the personnel management function or the organizational unit responsible for administering personnel programs.
Internal	An individuals or unit within the firm that receives services from other entities within the

Go to **Cram101.com** for the Practice Tests for this Chapter.

customer	organization is an internal customer.
Buyer	A buyer refers to a role in the buying center with formal authority and responsibility to select the supplier and negotiate the terms of the contract.
Innovation	Innovation refers to the first commercially successful introduction of a new product, the use of a new method of production, or the creation of a new form of business organization.
Market	A market is, as defined in economics, a social arrangement that allows buyers and sellers to discover information and carry out a voluntary exchange of goods or services.
Market opportunities	Market opportunities refer to areas where a company believes there are favorable demand trends, needs, and/or wants that are not being satisfied, and where it can compete effectively.
Firm	An organization that employs resources to produce a good or service for profit and owns and operates one or more plants is referred to as a firm.
Continuous improvement	The constant effort to eliminate waste, reduce response time, simplify the design of both products and processes, and improve quality and customer service is referred to as continuous improvement.
Hierarchy	A system of grouping people in an organization according to rank from the top down in which all subordinate managers must report to one person is called a hierarchy.
Trend	Trend refers to the long-term movement of an economic variable, such as its average rate of increase or decrease over enough years to encompass several business cycles.
Industry	A group of firms that produce identical or similar products is an industry. It is also used specifically to refer to an area of economic production focused on manufacturing which involves large amounts of capital investment before any profit can be realized, also called "heavy industry".
Technological change	The introduction of new methods of production or new products intended to increase the productivity of existing inputs or to raise marginal products is a technological change.
Honda	With more than 14 million internal combustion engines built each year, Honda is the largest engine-maker in the world. In 2004, the company began to produce diesel motors, which were both very quiet whilst not requiring particulate filters to pass pollution standards. It is arguable, however, that the foundation of their success is the motorcycle division.
DaimlerChrysler	In 2002, the merged company, DaimlerChrysler, appeared to run two independent product lines, with few signs of corporate integration. In 2003, however, it was alleged by the Detroit News that the "merger of equals" was, in fact, a takeover.
Compaq	Compaq was founded in February 1982 by Rod Canion, Jim Harris and Bill Murto, three senior managers from semiconductor manufacturer Texas Instruments. Each invested $1,000 to form the company. Their first venture capital came from Ben Rosen and Sevin-Rosen partners. It is often told that the architecture of the original PC was first sketched out on a placemat by the founders while dining in the Houston restaurant, House of Pies.
Marketing	Promoting and selling products or services to customers, or prospective customers, is referred to as marketing.
Competitiveness	Competitiveness usually refers to characteristics that permit a firm to compete effectively with other firms due to low cost or superior technology, perhaps internationally.
Production	The creation of finished goods and services using the factors of production: land, labor, capital, entrepreneurship, and knowledge.
Functional	A manager who is responsible for a department that performs a single functional task and has

manager	employees with similar training and skills is referred to as a functional manager.
Controller	Controller refers to the financial executive primarily responsible for management accounting and financial accounting. Also called chief accounting officer.
Corporate Strategy	Corporate strategy is concerned with the firm's choice of business, markets and activities and thus it defines the overall scope and direction of the business.
Appeal	Appeal refers to the act of asking an appellate court to overturn a decision after the trial court's final judgment has been entered.
Information system	An information system is a system whether automated or manual, that comprises people, machines, and/or methods organized to collect, process, transmit, and disseminate data that represent user information.
Administration	Administration refers to the management and direction of the affairs of governments and institutions; a collective term for all policymaking officials of a government; the execution and implementation of public policy.
Commodity	Could refer to any good, but in trade a commodity is usually a raw material or primary product that enters into international trade, such as metals or basic agricultural products.
Contract	A contract is a "promise" or an "agreement" that is enforced or recognized by the law. In the civil law, a contract is considered to be part of the general law of obligations.
Contribution	In business organization law, the cash or property contributed to a business by its owners is referred to as contribution.
Finished goods	Completed products awaiting sale are called finished goods. An item considered a finished good in a supplying plant might be considered a component or raw material in a receiving plant.
Raw material	Raw material refers to a good that has not been transformed by production; a primary product.
Purchase order	A form on which items or services needed by a business firm are specified and then communicated to the vendor is a purchase order.
Supplier evaluation	Supplier evaluation refers to a tool used by many firms to differentiate and discriminate among suppliers. A supplier evaluation often involves report cards where potential suppliers are rated based on different criteria such as quality, technical capability, or ability to meet schedule demands.
Negotiation	Negotiation is the process whereby interested parties resolve disputes, agree upon courses of action, bargain for individual or collective advantage, and/or attempt to craft outcomes which serve their mutual interests.
Evaluation	The consumer's appraisal of the product or brand on important attributes is called evaluation.
Inventory	Tangible property held for sale in the normal course of business or used in producing goods or services for sale is an inventory.
Inventory control	Inventory control, in the field of loss prevention, are systems designed to introduce technical barriers to shoplifting.
Overhead cost	An expenses of operating a business over and above the direct costs of producing a product is an overhead cost. They can include utilities (eg, electricity, telephone), advertizing and marketing, and any other costs not billed directly to the client or included in the price of the product.
Futures	Futures refer to contracts for the sale and future delivery of stocks or commodities, wherein either party may waive delivery, and receive or pay, as the case may be, the difference in

	market price at the time set for delivery.
Materials management	Materials management refers to the activity that controls the transmission of physical materials through the value chain, from procurement through production and into distribution.
Mission statement	Mission statement refers to an outline of the fundamental purposes of an organization.
Quality assurance	Those activities associated with assuring the quality of a product or service is called quality assurance.
Partnership	In the common law, a partnership is a type of business entity in which partners share with each other the profits or losses of the business undertaking in which they have all invested.
Bill of materials	A bill of materials describes a product in terms of its assemblies, sub-assemblies, and basic parts. Basically consisting of a list of parts, a bill of materials is an essential part of the design and manufacture of any product.
Bill of material	A bill of material is a list of all the materials needed to manufacture a product or product component.
Users	Users refer to people in the organization who actually use the product or service purchased by the buying center.
Control system	A control system is a device or set of devices that manage the behavior of other devices. Some devices or systems are not controllable.A control system is an interconnection of components connected or related in such a manner as to command, direct, or regulate itself or another system.
Proactive	To be proactive is to act before a situation becomes a source of confrontation or crisis. It is the opposite of "retroactive," which refers to actions taken after an event.
International trade	The export of goods and services from a country and the import of goods and services into a country is referred to as the international trade.
Countertrade	Countertrade is exchanging goods or services that are paid for, in whole or part, with other goods or services.
Insourcing	Insourcing refers to process of producing goods or providing services within the organization rather than purchasing those same goods or services from outside vendors.
Outsourcing	Outsourcing refers to a production activity that was previously done inside a firm or plant that is now conducted outside that firm or plant.
Vertical integration	Vertical integration refers to production of different stages of processing of a product within the same firm.
Integration	Economic integration refers to reducing barriers among countries to transactions and to movements of goods, capital, and labor, including harmonization of laws, regulations, and standards. Integrated markets theoretically function as a unified market.
Value analysis	Value analysis refers to a systematic appraisal of the design, quality, and performance of a product to reduce purchasing costs.
Exchange	The trade of things of value between buyer and seller so that each is better off after the trade is called the exchange.
Extension	Extension refers to an out-of-court settlement in which creditors agree to allow the firm more time to meet its financial obligations. A new repayment schedule will be developed, subject to the acceptance of creditors.
Performance	Performance improvement is the concept of measuring the output of a particular process or

improvement	procedure then modifying the process or procedure in order to increase the output, increase efficiency, or increase the effectiveness of the process or procedure.
Total quality control	A product-quality program in which the objective is complete elimination of product defects is called total quality control.
Product development	In business and engineering, new product development is the complete process of bringing a new product to market. There are two parallel aspects to this process : one involves product engineering ; the other marketing analysis. Marketers see new product development as the first stage in product life cycle management, engineers as part of Product Lifecycle Management.
Quality control	The measurement of products and services against set standards is referred to as quality control.
Assignment	A transfer of property or some right or interest is referred to as assignment.
Procurement	Procurement is the acquisition of goods or services at the best possible total cost of ownership, in the right quantity, at the right time, in the right place for the direct benefit or use of the governments, corporations, or individuals generally via, but not limited to a contract.
Research and development	The use of resources for the deliberate discovery of new information and ways of doing things, together with the application of that information in inventing new products or processes is referred to as research and development.
Organization structure	The system of task, reporting, and authority relationships within which the organization does its work is referred to as the organization structure.
Centralized authority	An organization structure in which decision-making authority is maintained at the top level of management at the company's headquarters is a centralized authority.
Business unit	The lowest level of the company which contains the set of functions that carry a product through its life span from concept through manufacture, distribution, sales and service is a business unit.
Capital	Capital generally refers to financial wealth, especially that used to start or maintain a business. In classical economics, capital is one of four factors of production, the others being land and labor and entrepreneurship.
Capital expenditure	A substantial expenditure that is used by a company to acquire or upgrade physical assets such as equipment, property, industrial buildings, including those which improve the quality and life of an asset is referred to as a capital expenditure.
Corporate level	Corporate level refers to level at which top management directs overall strategy for the entire organization.
Teamwork	That which occurs when group members work together in ways that utilize their skills well to accomplish a purpose is called teamwork.
Leadership	Management merely consists of leadership applied to business situations; or in other words: management forms a sub-set of the broader process of leadership.
Interpersonal skills	Interpersonal skills are used to communicate with, understand, and motivate individuals and groups.
Buying center	The group of people in an organization who participate in the buying process and share common goals, risks, and knowledge important to a purchase decision is referred to as buying center.
Centralization	A structural policy in which decision-making authority is concentrated at the top of the organizational hierarchy is referred to as centralization.

Outbound	Communications originating inside an organization and destined for customers, prospects, or other people outside the organization are called outbound.
Committee	A long-lasting, sometimes permanent team in the organization structure created to deal with tasks that recur regularly is the committee.
General Electric	In 1876, Thomas Alva Edison opened a new laboratory in Menlo Park, New Jersey. Out of the laboratory was to come perhaps the most famous invention of all—a successful development of the incandescent electric lamp. By 1890, Edison had organized his various businesses into the Edison General Electric Company.
Corporation	A legal entity chartered by a state or the Federal government that is distinct and separate from the individuals who own it is a corporation. This separation gives the corporation unique powers which other legal entities lack.
Controlling	A management function that involves determining whether or not an organization is progressing toward its goals and objectives, and taking corrective action if it is not is called controlling.
Electronic data interchange	Electronic data interchange refers to the direct exchange between organizations of data via a computer-to-computer interface.
Policy	Similar to a script in that a policy can be a less than completely rational decision-making method. Involves the use of a pre-existing set of decision steps for any problem that presents itself.
Standardization	Standardization, in the context related to technologies and industries, is the process of establishing a technical standard among competing entities in a market, where this will bring benefits without hurting competition.
Compliance	A type of influence process where a receiver accepts the position advocated by a source to obtain favorable outcomes or to avoid punishment is the compliance.
Context	The effect of the background under which a message often takes on more and richer meaning is a context. Context is especially important in cross-cultural interactions because some cultures are said to be high context or low context.
Gain	In finance, gain is a profit or an increase in value of an investment such as a stock or bond. Gain is calculated by fair market value or the proceeds from the sale of the investment minus the sum of the purchase price and all costs associated with it.
Appreciation	Appreciation refers to a rise in the value of a country's currency on the exchange market, relative either to a particular other currency or to a weighted average of other currencies. The currency is said to appreciate. Opposite of 'depreciation.' Appreciation can also refer to the increase in value of any asset.
Strategic plan	The formal document that presents the ways and means by which a strategic goal will be achieved is a strategic plan. A long-term flexible plan that does not regulate activities but rather outlines the means to achieve certain results, and provides the means to alter the course of action should the desired ends change.
Product design	Product Design is defined as the idea generation, concept development, testing and manufacturing or implementation of a physical object or service. It is possibly the evolution of former discipline name - Industrial Design.
Shares	Shares refer to an equity security, representing a shareholder's ownership of a corporation. Shares are one of a finite number of equal portions in the capital of a company, entitling the owner to a proportion of distributed, non-reinvested profits known as dividends and to a portion of the value of the company in case of liquidation.

Go to **Cram101.com** for the Practice Tests for this Chapter.

Decentralization	Decentralization is the process of redistributing decision-making closer to the point of service or action. This gives freedom to managers at lower levels of the organization to make decisions.
Total supply	Total supply refers to the supply schedule or the supply curve of all sellers of a good or service.
End user	End user refers to the ultimate user of a product or service.
Distribution	Distribution in economics, the manner in which total output and income is distributed among individuals or factors.
Organizational goals	Objectives that management seeks to achieve in pursuing the firm's purpose are organizational goals.
Interest	In finance and economics, interest is the price paid by a borrower for the use of a lender's money. In other words, interest is the amount of paid to "rent" money for a period of time.
Balance	In banking and accountancy, the outstanding balance is the amount of money owned, (or due), that remains in a deposit account (or a loan account) at a given date, after all past remittances, payments and withdrawal have been accounted for. It can be positive (then, in the balance sheet of a firm, it is an asset) or negative (a liability).
Cooperative	A business owned and controlled by the people who use it, producers, consumers, or workers with similar needs who pool their resources for mutual gain is called cooperative.
Tangible	Having a physical existence is referred to as the tangible. Personal property other than real estate, such as cars, boats, stocks, or other assets.
Channel	Channel, in communications (sometimes called communications channel), refers to the medium used to convey information from a sender (or transmitter) to a receiver.
Trust	An arrangement in which shareholders of independent firms agree to give up their stock in exchange for trust certificates that entitle them to a share of the trust's common profits.
Control activities	Control activities are the activities intended to prevent, detect, and correct errors and irregularities relating to business risks. Policies and procedures used by management to meet its objectives.
Sales forecast	Sales forecast refers to the maximum total sales of a product that a firm expects to sell during a specified time period under specified environmental conditions and its own marketing efforts.
Warehouse	Warehouse refers to a location, often decentralized, that a firm uses to store, consolidate, age, or mix stock; house product-recall programs; or ease tax burdens.
Promotion	Promotion refers to all the techniques sellers use to motivate people to buy products or services. An attempt by marketers to inform people about products and to persuade them to participate in an exchange.
Distribution center	Designed to facilitate the timely movement of goods and represent a very important part of a supply chain is a distribution center.
Inventory management	The planning, coordinating, and controlling activities related to the flow of inventory into, through, and out of an organization is referred to as inventory management.
Remainder	A remainder in property law is a future interest created in a transferee that is capable of becoming possessory upon the natural termination of a prior estate created by the same instrument.
Core	A core is the set of feasible allocations in an economy that cannot be improved upon by subset of the set of the economy's consumers (a coalition). In construction, when the force

in an element is within a certain center section, the core, the element will only be under compression.

Drawback	Drawback refers to rebate of import duties when the imported good is re-exported or used as input to the production of an exported good.
Motorola	The Six Sigma quality system was developed at Motorola even though it became most well known because of its use by General Electric. It was created by engineer Bill Smith, under the direction of Bob Galvin (son of founder Paul Galvin) when he was running the company.
External customers	Dealers, who buy products to sell to others, and ultimate customers, who buy products for their own personal use are referred to as external customers.
Logistics	Those activities that focus on getting the right amount of the right products to the right place at the right time at the lowest possible cost is referred to as logistics.
Reorganization	Reorganization occurs, among other instances, when one corporation acquires another in a merger or acquisition, a single corporation divides into two or more entities, or a corporation makes a substantial change in its capital structure.
Single sourcing	Single sourcing is the origination of any design, set of concepts, or any article real or insubstantial from a single, well defined source, either a person or an organization.
Option	A contract that gives the purchaser the option to buy or sell the underlying financial instrument at a specified price, called the exercise price or strike price, within a specific period of time.
Incentive	An incentive is any factor (financial or non-financial) that provides a motive for a particular course of action, or counts as a reason for preferring one choice to the alternatives.
Leverage	Leverage is using given resources in such a way that the potential positive or negative outcome is magnified. In finance, this generally refers to borrowing.
Performance requirement	Performance requirement refers to a requirement that an importer or exporter achieve some level of performance, in terms of exporting, domestic content, etc., in order to obtain an import or export license.
Economy	The income, expenditures, and resources that affect the cost of running a business and household are called an economy.
Economies of scale	In economics, returns to scale and economies of scale are related terms that describe what happens as the scale of production increases. They are different terms and not to be used interchangeably.
Labor	People's physical and mental talents and efforts that are used to help produce goods and services are called labor.
Financial control	A process in which a firm periodically compares its actual revenues, costs, and expenses with its projected ones is called financial control.
Collaboration	Collaboration occurs when the interaction between groups is very important to goal attainment and the goals are compatible. Wherein people work together —applying both to the work of individuals as well as larger collectives and societies.
Accounting	A system that collects and processes financial information about an organization and reports that information to decision makers is referred to as accounting.
Intranet	Intranet refers to a companywide network, closed to public access, that uses Internet-type technology. A set of communications links within one company that travel over the Internet but are closed to public access.

Corporate culture	The whole collection of beliefs, values, and behaviors of a firm that send messages to those within and outside the company about how business is done is the corporate culture.
Electronic mail	Electronic mail refers to electronic written communication between individuals using computers connected to the Internet.
Joint venture	Joint venture refers to an undertaking by two parties for a specific purpose and duration, taking any of several legal forms.
Business Week	Business Week is a business magazine published by McGraw-Hill. It was first published in 1929 under the direction of Malcolm Muir, who was serving as president of the McGraw-Hill Publishing company at the time. It is considered to be the standard both in industry and among students.
Organizational Behavior	The study of human behavior in organizational settings, the interface between human behavior and the organization, and the organization itself is called organizational behavior.
Journal	Book of original entry, in which transactions are recorded in a general ledger system, is referred to as a journal.
American Management Association	American Management Association International is the world's largest membership-based management development and executive training organization. Their products include instructor led seminars, workshops, conferences, customized corporate programs, online learning, books, newsletters, research surveys and reports.

Buyer	A buyer refers to a role in the buying center with formal authority and responsibility to select the supplier and negotiate the terms of the contract.
Supply	Supply is the aggregate amount of any material good that can be called into being at a certain price point; it comprises one half of the equation of supply and demand. In classical economic theory, a curve representing supply is one of the factors that produce price.
Contract	A contract is a "promise" or an "agreement" that is enforced or recognized by the law. In the civil law, a contract is considered to be part of the general law of obligations.
Management	Management characterizes the process of leading and directing all or part of an organization, often a business, through the deployment and manipulation of resources. Early twentieth-century management writer Mary Parker Follett defined management as "the art of getting things done through people."
Policy	Similar to a script in that a policy can be a less than completely rational decision-making method. Involves the use of a pre-existing set of decision steps for any problem that presents itself.
Purchasing	Purchasing refers to the function in a firm that searches for quality material resources, finds the best suppliers, and negotiates the best price for goods and services.
Regulation	Regulation refers to restrictions state and federal laws place on business with regard to the conduct of its activities.
Leadership	Management merely consists of leadership applied to business situations; or in other words: management forms a sub-set of the broader process of leadership.
Personnel	A collective term for all of the employees of an organization. Personnel is also commonly used to refer to the personnel management function or the organizational unit responsible for administering personnel programs.
Controlling	A management function that involves determining whether or not an organization is progressing toward its goals and objectives, and taking corrective action if it is not is called controlling.
Product development	In business and engineering, new product development is the complete process of bringing a new product to market. There are two parallel aspects to this process : one involves product engineering ; the other marketing analysis. Marketers see new product development as the first stage in product life cycle management, engineers as part of Product Lifecycle Management.
Innovation	Innovation refers to the first commercially successful introduction of a new product, the use of a new method of production, or the creation of a new form of business organization.
Conformance	A dimension of quality that refers to the extent to which a product lies within an allowable range of deviation from its specification is called the conformance.
Hierarchy	A system of grouping people in an organization according to rank from the top down in which all subordinate managers must report to one person is called a hierarchy.
Operation	A standardized method or technique that is performed repetitively, often on different materials resulting in different finished goods is called an operation.
Corporate policy	Dimension of social responsibility that refers to the position a firm takes on social and political issues is referred to as corporate policy.
Committee	A long-lasting, sometimes permanent team in the organization structure created to deal with tasks that recur regularly is the committee.
Business unit	The lowest level of the company which contains the set of functions that carry a product

through its life span from concept through manufacture, distribution, sales and service is a business unit.

Compliance A type of influence process where a receiver accepts the position advocated by a source to obtain favorable outcomes or to avoid punishment is the compliance.

Scope Scope of a project is the sum total of all projects products and their requirements or features.

Authority Authority in agency law, refers to an agent's ability to affect his principal's legal relations with third parties. Also used to refer to an actor's legal power or ability to do something. In addition, sometimes used to refer to a statute, case, or other legal source that justifies a particular result.

Interest In finance and economics, interest is the price paid by a borrower for the use of a lender's money. In other words, interest is the amount of paid to "rent" money for a period of time.

Grant Grant refers to an intergovernmental transfer of funds . Since the New Deal, state and local governments have become increasingly dependent upon federal grants for an almost infinite variety of programs.

Insurance Insurance refers to a system by which individuals can reduce their exposure to risk of large losses by spreading the risks among a large number of persons.

Estate An estate is the totality of the legal rights, interests, entitlements and obligations attaching to property. In the context of wills and probate, it refers to the totality of the property which the deceased owned or in which some interest was held.

Staff position A manager in a staff position has the authority and responsibility to advise people in the line positions but cannot issue direct orders to them.

Leverage Leverage is using given resources in such a way that the potential positive or negative outcome is magnified. In finance, this generally refers to borrowing.

Commodity Could refer to any good, but in trade a commodity is usually a raw material or primary product that enters into international trade, such as metals or basic agricultural products.

Negotiation Negotiation is the process whereby interested parties resolve disputes, agree upon courses of action, bargain for individual or collective advantage, and/or attempt to craft outcomes which serve their mutual interests.

Service Service refers to a "non tangible product" that is not embodied in a physical good and that typically effects some change in another product, person, or institution. Contrasts with good.

Long run In economic models, the long run time frame assumes no fixed factors of production. Firms can enter or leave the marketplace, and the cost (and availability) of land, labor, raw materials, and capital goods can be assumed to vary.

Manufacturing Production of goods primarily by the application of labor and capital to raw materials and other intermediate inputs, in contrast to agriculture, mining, forestry, fishing, and services a manufacturing.

Agent A person who makes economic decisions for another economic actor. A hired manager operates as an agent for a firm's owner.

Reciprocity An industrial buying practice in which two organizations agree to purchase each other's products and services is called reciprocity.

Technology The body of knowledge and techniques that can be used to combine economic resources to produce goods and services is called technology.

Bid	A bid price is a price offered by a buyer when he/she buys a good. In the context of stock trading on a stock exchange, the bid price is the highest price a buyer of a stock is willing to pay for a share of that given stock.
Competitor	Other organizations in the same industry or type of business that provide a good or service to the same set of customers is referred to as a competitor.
Corporate citizenship	A theory of responsibility that says a business has a responsibility to do good is corporate citizenship. Terms used in the business sector to refer to business giving, ie. business relationships and partnerships with not-for-profit organizations.
Subcontract	A subcontract is a contract that assigns part of an existing contract to a different party.
Administration	Administration refers to the management and direction of the affairs of governments and institutions; a collective term for all policymaking officials of a government; the execution and implementation of public policy.
Clean Air Act	A Clean Air Act describes one of a number of pieces of legislation relating to the reduction of smog and atmospheric pollution in general. The United States Congress passed the Clean Air Act in 1963, the Clean Air Act Amendment in 1966, the Clean Air Act Extension in 1970, and Clean Air Act Amendments in 1977 and 1990.
Industry	A group of firms that produce identical or similar products is an industry. It is also used specifically to refer to an area of economic production focused on manufacturing which involves large amounts of capital investment before any profit can be realized, also called "heavy industry".
Dow Chemical	Dow Chemical is the world's largest producer of plastics, including polystyrene, polyurethanes, polyethylene, polypropylene, and synthetic rubbers. It is also a major producer of the chemicals calcium chloride, ethylene oxide, and various acrylates, surfactants, and cellulose resins. It produces many agricultural chemicals.
Supplier evaluation	Supplier evaluation refers to a tool used by many firms to differentiate and discriminate among suppliers. A supplier evaluation often involves report cards where potential suppliers are rated based on different criteria such as quality, technical capability, or ability to meet schedule demands.
Evaluation	The consumer's appraisal of the product or brand on important attributes is called evaluation.
Corporation	A legal entity chartered by a state or the Federal government that is distinct and separate from the individuals who own it is a corporation. This separation gives the corporation unique powers which other legal entities lack.
Procurement	Procurement is the acquisition of goods or services at the best possible total cost of ownership, in the right quantity, at the right time, in the right place for the direct benefit or use of the governments, corporations, or individuals generally via, but not limited to a contract.
Firm	An organization that employs resources to produce a good or service for profit and owns and operates one or more plants is referred to as a firm.
Equity	Equity is the name given to the set of legal principles, in countries following the English common law tradition, which supplement strict rules of law where their application would operate harshly, so as to achieve what is sometimes referred to as "natural justice."
Revenue	Revenue is a U.S. business term for the amount of money that a company receives from its activities, mostly from sales of products and/or services to customers.
Optimum	Optimum refers to the best. Usually refers to a most preferred choice by consumers subject to

Go to **Cram101.com** for the Practice Tests for this Chapter.

	a budget constraint or a profit maximizing choice by firms or industry subject to a technological constraint.
Maturity	Maturity refers to the final payment date of a loan or other financial instrument, after which point no further interest or principal need be paid.
Trend	Trend refers to the long-term movement of an economic variable, such as its average rate of increase or decrease over enough years to encompass several business cycles.
Competitive bidding	A situation where two or more companies submit bids for a product, service, or project to a potential buyer is competitive bidding.
Strike	The withholding of labor services by an organized group of workers is referred to as a strike.
Ford	Ford is an American company that manufactures and sells automobiles worldwide. Ford introduced methods for large-scale manufacturing of cars, and large-scale management of an industrial workforce, especially elaborately engineered manufacturing sequences typified by the moving assembly lines.
Johnson Controls	Johnson Controls specializes in the design, manufacturing, and installation of automotive systems and nonresidential climate control systems. Its Controls Group also has a prominent facilities management division. It was founded in 1885 by professor Warren S. Johnson, inventor of the first electric room thermostat.
Liability	A liability is a present obligation of the enterprise arizing from past events, the settlement of which is expected to result in an outflow from the enterprise of resources embodying economic benefits.
Waiver	Waiver refers to an authorized deviation from the terms of a previously negotiated and legally binding agreement. Many countries have sought and obtained waivers from particular obligations of the GATT and WTO.
Product design	Product Design is defined as the idea generation, concept development, testing and manufacturing or implementation of a physical object or service. It is possibly the evolution of former discipline name - Industrial Design.
Marketing	Promoting and selling products or services to customers, or prospective customers, is referred to as marketing.
Patent	The legal right to the proceeds from and control over the use of an invented product or process, granted for a fixed period of time, usually 20 years. Patent is one form of intellectual property that is subject of the TRIPS agreement.
Financial liability	A financial liability is something that is owed to another party. This is typically contrasted with an asset which is something of value that is owned.
Production	The creation of finished goods and services using the factors of production: land, labor, capital, entrepreneurship, and knowledge.
Intranet	Intranet refers to a companywide network, closed to public access, that uses Internet-type technology. A set of communications links within one company that travel over the Internet but are closed to public access.
Brief	Brief refers to a statement of a party's case or legal arguments, usually prepared by an attorney. Also used to make legal arguments before appellate courts.
Best practice	Best practice is a management idea which asserts that there is a technique, method, process, activity, incentive or reward that is more effective at delivering a particular outcome than any other technique, method, process, etc.

Go to Cram101.com for the Practice Tests for this Chapter.

Benchmarking	The continuous process of comparing the levels of performance in producing products and services and executing activities against the best levels of performance is benchmarking.
Total cost	The sum of fixed cost and variable cost is referred to as total cost.
Assignment	A transfer of property or some right or interest is referred to as assignment.
Warrant	A warrant is a security that entitles the holder to buy or sell a certain additional quantity of an underlying security at an agreed-upon price, at the holder's discretion.
Vendor	A person who sells property to a vendee is a vendor. The words vendor and vendee are more commonly applied to the seller and purchaser of real estate, and the words seller and buyer are more commonly applied to the seller and purchaser of personal property.
Chrysler	The Chrysler Corporation was an American automobile manufacturer that existed independently from 1925–1998. The company was formed by Walter Percy Chrysler on June 6, 1925, with the remaining assets of Maxwell Motor Company.
Honda	With more than 14 million internal combustion engines built each year, Honda is the largest engine-maker in the world. In 2004, the company began to produce diesel motors, which were both very quiet whilst not requiring particulate filters to pass pollution standards. It is arguable, however, that the foundation of their success is the motorcycle division.
Purchase order	A form on which items or services needed by a business firm are specified and then communicated to the vendor is a purchase order.
Home Depot	Home Depot has recently added self checkout registers at most of its stores in North America. These automated kiosks allow the customer to scan the barcode of the item they wish to purchase, then insert money to pay for the items, and receive any change automatically. The customer no longer needs to interact with a store employee during checkout.
Preference	The act of a debtor in paying or securing one or more of his creditors in a manner more favorable to them than to other creditors or to the exclusion of such other creditors is a preference. In the absence of statute, a preference is perfectly good, but to be legal it must be bona fide, and not a mere subterfuge of the debtor to secure a future benefit to himself or to prevent the application of his property to his debts.
Balance	In banking and accountancy, the outstanding balance is the amount of money owned, (or due), that remains in a deposit account (or a loan account) at a given date, after all past remittances, payments and withdrawal have been accounted for. It can be positive (then, in the balance sheet of a firm, it is an asset) or negative (a liability).
Distribution	Distribution in economics, the manner in which total output and income is distributed among individuals or factors.
Audit	An examination of the financial reports to ensure that they represent what they claim and conform with generally accepted accounting principles is referred to as audit.
Independent audit	An evaluation and unbiased opinion about the accuracy of a company's financial statements conducted by an outside CPA is an independent audit.
Pledge	In law a pledge (also pawn) is a bailment of personal property as a security for some debt or engagement.
Rainforest Action Network	The Rainforest Action Network is an environmental organization based in San Francisco, California, USA. The Rainforest Action Network campaigns for the forests, their inhabitants and the natural systems that sustain life by transforming the global marketplace through grassroots organizing, education and non-violent direct action.
License	A license in the sphere of Intellectual Property Rights (IPR) is a document, contract or agreement giving permission or the 'right' to a legally-definable entity to do something

	(such as manufacture a product or to use a service), or to apply something (such as a trademark), with the objective of achieving commercial gain.
Market	A market is, as defined in economics, a social arrangement that allows buyers and sellers to discover information and carry out a voluntary exchange of goods or services.
Fund	Independent accounting entity with a self-balancing set of accounts segregated for the purposes of carrying on specific activities is referred to as a fund.
Sustainable development	Economic development that is achieved without undermining the incomes, resources, or environment of future generations is called sustainable development.
Nike	Because Nike creates goods for a wide range of sports, they have competition from every sports and sports fashion brand there is. Nike has no direct competitors because there is no single brand which can compete directly with their range of sports and non-sports oriented gear, except for Reebok.

Purchasing	Purchasing refers to the function in a firm that searches for quality material resources, finds the best suppliers, and negotiates the best price for goods and services.
Concurrent engineering	The simultaneous performance of product design and process design is concurrent engineering. Typically, concurrent engineering involves the formation of cross-functional teams. This allows engineers and managers of different disciplines to work together simultaneously in developing product and process designs.
Marketing	Promoting and selling products or services to customers, or prospective customers, is referred to as marketing.
Historical cost	In accounting terminology, historical cost describes the original cost of an asset at the time of purchase or payment as opposed to its market value
Target cost	The projected long-run product cost that will enable a firm to enter and remain in the market for the product and compete successfully with the firm's competitors is referred to as target cost.
Supply	Supply is the aggregate amount of any material good that can be called into being at a certain price point; it comprises one half of the equation of supply and demand. In classical economic theory, a curve representing supply is one of the factors that produce price.
Liaison	An individual who serves as a bridge between groups, tying groups together and facilitating the communication flow needed to integrate group activities is a liaison.
Contract	A contract is a "promise" or an "agreement" that is enforced or recognized by the law. In the civil law, a contract is considered to be part of the general law of obligations.
Management	Management characterizes the process of leading and directing all or part of an organization, often a business, through the deployment and manipulation of resources. Early twentieth-century management writer Mary Parker Follett defined management as "the art of getting things done through people."
Personnel	A collective term for all of the employees of an organization. Personnel is also commonly used to refer to the personnel management function or the organizational unit responsible for administering personnel programs.
Cost management	The approaches and activities of managers in short-run and long-run planning and control decisions that increase value for customers and lower costs of products and services are called cost management.
Brainstorming	Brainstorming refers to a technique designed to overcome our natural tendency to evaluate and criticize ideas and thereby reduce the creative output of those ideas. People are encouraged to produce ideas/options without criticizing, often at a very fast pace to minimize our natural tendency to criticize.
Product cost	Product cost refers to sum of the costs assigned to a product for a specific purpose. A concept used in applying the cost plus approach to product pricing in which only the costs of manufacturing the product are included in the cost amount to which the markup is added.
Competitive advantage	A business is said to have a competitive advantage when its unique strengths, often based on cost, quality, time, and innovation, offer consumers a greater percieved value and there by differtiating it from its competitors.
Sustainable competitive advantage	A strength, relative to competitors, in the markets served and the products offered is referred to as the sustainable competitive advantage.
Contribution	In business organization law, the cash or property contributed to a business by its owners is referred to as contribution.

Go to **Cram101.com** for the Practice Tests for this Chapter.

Exchange	The trade of things of value between buyer and seller so that each is better off after the trade is called the exchange.
Operation	A standardized method or technique that is performed repetitively, often on different materials resulting in different finished goods is called an operation.
Firm	An organization that employs resources to produce a good or service for profit and owns and operates one or more plants is referred to as a firm.
Operations strategy	Operations strategy refers to the recognition of the importance of operations to the firm's success and the involvement of operations managers in the organization's strategic planning.
Production	The creation of finished goods and services using the factors of production: land, labor, capital, entrepreneurship, and knowledge.
Manufacturing	Production of goods primarily by the application of labor and capital to raw materials and other intermediate inputs, in contrast to agriculture, mining, forestry, fishing, and services a manufacturing.
Total quality management	The broad set of management and control processes designed to focus an entire organization and all of its employees on providing products or services that do the best possible job of satisfying the customer is called total quality management.
Quality management	Quality management is a method for ensuring that all the activities necessary to design, develop and implement a product or service are effective and efficient with respect to the system and its performance.
Product design	Product Design is defined as the idea generation, concept development, testing and manufacturing or implementation of a physical object or service. It is possibly the evolution of former discipline name - Industrial Design.
Buyer	A buyer refers to a role in the buying center with formal authority and responsibility to select the supplier and negotiate the terms of the contract.
Teamwork	That which occurs when group members work together in ways that utilize their skills well to accomplish a purpose is called teamwork.
Product development	In business and engineering, new product development is the complete process of bringing a new product to market. There are two parallel aspects to this process : one involves product engineering ; the other marketing analysis. Marketers see new product development as the first stage in product life cycle management, engineers as part of Product Lifecycle Management.
Regular meeting	A meeting held by the board of directors that is held at regular intervals at the time and place established in the bylaws is called a regular meeting.
Trust	An arrangement in which shareholders of independent firms agree to give up their stock in exchange for trust certificates that entitle them to a share of the trust's common profits.
Service	Service refers to a "non tangible product" that is not embodied in a physical good and that typically effects some change in another product, person, or institution. Contrasts with good.
Technology	The body of knowledge and techniques that can be used to combine economic resources to produce goods and services is called technology.
Accounting	A system that collects and processes financial information about an organization and reports that information to decision makers is referred to as accounting.
Control system	A control system is a device or set of devices that manage the behavior of other devices. Some devices or systems are not controllable.A control system is an interconnection of

Go to **Cram101.com** for the Practice Tests for this Chapter.

	components connected or related in such a manner as to command, direct, or regulate itself or another system.
Accounts payable	A written record of all vendors to whom the business firm owes money is referred to as accounts payable.
Cost accounting	Cost accounting measures and reports financial and nonfinancial information relating to the cost of acquiring or consuming resources in an organization. It provides information for both management accounting and financial accounting.
Total cost	The sum of fixed cost and variable cost is referred to as total cost.
Performance measurement	The process by which someone evaluates an employee's work behaviors by measurement and comparison with previously established standards, documents the results, and communicates the results to the employee is called performance measurement.
Antitrust	Government intervention to alter market structure or prevent abuse of market power is called antitrust.
Property	Assets defined in the broadest legal sense. Property includes the unrealized receivables of a cash basis taxpayer, but not services rendered.
Liability	A liability is a present obligation of the enterprise arizing from past events, the settlement of which is expected to result in an outflow from the enterprise of resources embodying economic benefits.
Patent	The legal right to the proceeds from and control over the use of an invented product or process, granted for a fixed period of time, usually 20 years. Patent is one form of intellectual property that is subject of the TRIPS agreement.
Intellectual property	In law, intellectual property is an umbrella term for various legal entitlements which attach to certain types of information, ideas, or other intangibles in their expressed form. The holder of this legal entitlement is generally entitled to exercise various exclusive rights in relation to its subject matter.
Product liability	Part of tort law that holds businesses liable for harm that results from the production, design, sale, or use of products they market is referred to as product liability.
Escape clause	The portion of a legal text that permits departure from ts provisions in the event of specified adverse circumstances is the escape clause.
Commerce	Commerce is the exchange of something of value between two entities. It is the central mechanism from which capitalism is derived.
Electronic commerce	Electronic commerce or e-commerce, refers to any activity that uses some form of electronic communication in the inventory, exchange, advertisement, distribution, and payment of goods and services.
Regulation	Regulation refers to restrictions state and federal laws place on business with regard to the conduct of its activities.
Administration	Administration refers to the management and direction of the affairs of governments and institutions; a collective term for all policymaking officials of a government; the execution and implementation of public policy.
Occupational Safety and Health Administration	The United States Occupational Safety and Health Administration is an agency of the United States Department of Labor. It was created by Congress under the Occupational Safety and Health Act, signed by President Richard M. Nixon, on December 29, 1970.
Authority	Authority in agency law, refers to an agent's ability to affect his principal's legal

	relations with third parties. Also used to refer to an actor's legal power or ability to do something. In addition, sometimes used to refer to a statute, case, or other legal source that justifies a particular result.
Policy	Similar to a script in that a policy can be a less than completely rational decision-making method. Involves the use of a pre-existing set of decision steps for any problem that presents itself.
Federal government	Federal government refers to the government of the United States, as distinct from the state and local governments.
Environmental protection agency	An administrative agency created by Congress in 1970 to coordinate the implementation and enforcement of the federal environmental protection laws is referred to as the Environmental Protection Agency or EPA.
Public policy	Decision making by government. Governments are constantly concerned about what they should or should not do. And whatever they do or do not do is public policy. public program All those activities designed to implement a public policy; often this calls for the creation of organizations, public agencies, and bureaus.
Budget	Budget refers to an account, usually for a year, of the planned expenditures and the expected receipts of an entity. For a government, the receipts are tax revenues.
Industry	A group of firms that produce identical or similar products is an industry. It is also used specifically to refer to an area of economic production focused on manufacturing which involves large amounts of capital investment before any profit can be realized, also called "heavy industry".
Bid	A bid price is a price offered by a buyer when he/she buys a good. In the context of stock trading on a stock exchange, the bid price is the highest price a buyer of a stock is willing to pay for a share of that given stock.
Profit	Profit refers to the return to the resource entrepreneurial ability; total revenue minus total cost.
Innovation	Innovation refers to the first commercially successful introduction of a new product, the use of a new method of production, or the creation of a new form of business organization.
Performance improvement	Performance improvement is the concept of measuring the output of a particular process or procedure then modifying the process or procedure in order to increase the output, increase efficiency, or increase the effectiveness of the process or procedure.
Gain	In finance, gain is a profit or an increase in value of an investment such as a stock or bond. Gain is calculated by fair market value or the proceeds from the sale of the investment minus the sum of the purchase price and all costs associated with it.
Incentive	An incentive is any factor (financial or non-financial) that provides a motive for a particular course of action, or counts as a reason for preferring one choice to the alternatives.
Risk sharing	The distribution of financial risk among parties furnishing a service is called risk sharing.
Quality assurance	Those activities associated with assuring the quality of a product or service is called quality assurance.
Supply chain	Supply chain refers to the flow of goods, services, and information from the initial sources of materials and services to the delivery of products to consumers.
Leadership	Management merely consists of leadership applied to business situations; or in other words: management forms a sub-set of the broader process of leadership.

Prototype	A prototype is built to test the function of a new design before starting production of a product.
Honda	With more than 14 million internal combustion engines built each year, Honda is the largest engine-maker in the world. In 2004, the company began to produce diesel motors, which were both very quiet whilst not requiring particulate filters to pass pollution standards. It is arguable, however, that the foundation of their success is the motorcycle division.
Productivity	Productivity refers to the total output of goods and services in a given period of time divided by work hours.
General Motors	General Motors is the world's largest automaker. Founded in 1908, today it employs about 327,000 people around the world. With global headquarters in Detroit, it manufactures its cars and trucks in 33 countries.
Competitor	Other organizations in the same industry or type of business that provide a good or service to the same set of customers is referred to as a competitor.
Shares	Shares refer to an equity security, representing a shareholder's ownership of a corporation. Shares are one of a finite number of equal portions in the capital of a company, entitling the owner to a proportion of distributed, non-reinvested profits known as dividends and to a portion of the value of the company in case of liquidation.
DaimlerChrysler	In 2002, the merged company, DaimlerChrysler, appeared to run two independent product lines, with few signs of corporate integration. In 2003, however, it was alleged by the Detroit News that the "merger of equals" was, in fact, a takeover.
Proprietary	Proprietary indicates that a party, or proprietor, exercises private ownership, control or use over an item of property, usually to the exclusion of other parties. Where a party, holds or claims proprietary interests in relation to certain types of property (eg. a creative literary work, or software), that property may also be the subject of intellectual property law (eg. copyright or patents).
Interest	In finance and economics, interest is the price paid by a borrower for the use of a lender's money. In other words, interest is the amount of paid to "rent" money for a period of time.
Leverage	Leverage is using given resources in such a way that the potential positive or negative outcome is magnified. In finance, this generally refers to borrowing.
Resistance to change	Resistance to change refers to an attitude or behavior that shows unwillingness to make or support a change.
Performance requirement	Performance requirement refers to a requirement that an importer or exporter achieve some level of performance, in terms of exporting, domestic content, etc., in order to obtain an import or export license.
Product life cycle	Product life cycle refers to a series of phases in a product's sales and cash flows over time; these phases, in order of occurrence, are introductory, growth, maturity, and decline.
Market	A market is, as defined in economics, a social arrangement that allows buyers and sellers to discover information and carry out a voluntary exchange of goods or services.
Collaboration	Collaboration occurs when the interaction between groups is very important to goal attainment and the goals are compatible. Wherein people work together —applying both to the work of individuals as well as larger collectives and societies.
Trend	Trend refers to the long-term movement of an economic variable, such as its average rate of increase or decrease over enough years to encompass several business cycles.
Competitive bidding	A situation where two or more companies submit bids for a product, service, or project to a potential buyer is competitive bidding.

Extension	Extension refers to an out-of-court settlement in which creditors agree to allow the firm more time to meet its financial obligations. A new repayment schedule will be developed, subject to the acceptance of creditors.
Chrysler	The Chrysler Corporation was an American automobile manufacturer that existed independently from 1925–1998. The company was formed by Walter Percy Chrysler on June 6, 1925, with the remaining assets of Maxwell Motor Company.
Design phase	The phase in the instructional system design process where learning objectives, tests, and the required skills and knowledge for a task are constructed and sequenced is the design phase.
Capital	Capital generally refers to financial wealth, especially that used to start or maintain a business. In classical economics, capital is one of four factors of production, the others being land and labor and entrepreneurship.
Pact	Pact refers to a set of principles endorsed by 21 of the largest U.S. ad agencies aimed at improving the research used in preparing and testing ads, providing a better creative product for clients, and controlling the cost of TV commercials.
Strategic alliance	Strategic alliance refers to a long-term partnership between two or more companies established to help each company build competitive market advantages.
Senior management	Senior management is generally a team of individuals at the highest level of organizational management who have the day-to-day responsibilities of managing a corporation.
Alignment	Term that refers to optimal coordination among disparate departments and divisions within a firm is referred to as alignment.
Appeal	Appeal refers to the act of asking an appellate court to overturn a decision after the trial court's final judgment has been entered.
Consideration	Consideration in contract law, a basic requirement for an enforceable agreement under traditional contract principles, defined in this text as legal value, bargained for and given in exchange for an act or promise. In corporation law, cash or property contributed to a corporation in exchange for shares, or a promise to contribute such cash or property.
Conflict resolution	Conflict resolution is the process of resolving a dispute or a conflict. Successful conflict resolution occurs by providing each side's needs, and adequately addressing their interests so that they are each satisfied with the outcome. Conflict resolution aims to end conflicts before they start or lead to physical fighting.
Logistics	Those activities that focus on getting the right amount of the right products to the right place at the right time at the lowest possible cost is referred to as logistics.
Organizational structure	Organizational structure is the way in which the interrelated groups of an organization are constructed. From a managerial point of view the main concerns are ensuring effective communication and coordination.
Assignment	A transfer of property or some right or interest is referred to as assignment.
Company culture	Company culture is the term given to the values and practices shared by the employees of a firm.
Specific performance	A contract remedy whereby the defendant is ordered to perform according to the terms of his contract is referred to as specific performance.
Stakeholder	A stakeholder is an individual or group with a vested interest in or expectation for organizational performance. Usually stakeholders can either have an effect on or are affected by an organization.

Synergy	Corporate synergy occurs when corporations interact congruently. A corporate synergy refers to a financial benefit that a corporation expects to realize when it merges with or acquires another corporation.
Synergistic effect	In media buying, combining a number of complementary types of media that create advertising awareness greater than the sum of each is called synergistic effect.
Drawback	Drawback refers to rebate of import duties when the imported good is re-exported or used as input to the production of an exported good.
Groupthink	Groupthink is a situation in which pressures for cohesion and togetherness are so strong as to produce narrowly considered and bad decisions; this can be especially true via conformity pressures in groups.
Evaluation	The consumer's appraisal of the product or brand on important attributes is called evaluation.
Procurement	Procurement is the acquisition of goods or services at the best possible total cost of ownership, in the right quantity, at the right time, in the right place for the direct benefit or use of the governments, corporations, or individuals generally via, but not limited to a contract.
Accord	An agreement whereby the parties agree to accept something different in satisfaction of the original contract is an accord.
BMW	BMW is an independent German company and manufacturer of automobiles and motorcycles. BMW is the world's largest premium carmaker and is the parent company of the BMW MINI and Rolls-Royce car brands, and, formerly, Rover.
Investment	Investment refers to spending for the production and accumulation of capital and additions to inventories. In a financial sense, buying an asset with the expectation of making a return.
Ford	Ford is an American company that manufactures and sells automobiles worldwide. Ford introduced methods for large-scale manufacturing of cars, and large-scale management of an industrial workforce, especially elaborately engineered manufacturing sequences typified by the moving assembly lines.
Labor	People's physical and mental talents and efforts that are used to help produce goods and services are called labor.
Joint venture	Joint venture refers to an undertaking by two parties for a specific purpose and duration, taking any of several legal forms.
Negotiation	Negotiation is the process whereby interested parties resolve disputes, agree upon courses of action, bargain for individual or collective advantage, and/or attempt to craft outcomes which serve their mutual interests.
Remainder	A remainder in property law is a future interest created in a transferee that is capable of becoming possessory upon the natural termination of a prior estate created by the same instrument.
Points	Loan origination fees that may be deductible as interest by a buyer of property. A seller of property who pays points reduces the selling price by the amount of the points paid for the buyer.
Brief	Brief refers to a statement of a party's case or legal arguments, usually prepared by an attorney. Also used to make legal arguments before appellate courts.
Effective communication	When the intended meaning equals the perceived meaning it is called effective communication.

Go to **Cram101.com** for the Practice Tests for this Chapter.

Project management	Project management is the discipline of organizing and managing resources in such a way that these resources deliver all the work required to complete a project within defined scope, time, and cost constraints.
Consensus decision making	Consensus decision making is a decision process that not only seeks the agreement of most participants, but also to resolve or mitigate the objections of the minority to achieve the most agreeable decision.
Frequency	Frequency refers to the speed of the up and down movements of a fluctuating economic variable; that is, the number of times per unit of time that the variable completes a cycle of up and down movement.
Holding	The holding is a court's determination of a matter of law based on the issue presented in the particular case. In other words: under this law, with these facts, this result.
Performance target	A task established for an employee that provides the comparative basis for performance appraisal is a performance target.
Warrant	A warrant is a security that entitles the holder to buy or sell a certain additional quantity of an underlying security at an agreed-upon price, at the holder's discretion.
Process improvement	Process improvement is the activity of elevating the performance of a process, especially that of a business process with regard to its goal.
Quality improvement	Quality is inversely proportional to variability thus quality Improvement is the reduction of variability in products and processes.
Competitiveness	Competitiveness usually refers to characteristics that permit a firm to compete effectively with other firms due to low cost or superior technology, perhaps internationally.
Integration	Economic integration refers to reducing barriers among countries to transactions and to movements of goods, capital, and labor, including harmonization of laws, regulations, and standards. Integrated markets theoretically function as a unified market.
Realization	Realization is the sale of assets when an entity is being liquidated.
New product development	New product development is the complete process of bringing a new product to market. There are two parallel aspects to this process : one involves product engineering ; the other marketing analysis.
Process innovation	The development and use of new or improved production or distribution methods is called process innovation. It is an approach in business process reengineering by which radical changes are made through innovations.
Market share	That fraction of an industry's output accounted for by an individual firm or group of firms is called market share.
Premium	Premium refers to the fee charged by an insurance company for an insurance policy. The rate of losses must be relatively predictable: In order to set the premium (prices) insurers must be able to estimate them accurately.
Critical success factor	Critical Success Factor is a business term for an element which is necessary for an organization or project to achieve its mission.
Success factor	The term success factor refers to the characteristics necessary for high performance; knowledge, skills, abilities, behaviors.
Research and development	The use of resources for the deliberate discovery of new information and ways of doing things, together with the application of that information in inventing new products or processes is referred to as research and development.
Compaq	Compaq was founded in February 1982 by Rod Canion, Jim Harris and Bill Murto, three senior

managers from semiconductor manufacturer Texas Instruments. Each invested $1,000 to form the company. Their first venture capital came from Ben Rosen and Sevin-Rosen partners. It is often told that the architecture of the original PC was first sketched out on a placemat by the founders while dining in the Houston restaurant, House of Pies.

Digital Equipment Corporation	Digital Equipment Corporation was a pioneering company in the American computer industry. Its PDP and VAX products were arguably the most popular mini-computers for the scientific and engineering communities during the 70s and 80s.
Corporation	A legal entity chartered by a state or the Federal government that is distinct and separate from the individuals who own it is a corporation. This separation gives the corporation unique powers which other legal entities lack.
Manufacturing costs	Costs incurred in a manufacturing process, which consist of direct material, direct labor, and manufacturing overhead are referred to as manufacturing costs.
Basic research	Involves discovering new knowledge rather than solving specific problems is called basic research.
Convergence	The blending of various facets of marketing functions and communication technology to create more efficient and expanded synergies is a convergence.
Time horizon	A time horizon is a fixed point of time in the future at which point certain processes will be evaluated or assumed to end. It is necessary in an accounting, finance or risk management regime to assign such a fixed horizon time so that alternatives can be evaluated for performance over the same period of time.
Planning horizon	The length of time it takes to conceive, develop, and complete a project and to recover the cost of the project on a discounted cash flow basis is referred to as planning horizon.
Assessment	Collecting information and providing feedback to employees about their behavior, communication style, or skills is an assessment.
Inventory	Tangible property held for sale in the normal course of business or used in producing goods or services for sale is an inventory.
Credit	Credit refers to a recording as positive in the balance of payments, any transaction that gives rise to a payment into the country, such as an export, the sale of an asset, or borrowing from abroad.
Finished goods	Completed products awaiting sale are called finished goods. An item considered a finished good in a supplying plant might be considered a component or raw material in a receiving plant.
Integration process	The way information such as product knowledge, meanings, and beliefs is combined to evaluate two or more alternatives is referred to as an integration process.
Product cycle	Product cycle refers to the life cycle of a new product, which first can be produced only in the country where it was developed, then as it becomes standardized and more familiar, can be produced in other countries and exported back to where it started.
Intel	Intel Corporation, founded in 1968 and based in Santa Clara, California, USA, is the world's largest semiconductor company. Intel is best known for its PC microprocessors, where it maintains roughly 80% market share.
Business strategy	Business strategy, which refers to the aggregated operational strategies of single business firm or that of an SBU in a diversified corporation refers to the way in which a firm competes in its chosen arenas.
Honeywell	Honeywell is a major American multinational corporation that produces electronic control systems and automation equipment. It is a major supplier of engineering services and avionics

for NASA, Boeing and the United States Department of Defense.

Commodity	Could refer to any good, but in trade a commodity is usually a raw material or primary product that enters into international trade, such as metals or basic agricultural products.
Revenue	Revenue is a U.S. business term for the amount of money that a company receives from its activities, mostly from sales of products and/or services to customers.
Business unit	The lowest level of the company which contains the set of functions that carry a product through its life span from concept through manufacture, distribution, sales and service is a business unit.
Journal	Book of original entry, in which transactions are recorded in a general ledger system, is referred to as a journal.
Variable	A variable is something measured by a number; it is used to analyze what happens to other things when the size of that number changes.
Correlation	A correlation is the measure of the extent to which two economic or statistical variables move together, normalized so that its values range from -1 to +1. It is defined as the covariance of the two variables divided by the square root of the product of their variances.
Punitive	Damages designed to punish flagrant wrongdoers and to deter them and others from engaging in similar conduct in the future are called punitive.
Mistake	In contract law a mistake is incorrect understanding by one or more parties to a contract and may be used as grounds to invalidate the agreement. Common law has identified three different types of mistake in contract: unilateral mistake, mutual mistake, and common mistake.
Target price	Target price refers to estimated price for a product or service that potential customers will
Complaint	The pleading in a civil case in which the plaintiff states his claim and requests relief is called complaint. In the common law, it is a formal legal document that sets out the basic facts and legal reasons that the filing party (the plaintiffs) believes are sufficient to support a claim against another person, persons, entity or entities (the defendants) that entitles the plaintiff(s) to a remedy (either money damages or injunctive relief).
Materials management	Materials management refers to the activity that controls the transmission of physical materials through the value chain, from procurement through production and into distribution.
Best practice	Best practice is a management idea which asserts that there is a technique, method, process, activity, incentive or reward that is more effective at delivering a particular outcome than any other technique, method, process, etc.

Industry	A group of firms that produce identical or similar products is an industry. It is also used specifically to refer to an area of economic production focused on manufacturing which involves large amounts of capital investment before any profit can be realized, also called "heavy industry".
Best practice	Best practice is a management idea which asserts that there is a technique, method, process, activity, incentive or reward that is more effective at delivering a particular outcome than any other technique, method, process, etc.
Journal	Book of original entry, in which transactions are recorded in a general ledger system, is referred to as a journal.
Tactic	A short-term immediate decision that, in its totality, leads to the achievement of strategic goals is called a tactic.
Supply	Supply is the aggregate amount of any material good that can be called into being at a certain price point; it comprises one half of the equation of supply and demand. In classical economic theory, a curve representing supply is one of the factors that produce price.
Product development	In business and engineering, new product development is the complete process of bringing a new product to market. There are two parallel aspects to this process : one involves product engineering ; the other marketing analysis. Marketers see new product development as the first stage in product life cycle management, engineers as part of Product Lifecycle Management.
Business strategy	Business strategy, which refers to the aggregated operational strategies of single business firm or that of an SBU in a diversified corporation refers to the way in which a firm competes in its chosen arenas.
Supply chain	Supply chain refers to the flow of goods, services, and information from the initial sources of materials and services to the delivery of products to consumers.
Innovation	Innovation refers to the first commercially successful introduction of a new product, the use of a new method of production, or the creation of a new form of business organization.
Productivity	Productivity refers to the total output of goods and services in a given period of time divided by work hours.
Purchasing	Purchasing refers to the function in a firm that searches for quality material resources, finds the best suppliers, and negotiates the best price for goods and services.
Management	Management characterizes the process of leading and directing all or part of an organization, often a business, through the deployment and manipulation of resources. Early twentieth-century management writer Mary Parker Follett defined management as "the art of getting things done through people."
Critical success factor	Critical Success Factor is a business term for an element which is necessary for an organization or project to achieve its mission.
Materials management	Materials management refers to the activity that controls the transmission of physical materials through the value chain, from procurement through production and into distribution.
Success factor	The term success factor refers to the characteristics necessary for high performance; knowledge, skills, abilities, behaviors.
Training and development	All attempts to improve productivity by increasing an employee's ability to perform is training and development.
Competitive advantage	A business is said to have a competitive advantage when its unique strengths, often based on cost, quality, time, and innovation, offer consumers a greater percieved value and there by differtiating it from its competitors.

New product development	New product development is the complete process of bringing a new product to market. There are two parallel aspects to this process : one involves product engineering ; the other marketing analysis.
Concurrent engineering	The simultaneous performance of product design and process design is concurrent engineering. Typically, concurrent engineering involves the formation of cross-functional teams. This allows engineers and managers of different disciplines to work together simultaneously in developing product and process designs.
Reengineering	The fundamental rethinking and redesign of business processes to achieve improvements in critical measures of performance, such as cost, quality, service, speed, and customer satisfaction is referred to as reengineering.
Technology	The body of knowledge and techniques that can be used to combine economic resources to produce goods and services is called technology.
AlliedSignal	AlliedSignal was created through a 1985 merger of Allied Chemical & Dye Corportation and Signal Oil, the company renamed to AlliedSignal on September 19, 1985. The company's involvement in aerospace stems from a previous merger between Signal Oil and the Garrett Corporation in 1968. After that merger, aviation became the company's largest division. In 1999. AlliedSignal acquired Honeywell and took its more-recognizable name.
Discount	The difference between the face value of a bond and its selling price, when a bond is sold for less than its face value it's referred to as a discount.
Commodity	Could refer to any good, but in trade a commodity is usually a raw material or primary product that enters into international trade, such as metals or basic agricultural products.
Manufacturing	Production of goods primarily by the application of labor and capital to raw materials and other intermediate inputs, in contrast to agriculture, mining, forestry, fishing, and services a manufacturing.
Raw material	Raw material refers to a good that has not been transformed by production; a primary product.
Contract	A contract is a "promise" or an "agreement" that is enforced or recognized by the law. In the civil law, a contract is considered to be part of the general law of obligations.
Total quality management	The broad set of management and control processes designed to focus an entire organization and all of its employees on providing products or services that do the best possible job of satisfying the customer is called total quality management.
Quality management	Quality management is a method for ensuring that all the activities necessary to design, develop and implement a product or service are effective and efficient with respect to the system and its performance.
Inflation	An increase in the overall price level of an economy, usually as measured by the CPI or by the implicit price deflator is called inflation.
Adjusted for inflation	Adjusted for inflation refers to correcting for price changes to yield an equivalent real rate, or real non-inflationary number. The adjustment divides nominal amounts for different years by price indices for those years -- eg the CPI or the implicit price deflator -- and multiplies by 100. This converts to real values, ie valued at the prices of the base year for the price index.
Total cost	The sum of fixed cost and variable cost is referred to as total cost.
Inventory	Tangible property held for sale in the normal course of business or used in producing goods or services for sale is an inventory.
Frequency	Frequency refers to the speed of the up and down movements of a fluctuating economic variable; that is, the number of times per unit of time that the variable completes a cycle

of up and down movement.

Service	Service refers to a "non tangible product" that is not embodied in a physical good and that typically effects some change in another product, person, or institution. Contrasts with good.
Scope	Scope of a project is the sum total of all projects products and their requirements or features.
Procurement	Procurement is the acquisition of goods or services at the best possible total cost of ownership, in the right quantity, at the right time, in the right place for the direct benefit or use of the governments, corporations, or individuals generally via, but not limited to a contract.
Forming	The first stage of team development, where the team is formed and the objectives for the team are set is referred to as forming.
Partnership	In the common law, a partnership is a type of business entity in which partners share with each other the profits or losses of the business undertaking in which they have all invested.
Business unit	The lowest level of the company which contains the set of functions that carry a product through its life span from concept through manufacture, distribution, sales and service is a business unit.
Total supply	Total supply refers to the supply schedule or the supply curve of all sellers of a good or service.
Supply chain management	Supply chain management deals with the planning and execution issues involved in managing a supply chain. Supply chain management spans all movement and storage of raw materials, work-in-process inventory, and finished goods from point-of-origin to point-of-consumption.
Operational excellence	Operational excellence is a goal of conducting business in a manner that improves quality, obtains higher yields, faster throughput, and less waste.
Lean manufacturing	The production of goods using less of everything compared to mass production is called lean manufacturing.
Human resources	Human resources refers to the individuals within the firm, and to the portion of the firm's organization that deals with hiring, firing, training, and other personnel issues.
Continuous improvement	The constant effort to eliminate waste, reduce response time, simplify the design of both products and processes, and improve quality and customer service is referred to as continuous improvement.
Honeywell	Honeywell is a major American multinational corporation that produces electronic control systems and automation equipment. It is a major supplier of engineering services and avionics for NASA, Boeing and the United States Department of Defense.
Enterprise	Enterprise refers to another name for a business organization. Other similar terms are business firm, sometimes simply business, sometimes simply firm, as well as company, and entity.
Corporate Strategy	Corporate strategy is concerned with the firm's choice of business, markets and activities and thus it defines the overall scope and direction of the business.
Action plan	Action plan refers to a written document that includes the steps the trainee and manager will take to ensure that training transfers to the job.
Downsizing	The process of eliminating managerial and non-managerial positions are called downsizing.
Operation	A standardized method or technique that is performed repetitively, often on different materials resulting in different finished goods is called an operation.

Economic growth	Economic growth refers to the increase over time in the capacity of an economy to produce goods and services and to improve the well-being of its citizens.
Bankruptcy	Bankruptcy is a legally declared inability or impairment of ability of an individual or organization to pay their creditors.
Market	A market is, as defined in economics, a social arrangement that allows buyers and sellers to discover information and carry out a voluntary exchange of goods or services.
Policy	Similar to a script in that a policy can be a less than completely rational decision-making method. Involves the use of a pre-existing set of decision steps for any problem that presents itself.
Customer satisfaction	Customer satisfaction is a business term which is used to capture the idea of measuring how satisfied an enterprise's customers are with the organization's efforts in a marketplace.
Stakeholder	A stakeholder is an individual or group with a vested interest in or expectation for organizational performance. Usually stakeholders can either have an effect on or are affected by an organization.
Competitor	Other organizations in the same industry or type of business that provide a good or service to the same set of customers is referred to as a competitor.
Revenue	Revenue is a U.S. business term for the amount of money that a company receives from its activities, mostly from sales of products and/or services to customers.
Profit	Profit refers to the return to the resource entrepreneurial ability; total revenue minus total cost.
Interest	In finance and economics, interest is the price paid by a borrower for the use of a lender's money. In other words, interest is the amount of paid to "rent" money for a period of time.
Margin	A deposit by a buyer in stocks with a seller or a stockbroker, as security to cover fluctuations in the market in reference to stocks that the buyer has purchased but for which he has not paid is a margin. Commodities are also traded on margin.
Global competition	Global competition exists when competitive conditions across national markets are linked strongly enough to form a true international market and when leading competitors compete head to head in many different countries.
Profit margin	Profit margin is a measure of profitability. It is calculated using a formula and written as a percentage or a number. Profit margin = Net income before tax and interest / Revenue.
Shareholder	A shareholder is an individual or company (including a corporation) that legally owns one or more shares of stock in a joined stock company.
Process reengineering	Process reengineering refers to the total rethinking and redesign of organizational process to improve performance and innovation; involves analyzing, streamlining, and reconfiguring actions and tasks to achieve work goals.
Motorola	The Six Sigma quality system was developed at Motorola even though it became most well known because of its use by General Electric. It was created by engineer Bill Smith, under the direction of Bob Galvin (son of founder Paul Galvin) when he was running the company.
Ford	Ford is an American company that manufactures and sells automobiles worldwide. Ford introduced methods for large-scale manufacturing of cars, and large-scale management of an industrial workforce, especially elaborately engineered manufacturing sequences typified by the moving assembly lines.
Toyota	Toyota is a Japanese multinational corporation that manufactures automobiles, trucks and buses. Toyota is the world's second largest automaker by sales. Toyota also provides

Go to **Cram101.com** for the Practice Tests for this Chapter.

	financial services through its subsidiary, Toyota Financial Services, and participates in other lines of business.
Option	A contract that gives the purchaser the option to buy or sell the underlying financial instrument at a specified price, called the exercise price or strike price, within a specific period of time.
Asset	An item of property, such as land, capital, money, a share in ownership, or a claim on others for future payment, such as a bond or a bank deposit is an asset.
Return on Assets	The Return on Assets percentage shows how profitable a company's assets are in generating revenue.
Firm	An organization that employs resources to produce a good or service for profit and owns and operates one or more plants is referred to as a firm.
Labor	People's physical and mental talents and efforts that are used to help produce goods and services are called labor.
Internal customer	An individuals or unit within the firm that receives services from other entities within the organization is an internal customer.
Categorizing	The act of placing strengths and weaknesses into categories in generic internal assessment is called categorizing.
Strategic planning	The process of determining the major goals of the organization and the policies and strategies for obtaining and using resources to achieve those goals is called strategic planning.
Strategic plan	The formal document that presents the ways and means by which a strategic goal will be achieved is a strategic plan. A long-term flexible plan that does not regulate activities but rather outlines the means to achieve certain results, and provides the means to alter the course of action should the desired ends change.
Contribution	In business organization law, the cash or property contributed to a business by its owners is referred to as contribution.
Alignment	Term that refers to optimal coordination among disparate departments and divisions within a firm is referred to as alignment.
Proactive	To be proactive is to act before a situation becomes a source of confrontation or crisis. It is the opposite of "retroactive," which refers to actions taken after an event.
Marketing	Promoting and selling products or services to customers, or prospective customers, is referred to as marketing.
Specificity	The property that a policy measure applies to one or a group of enterprises or industries, as opposed to all industries, is called specificity.
Warranty	An obligation of a company to replace defective goods or correct any deficiencies in performance or quality of a product is called a warranty.
Functional strategy	A functional strategy is a strategy implemented by each functional area of the organization to support the organization's business strategy.
Complement	A good that is used in conjunction with another good is a complement. For example, cameras and film would complement eachother.
Trend	Trend refers to the long-term movement of an economic variable, such as its average rate of increase or decrease over enough years to encompass several business cycles.
Consideration	Consideration in contract law, a basic requirement for an enforceable agreement under

traditional contract principles, defined in this text as legal value, bargained for and given in exchange for an act or promise. In corporation law, cash or property contributed to a corporation in exchange for shares, or a promise to contribute such cash or property.

Mission statement	Mission statement refers to an outline of the fundamental purposes of an organization.
Distribution	Distribution in economics, the manner in which total output and income is distributed among individuals or factors.
Premium	Premium refers to the fee charged by an insurance company for an insurance policy. The rate of losses must be relatively predictable: In order to set the premium (prices) insurers must be able to estimate them accurately.
Information technology	Information technology refers to technology that helps companies change business by allowing them to use new methods.
Senior management	Senior management is generally a team of individuals at the highest level of organizational management who have the day-to-day responsibilities of managing a corporation.
Teamwork	That which occurs when group members work together in ways that utilize their skills well to accomplish a purpose is called teamwork.
Fiscal year	A fiscal year is a 12-month period used for calculating annual ("yearly") financial reports in businesses and other organizations. In many jurisdictions, regulatory laws regarding accounting require such reports once per twelve months, but do not require that the twelve months constitute a calendar year (i.e. January to December).
Personnel	A collective term for all of the employees of an organization. Personnel is also commonly used to refer to the personnel management function or the organizational unit responsible for administering personnel programs.
Portfolio	In finance, a portfolio is a collection of investments held by an institution or a private individual. Holding but not always a portfolio is part of an investment and risk-limiting strategy called diversification. By owning several assets, certain types of risk (in particular specific risk) can be reduced.
Gap	In December of 1995, Gap became the first major North American retailer to accept independent monitoring of the working conditions in a contract factory producing its garments. Gap is the largest specialty retailer in the United States.
Gap analysis	A measurement of the sensitivity of bank profits to changes in interest rates, calculated by subtracting the amount of rate-sensitive liabilities from the amount of rate-sensitive assets is referred to as gap analysis.
Acquisition	A company's purchase of the property and obligations of another company is an acquisition.
Switching costs	Switching costs is a term used in microeconomics, strategic management, and marketing to describe any impediment to a customer's changing of suppliers. In many markets, consumers are forced to incur costs when switching from one supplier to another. These costs are called switching costs and can come in many different shapes.
Users	Users refer to people in the organization who actually use the product or service purchased by the buying center.
Possession	Possession refers to respecting real property, exclusive dominion and control such as owners of like property usually exercise over it. Manual control of personal property either as owner or as one having a qualified right in it.
Market research	Market research is the process of systematic gathering, recording and analyzing of data about customers, competitors and the market. Market research can help create a business plan,

Go to **Cram101.com** for the Practice Tests for this Chapter.

launch a new product or service, fine tune existing products and services, expand into new markets etc. It can be used to determine which portion of the population will purchase the product/service, based on variables like age, gender, location and income level. It can be found out what market characteristics your target market has.

Bid	A bid price is a price offered by a buyer when he/she buys a good. In the context of stock trading on a stock exchange, the bid price is the highest price a buyer of a stock is willing to pay for a share of that given stock.
Leverage	Leverage is using given resources in such a way that the potential positive or negative outcome is magnified. In finance, this generally refers to borrowing.
Yield	The interest rate that equates a future value or an annuity to a given present value is a yield.
Average fixed Cost	Average fixed cost refers to total fixed cost divided by the number of units of output; a per-unit measure of fixed costs.
Fixed cost	The cost that a firm bears if it does not produce at all and that is independent of its output. The presence of a fixed cost tends to imply increasing returns to scale. Contrasts with variable cost.
Variable	A variable is something measured by a number; it is used to analyze what happens to other things when the size of that number changes.
Variable cost	The portion of a firm or industry's cost that changes with output, in contrast to fixed cost is referred to as variable cost.
Consolidation	The combination of two or more firms, generally of equal size and market power, to form an entirely new entity is a consolidation.
Performance improvement	Performance improvement is the concept of measuring the output of a particular process or procedure then modifying the process or procedure in order to increase the output, increase efficiency, or increase the effectiveness of the process or procedure.
Cost driver	Cost driver refers to a factor related to an activity that changes the volume or characteristics of that activity, and in doing so changes its costs. An activity can have more than one cost driver.
Customer service	The ability of logistics management to satisfy users in terms of time, dependability, communication, and convenience is called the customer service.
Market leader	The market leader is dominant in its industry. It has substantial market share and often extensive distribution arrangements with retailers. It typically is the industry leader in developing innovative new business models and new products (although not always).
Strategy execution	The managerial exercise of supervizing the ongoing pursuit of strategy, implementing it, improving the efficiency with which it is executed, and showing measurable progress in achieving the targeted results is strategy execution.
Negotiation	Negotiation is the process whereby interested parties resolve disputes, agree upon courses of action, bargain for individual or collective advantage, and/or attempt to craft outcomes which serve their mutual interests.
Performance measurement	The process by which someone evaluates an employee's work behaviors by measurement and comparison with previously established standards, documents the results, and communicates the results to the employee is called performance measurement.
Audit	An examination of the financial reports to ensure that they represent what they claim and conform with generally accepted accounting principles is referred to as audit.

Design of experiments	A practical application of a statistical tool that enables low cost experimental methods to optimise the performance of products and processes during development is the design of experiments.
Statistical process control	Statistical process control is a method for achieving quality control in manufacturing processes. It is a set of methods using statistical tools such as mean, variance and others, to detect whether the process observed is under control.
Quality audit	Quality audit means a systematic, independent examination of a quality system. A quality audit is typically performed at defined intervals and ensures that the institution has clearly-defined internal quality monitoring procedures linked to effective action. The checking determines if the quality system complies with applicable regulations or standards The process involves assessing the standard operating procedures (SOP's) for compliance to the regulations, and also assessing the actual process and results against what is stated in the SOP.
Quality control	The measurement of products and services against set standards is referred to as quality control.
Finished goods	Completed products awaiting sale are called finished goods. An item considered a finished good in a supplying plant might be considered a component or raw material in a receiving plant.
Gain	In finance, gain is a profit or an increase in value of an investment such as a stock or bond. Gain is calculated by fair market value or the proceeds from the sale of the investment minus the sum of the purchase price and all costs associated with it.
Countertrade	Countertrade is exchanging goods or services that are paid for, in whole or part, with other goods or services.
Domestic	From or in one's own country. A domestic producer is one that produces inside the home country. A domestic price is the price inside the home country. Opposite of 'foreign' or 'world.'.
Buyer	A buyer refers to a role in the buying center with formal authority and responsibility to select the supplier and negotiate the terms of the contract.
Logistics	Those activities that focus on getting the right amount of the right products to the right place at the right time at the lowest possible cost is referred to as logistics.
Relevant cost	A relevant cost refers to expected future costs that differ among alternative courses of action being considered. A cost that will be affected by taking a particular decision.
Toshiba	Toshiba is a Japanese high technology electrical and electronics manufacturing firm, headquartered in Tokyo, Japan. It is the 7th largest integrated manufacturer of electric and electronic equipment in the world.
Bottom line	The bottom line is net income on the last line of a income statement.
Preference	The act of a debtor in paying or securing one or more of his creditors in a manner more favorable to them than to other creditors or to the exclusion of such other creditors is a preference. In the absence of statute, a preference is perfectly good, but to be legal it must be bona fide, and not a mere subterfuge of the debtor to secure a future benefit to himself or to prevent the application of his property to his debts.
Base year	The year used as the basis for comparison by a price index such as the CPI. The index for any year is the average of prices for that year compared to the base year; e.g., 110 means that prices are 10% higher than in the base year.
Property	Assets defined in the broadest legal sense. Property includes the unrealized receivables of a

Go to **Cram101.com** for the Practice Tests for this Chapter.

cash basis taxpayer, but not services rendered.

Intellectual property	In law, intellectual property is an umbrella term for various legal entitlements which attach to certain types of information, ideas, or other intangibles in their expressed form. The holder of this legal entitlement is generally entitled to exercise various exclusive rights in relation to its subject matter.
Production	The creation of finished goods and services using the factors of production: land, labor, capital, entrepreneurship, and knowledge.
Product development teams	Combinations of work teams and problem-solving teams that create new designs for products or services that will satisfy customer needs are product development teams.
Simultaneous engineering	A way of simultaneously designing products, and the processes for manufacturing those products, through the use of cross functional teams to assure manufacturability and to reduce cycle time is called simultaneous engineering.
Variance	Variance refers to a measure of how much an economic or statistical variable varies across values or observations. Its calculation is the same as that of the covariance, being the covariance of the variable with itself.
Cost variance	The difference between the actual and budgeted cost of work performed is called cost variance.
Complaint	The pleading in a civil case in which the plaintiff states his claim and requests relief is called complaint. In the common law, it is a formal legal document that sets out the basic facts and legal reasons that the filing party (the plaintiffs) believes are sufficient to support a claim against another person, persons, entity or entities (the defendants) that entitles the plaintiff(s) to a remedy (either money damages or injunctive relief).
Purchase order	A form on which items or services needed by a business firm are specified and then communicated to the vendor is a purchase order.
Information system	An information system is a system whether automated or manual, that comprises people, machines, and/or methods organized to collect, process, transmit, and disseminate data that represent user information.
Single sourcing	Single sourcing is the origination of any design, set of concepts, or any article real or insubstantial from a single, well defined source, either a person or an organization.
Integration	Economic integration refers to reducing barriers among countries to transactions and to movements of goods, capital, and labor, including harmonization of laws, regulations, and standards. Integrated markets theoretically function as a unified market.
Competitive Strategy	An outline of how a business intends to compete with other firms in the same industry is called competitive strategy.
Channel	Channel, in communications (sometimes called communications channel), refers to the medium used to convey information from a sender (or transmitter) to a receiver.
Accounting	A system that collects and processes financial information about an organization and reports that information to decision makers is referred to as accounting.
Organizational structure	Organizational structure is the way in which the interrelated groups of an organization are constructed. From a managerial point of view the main concerns are ensuring effective communication and coordination.
Customer focus	Customer focus acknowledges that the more a company understands and meets the real needs of its consumers, the more likely it is to have happy customers who come back for more, and tell their friends.

Household	An economic unit that provides the economy with resources and uses the income received to purchase goods and services that satisfy economic wants is called household.
Average product	The average product of a factor (i.e. labor, capital, etc.) in a firm or industry is its output divided by the amount of the factor employed. The total quantity of output divided the total quantity of some input.
Competitiveness	Competitiveness usually refers to characteristics that permit a firm to compete effectively with other firms due to low cost or superior technology, perhaps internationally.
Insourcing	Insourcing refers to process of producing goods or providing services within the organization rather than purchasing those same goods or services from outside vendors.
Core	A core is the set of feasible allocations in an economy that cannot be improved upon by subset of the set of the economy's consumers (a coalition). In construction, when the force in an element is within a certain center section, the core, the element will only be under compression.
Outsourcing	Outsourcing refers to a production activity that was previously done inside a firm or plant that is now conducted outside that firm or plant.
Value chain	The sequence of business functions in which usefulness is added to the products or services of a company is a value chain.
Exxon	Exxon formally replaced the Esso, Enco, and Humble brands on January 1, 1973, in the USA. The name Esso, pronounced S-O, attracted protests from other Standard Oil spinoffs because of its similarity to the name of the parent company, Standard Oil.
Sole source	A sole source is a supplier that is the only source for a contract item.
Corporation	A legal entity chartered by a state or the Federal government that is distinct and separate from the individuals who own it is a corporation. This separation gives the corporation unique powers which other legal entities lack.
Warehouse	Warehouse refers to a location, often decentralized, that a firm uses to store, consolidate, age, or mix stock; house product-recall programs; or ease tax burdens.
Stock	In financial terminology, stock is the capital raized by a corporation, through the issuance and sale of shares.
Trust	An arrangement in which shareholders of independent firms agree to give up their stock in exchange for trust certificates that entitle them to a share of the trust's common profits.
Strategic management	A philosophy of management that links strategic planning with dayto-day decision making. Strategic management seeks a fit between an organization's external and internal environments.
Strategy implementation	Strategy implementation refers to the process of devising structures and allocating resources to enact the strategy a company has chosen.
Logistics Management	Logistics management refers to the practice of organizing the cost-effective flow of raw materials, in-process inventory, finished goods, and related information from point of origin to point of consumption to satisfy customer requirements.

Supply	Supply is the aggregate amount of any material good that can be called into being at a certain price point; it comprises one half of the equation of supply and demand. In classical economic theory, a curve representing supply is one of the factors that produce price.
Customer focus	Customer focus acknowledges that the more a company understands and meets the real needs of its consumers, the more likely it is to have happy customers who come back for more, and tell their friends.
Supply chain	Supply chain refers to the flow of goods, services, and information from the initial sources of materials and services to the delivery of products to consumers.
Purchasing	Purchasing refers to the function in a firm that searches for quality material resources, finds the best suppliers, and negotiates the best price for goods and services.
Competitor	Other organizations in the same industry or type of business that provide a good or service to the same set of customers is referred to as a competitor.
Users	Users refer to people in the organization who actually use the product or service purchased by the buying center.
Core	A core is the set of feasible allocations in an economy that cannot be improved upon by subset of the set of the economy's consumers (a coalition). In construction, when the force in an element is within a certain center section, the core, the element will only be under compression.
Production	The creation of finished goods and services using the factors of production: land, labor, capital, entrepreneurship, and knowledge.
Distribution	Distribution in economics, the manner in which total output and income is distributed among individuals or factors.
Outsourcing	Outsourcing refers to a production activity that was previously done inside a firm or plant that is now conducted outside that firm or plant.
Cost of goods sold	In accounting, the cost of goods sold describes the direct expenses incurred in producing a particular good for sale, including the actual cost of materials that comprise the good, and direct labor expense in putting the good in salable condition.
Logistics	Those activities that focus on getting the right amount of the right products to the right place at the right time at the lowest possible cost is referred to as logistics.
Net profit	Net profit is an accounting term which is commonly used in business. It is equal to the gross revenue for a given time period minus associated expenses.
Profit	Profit refers to the return to the resource entrepreneurial ability; total revenue minus total cost.
Restructuring	Restructuring is the corporate management term for the act of partially dismantling and reorganizing a company for the purpose of making it more efficient and therefore more profitable.
Insourcing	Insourcing refers to process of producing goods or providing services within the organization rather than purchasing those same goods or services from outside vendors.
Service	Service refers to a "non tangible product" that is not embodied in a physical good and that typically effects some change in another product, person, or institution. Contrasts with good.
Trend	Trend refers to the long-term movement of an economic variable, such as its average rate of increase or decrease over enough years to encompass several business cycles.
Ford	Ford is an American company that manufactures and sells automobiles worldwide. Ford

introduced methods for large-scale manufacturing of cars, and large-scale management of an industrial workforce, especially elaborately engineered manufacturing sequences typified by the moving assembly lines.

Acquisition	A company's purchase of the property and obligations of another company is an acquisition.
Henry Ford	Henry Ford was the founder of the Ford Motor Company. His introduction of the Model T automobile revolutionized transportation and American industry.
Vertical integration	Vertical integration refers to production of different stages of processing of a product within the same firm.
Integration	Economic integration refers to reducing barriers among countries to transactions and to movements of goods, capital, and labor, including harmonization of laws, regulations, and standards. Integrated markets theoretically function as a unified market.
Industry	A group of firms that produce identical or similar products is an industry. It is also used specifically to refer to an area of economic production focused on manufacturing which involves large amounts of capital investment before any profit can be realized, also called "heavy industry".
Gain	In finance, gain is a profit or an increase in value of an investment such as a stock or bond. Gain is calculated by fair market value or the proceeds from the sale of the investment minus the sum of the purchase price and all costs associated with it.
Technology	The body of knowledge and techniques that can be used to combine economic resources to produce goods and services is called technology.
Market	A market is, as defined in economics, a social arrangement that allows buyers and sellers to discover information and carry out a voluntary exchange of goods or services.
Analyst	Analyst refers to a person or tool with a primary function of information analysis, generally with a more limited, practical and short term set of goals than a researcher.
Value added	The value of output minus the value of all intermediate inputs, representing therefore the contribution of, and payments to, primary factors of production a value added.
Channel	Channel, in communications (sometimes called communications channel), refers to the medium used to convey information from a sender (or transmitter) to a receiver.
Inventory	Tangible property held for sale in the normal course of business or used in producing goods or services for sale is an inventory.
Buyer	A buyer refers to a role in the buying center with formal authority and responsibility to select the supplier and negotiate the terms of the contract.
Expense	In accounting, an expense represents an event in which an asset is used up or a liability is incurred. In terms of the accounting equation, expenses reduce owners' equity.
Procurement	Procurement is the acquisition of goods or services at the best possible total cost of ownership, in the right quantity, at the right time, in the right place for the direct benefit or use of the governments, corporations, or individuals generally via, but not limited to a contract.
Wage	The payment for the service of a unit of labor, per unit time. In trade theory, it is the only payment to labor, usually unskilled labor. In empirical work, wage data may exclude other compenzation, which must be added to get the total cost of employment.
Developing country	Developing country refers to a country whose per capita income is low by world standards. Same as LDC. As usually used, it does not necessarily connote that the country's income is rising.

World Trade Organization	The World Trade Organization is an international, multilateral organization, which sets the rules for the global trading system and resolves disputes between its member states, all of whom are signatories to its approximately 30 agreements.
Free trade	Free trade refers to a situation in which there are no artificial barriers to trade, such as tariffs and quotas. Usually used, often only implicitly, with frictionless trade, so that it implies that there are no barriers to trade of any kind.
Labor law	Labor law is the body of laws, administrative rulings, and precedents which addresses the legal rights of, and restrictions on, workers and their organizations.
Labor	People's physical and mental talents and efforts that are used to help produce goods and services are called labor.
Child labor	Originally, the employment of children in a manner detrimental to their health and social development. Now that the law contains strong child labor prohibitions, the term refers to the employment of children below the legal age limit.
Variable	A variable is something measured by a number; it is used to analyze what happens to other things when the size of that number changes.
Firm	An organization that employs resources to produce a good or service for profit and owns and operates one or more plants is referred to as a firm.
Continuous improvement	The constant effort to eliminate waste, reduce response time, simplify the design of both products and processes, and improve quality and customer service is referred to as continuous improvement.
Competitiveness	Competitiveness usually refers to characteristics that permit a firm to compete effectively with other firms due to low cost or superior technology, perhaps internationally.
Total cost	The sum of fixed cost and variable cost is referred to as total cost.
Investment	Investment refers to spending for the production and accumulation of capital and additions to inventories. In a financial sense, buying an asset with the expectation of making a return.
Operation	A standardized method or technique that is performed repetitively, often on different materials resulting in different finished goods is called an operation.
Marketing	Promoting and selling products or services to customers, or prospective customers, is referred to as marketing.
Utility	Utility refers to the want-satisfying power of a good or service; the satisfaction or pleasure a consumer obtains from the consumption of a good or service.
Customer satisfaction	Customer satisfaction is a business term which is used to capture the idea of measuring how satisfied an enterprise's customers are with the organization's efforts in a marketplace.
Outplacement	The process of placing employees in other positions or training once they have been separated from a job is outplacement. It helps people regain employment elsewhere.
Accounting	A system that collects and processes financial information about an organization and reports that information to decision makers is referred to as accounting.
Commodity	Could refer to any good, but in trade a commodity is usually a raw material or primary product that enters into international trade, such as metals or basic agricultural products.
Consideration	Consideration in contract law, a basic requirement for an enforceable agreement under traditional contract principles, defined in this text as legal value, bargained for and given in exchange for an act or promise. In corporation law, cash or property contributed to a corporation in exchange for shares, or a promise to contribute such cash or property.

Core competency	A company's core competency are things that a firm can (alsosns) do well and that meet the following three conditions. 1. It provides customer benefits, 2. It is hard for competitors to imitate, and 3. it can be leveraged widely to many products and market. A core competency can take various forms, including technical/subject matter knowhow, a reliable process, and/or close relationships with customers and suppliers. It may also include product development or culture such as employee dedication. Modern business theories suggest that most activities that are not part of a company's core competency should be outsourced.
Business strategy	Business strategy, which refers to the aggregated operational strategies of single business firm or that of an SBU in a diversified corporation refers to the way in which a firm competes in its chosen arenas.
Jack Welch	In 1986, GE acquired NBC. During the 90s, Jack Welch helped to modernize GE by emphasizing a shift from manufacturing to services. He also made hundreds of acquisitions and made a push to dominate markets abroad. Welch adopted the Six Sigma quality program in late 1995.
Policy	Similar to a script in that a policy can be a less than completely rational decision-making method. Involves the use of a pre-existing set of decision steps for any problem that presents itself.
General Electric	In 1876, Thomas Alva Edison opened a new laboratory in Menlo Park, New Jersey. Out of the laboratory was to come perhaps the most famous invention of all—a successful development of the incandescent electric lamp. By 1890, Edison had organized his various businesses into the Edison General Electric Company.
Business unit	The lowest level of the company which contains the set of functions that carry a product through its life span from concept through manufacture, distribution, sales and service is a business unit.
Innovation	Innovation refers to the first commercially successful introduction of a new product, the use of a new method of production, or the creation of a new form of business organization.
Economics	The social science dealing with the use of scarce resources to obtain the maximum satisfaction of society's virtually unlimited economic wants is an economics.
Asset	An item of property, such as land, capital, money, a share in ownership, or a claim on others for future payment, such as a bond or a bank deposit is an asset.
Capital	Capital generally refers to financial wealth, especially that used to start or maintain a business. In classical economics, capital is one of four factors of production, the others being land and labor and entrepreneurship.
Intellectual capital	Intellectual capital makes an organization worth more than its balance sheet value. For many years, intellectual capital and goodwill meant the same thing. Today, intellectual capital management is far broader. It seeks to explain how knowledge, collaboration, and process-engagement create decisions and actions that lead to cost allocations, productivity, and finally financial performance.
Physical asset	A physical asset is an item of economic value that has a tangible or material existence. A physical asset usually refers to cash, equipment, inventory and properties owned by a business.
Economic efficiency	Economic efficiency refers to the use of the minimum necessary resources to obtain the socially optimal amounts of goods and services; entails both productive efficiency and allocative efficiency.
Technology life cycle	Most new technologies follow a similar technology life cycle. This is similar to a product life cycle, but applies to an entire technology, or a generation of a technology. Technology adoption is the most common phenomenon driving the evolution of industries along the industry

Go to **Cram101.com** for the Practice Tests for this Chapter.

	lifecycle.
Payback	A value that indicates the time period required to recoup an initial investment is a payback. The payback does not include the time-value-of-money concept.
Payback period	The amount of time required for a project's after-tax cash inflows to accumulate to an amount that covers the initial investment is a payback period.
Alignment	Term that refers to optimal coordination among disparate departments and divisions within a firm is referred to as alignment.
Maturity	Maturity refers to the final payment date of a loan or other financial instrument, after which point no further interest or principal need be paid.
Assessment	Collecting information and providing feedback to employees about their behavior, communication style, or skills is an assessment.
Functional strategy	A functional strategy is a strategy implemented by each functional area of the organization to support the organization's business strategy.
Harvard Business Review	Harvard Business Review is a research-based magazine written for business practitioners, it claims a high ranking business readership and enjoys the reverence of academics, executives, and management consultants. It has been the frequent publishing home for well known scholars and management thinkers.
Polaroid	The Polaroid Corporation was founded in 1937 by Edwin H. Land. It is most famous for its instant film cameras, which reached the market in 1948, and continue to be the company's flagship product line.
Leverage	Leverage is using given resources in such a way that the potential positive or negative outcome is magnified. In finance, this generally refers to borrowing.
Competitive advantage	A business is said to have a competitive advantage when its unique strengths, often based on cost, quality, time, and innovation, offer consumers a greater percieved value and there by diffentiating it from its competitors.
Licensing	Licensing is a form of strategic alliance which involves the sale of a right to use certain proprietary knowledge (so called intellectual property) in a defined way.
Capital budgeting	Capital budgeting is the planning process used to determine a firm's long term investments such as new machinery, replacement machinery, new plants, new products, and research and development projects.
Invoice	The itemized bill for a transaction, stating the nature of the transaction and its cost. In international trade, the invoice price is often the preferred basis for levying an ad valorem tariff.
Cost driver	Cost driver refers to a factor related to an activity that changes the volume or characteristics of that activity, and in doing so changes its costs. An activity can have more than one cost driver.
Unit cost	Unit cost refers to cost computed by dividing some amount of total costs by the related number of units. Also called average cost.
Total variable Cost	The total of all costs that vary with output in the short run is called total variable cost.
Variable cost	The portion of a firm or industry's cost that changes with output, in contrast to fixed cost is referred to as variable cost.
Direct labor	The earnings of employees who work directly on the products being manufactured are direct labor.

Overhead cost	An expenses of operating a business over and above the direct costs of producing a product is an overhead cost. They can include utilities (eg, electricity, telephone), advertizing and marketing, and any other costs not billed directly to the client or included in the price of the product.
Direct cost	A direct cost is a cost that can be identified specifically with a particular sponsored project, an instructional activity, or any other institutional activity, or that can be directly assigned to such activities relatively easily with a high degree of accuracy.
Property	Assets defined in the broadest legal sense. Property includes the unrealized receivables of a cash basis taxpayer, but not services rendered.
Research and development	The use of resources for the deliberate discovery of new information and ways of doing things, together with the application of that information in inventing new products or processes is referred to as research and development.
Advertising	Advertising refers to paid, nonpersonal communication through various media by organizations and individuals who are in some way identified in the advertising message.
Fixed cost	The cost that a firm bears if it does not produce at all and that is independent of its output. The presence of a fixed cost tends to imply increasing returns to scale. Contrasts with variable cost.
Contract	A contract is a "promise" or an "agreement" that is enforced or recognized by the law. In the civil law, a contract is considered to be part of the general law of obligations.
Staffing	Staffing refers to a management function that includes hiring, motivating, and retaining the best people available to accomplish the company's objectives.
Management	Management characterizes the process of leading and directing all or part of an organization, often a business, through the deployment and manipulation of resources. Early twentieth-century management writer Mary Parker Follett defined management as "the art of getting things done through people."
Vendor	A person who sells property to a vendee is a vendor. The words vendor and vendee are more commonly applied to the seller and purchaser of real estate, and the words seller and buyer are more commonly applied to the seller and purchaser of personal property.
Browser	A program that allows a user to connect to the World Wide Web by simply typing in a URL is a browser.
Managing director	Managing director is the term used for the chief executive of many limited companies in the United Kingdom, Commonwealth and some other English speaking countries. The title reflects their role as both a member of the Board of Directors but also as the senior manager.
Capital expenditures	Major investments in long-term assets such as land, buildings, equipment, or research and development are referred to as capital expenditures.
Capital expenditure	A substantial expenditure that is used by a company to acquire or upgrade physical assets such as equipment, property, industrial buildings, including those which improve the quality and life of an asset is referred to as a capital expenditure.
Product life cycle	Product life cycle refers to a series of phases in a product's sales and cash flows over time; these phases, in order of occurrence, are introductory, growth, maturity, and decline.
Depreciation	Depreciation is an accounting and finance term for the method of attributing the cost of an asset across the useful life of the asset. Depreciation is a reduction in the value of a currency in floating exchange rate.
Useful life	The length of service of a productive facility or piece of equipment is its useful life. The period of time during which an asset will have economic value and be usable.

Go to **Cram101.com** for the Practice Tests for this Chapter.

Transfer price	Transfer price refers to the price one subunit charges for a product or service supplied to another subunit of the same organization.
Evaluation	The consumer's appraisal of the product or brand on important attributes is called evaluation.
Bid	A bid price is a price offered by a buyer when he/she buys a good. In the context of stock trading on a stock exchange, the bid price is the highest price a buyer of a stock is willing to pay for a share of that given stock.
Purchase order	A form on which items or services needed by a business firm are specified and then communicated to the vendor is a purchase order.
Fringe benefits	The rewards other than wages that employees receive from their employers and that include pensions, medical and dental insurance, paid vacations, and sick leaves are referred to as fringe benefits.
Fringe benefit	Benefits such as sick-leave pay, vacation pay, pension plans, and health plans that represent additional compenzation to employees beyond base wages is a fringe benefit.
Comptroller	A comptroller is an official who supervises expenditures. Comptrollers include both royal-household officials and public comptrollers who audit government accounts and sometimes certify expenditures.
Relevant cost	A relevant cost refers to expected future costs that differ among alternative courses of action being considered. A cost that will be affected by taking a particular decision.
Proprietary	Proprietary indicates that a party, or proprietor, exercises private ownership, control or use over an item of property, usually to the exclusion of other parties. Where a party, holds or claims proprietary interests in relation to certain types of property (eg. a creative literary work, or software), that property may also be the subject of intellectual property law (eg. copyright or patents).
Factors of production	Economic resources: land, capital, labor, and entrepreneurial ability are called factors of production.
Scope	Scope of a project is the sum total of all projects products and their requirements or features.
Economy	The income, expenditures, and resources that affect the cost of running a business and household are called an economy.
Economies of scale	In economics, returns to scale and economies of scale are related terms that describe what happens as the scale of production increases. They are different terms and not to be used interchangeably.
Motorola	The Six Sigma quality system was developed at Motorola even though it became most well known because of its use by General Electric. It was created by engineer Bill Smith, under the direction of Bob Galvin (son of founder Paul Galvin) when he was running the company.
Intel	Intel Corporation, founded in 1968 and based in Santa Clara, California, USA, is the world's largest semiconductor company. Intel is best known for its PC microprocessors, where it maintains roughly 80% market share.
Average cost	Average cost is equal to total cost divided by the number of goods produced (Quantity-Q). It is also equal to the sum of average variable costs (total variable costs divided by Q) plus average fixed costs (total fixed costs divided by Q).
Matching	Matching refers to an accounting concept that establishes when expenses are recognized. Expenses are matched with the revenues they helped to generate and are recognized when those revenues are recognized.

Return on investment	Return on investment refers to the return a businessperson gets on the money he and other owners invest in the firm; for example, a business that earned $100 on a $1,000 investment would have a ROI of 10 percent: 100 divided by 1000.
Revenue	Revenue is a U.S. business term for the amount of money that a company receives from its activities, mostly from sales of products and/or services to customers.
Dell Computer	Dell Computer, formerly PC's Limited, was founded on the principle that by selling personal computer systems directly to customers, PC's Limited could best understand their needs and provide the most effective computing solutions to meet those needs.
Fixed asset	Fixed asset, also known as property, plant, and equipment (PP&E), is a term used in accountancy for assets and property which cannot easily be converted into cash. This can be compared with current assets such as cash or bank accounts, which are described as liquid assets. In most cases, only tangible assets are referred to as fixed.
Management team	A management team is directly responsible for managing the day-to-day operations (and profitability) of a company.
Personnel	A collective term for all of the employees of an organization. Personnel is also commonly used to refer to the personnel management function or the organizational unit responsible for administering personnel programs.
Apple Computer	Apple Computer has been a major player in the evolution of personal computing since its founding in 1976. The Apple II microcomputer, introduced in 1977, was a hit with home users.
Corporation	A legal entity chartered by a state or the Federal government that is distinct and separate from the individuals who own it is a corporation. This separation gives the corporation unique powers which other legal entities lack.
Balance	In banking and accountancy, the outstanding balance is the amount of money owned, (or due), that remains in a deposit account (or a loan account) at a given date, after all past remittances, payments and withdrawal have been accounted for. It can be positive (then, in the balance sheet of a firm, it is an asset) or negative (a liability).
Cisco Systems	While Cisco Systems was not the first company to develop and sell a router (a device that forwards computer traffic from one network to another), it did create the first commercially successful multi-protocol router to allow previously incompatible computers to communicate using different network protocols.
Negotiation	Negotiation is the process whereby interested parties resolve disputes, agree upon courses of action, bargain for individual or collective advantage, and/or attempt to craft outcomes which serve their mutual interests.
Partnership	In the common law, a partnership is a type of business entity in which partners share with each other the profits or losses of the business undertaking in which they have all invested.
Leadership	Management merely consists of leadership applied to business situations; or in other words: management forms a sub-set of the broader process of leadership.
Hierarchy	A system of grouping people in an organization according to rank from the top down in which all subordinate managers must report to one person is called a hierarchy.
Product line	A group of products that are physically similar or are intended for a similar market are called the product line.
Benchmarking	The continuous process of comparing the levels of performance in producing products and services and executing activities against the best levels of performance is benchmarking.
Learning curve	Learning curve is a function that measures how labor-hours per unit decline as units of production increase because workers are learning and becoming better at their jobs.

Go to **Cram101.com** for the Practice Tests for this Chapter.

Competitive disadvantage	A situation in which a firm is not implementing using strategies that are being used by competing organizations is competitive disadvantage.
Management control	That aspect of management concerned with the comparison of actual versus planned performance as well as the development and implementation of procedures to correct substandard performance is called management control.
Joint venture	Joint venture refers to an undertaking by two parties for a specific purpose and duration, taking any of several legal forms.
Product design	Product Design is defined as the idea generation, concept development, testing and manufacturing or implementation of a physical object or service. It is possibly the evolution of former discipline name - Industrial Design.
Abstraction	Abstraction is a model building simplification process that refers to retaining only the essential facts, and the elimination of irrelevant and non-economic facts, to obtain an economic principle.
Cost advantage	Possession of a lower cost of production or operation than a competing firm or country is cost advantage.
Labor productivity	In labor economics labor productivity is a measure of the efficiency of the labor force. It is usually measured as output per hour of all people. When comparing labor productivity one mostly looks at the change over time.
Productivity	Productivity refers to the total output of goods and services in a given period of time divided by work hours.
Performance improvement	Performance improvement is the concept of measuring the output of a particular process or procedure then modifying the process or procedure in order to increase the output, increase efficiency, or increase the effectiveness of the process or procedure.
Performance measurement	The process by which someone evaluates an employee's work behaviors by measurement and comparison with previously established standards, documents the results, and communicates the results to the employee is called performance measurement.
Control system	A control system is a device or set of devices that manage the behavior of other devices. Some devices or systems are not controllable.A control system is an interconnection of components connected or related in such a manner as to command, direct, or regulate itself or another system.
Discount	The difference between the face value of a bond and its selling price, when a bond is sold for less than its face value it's referred to as a discount.
Consumption	In Keynesian economics consumption refers to personal consumption expenditure, i.e., the purchase of currently produced goods and services out of income, out of savings (net worth), or from borrowed funds. It refers to that part of disposable income that does not go to saving.
Data mining	The extraction of hidden predictive information from large databases is referred to as data mining.
Customer service	The ability of logistics management to satisfy users in terms of time, dependability, communication, and convenience is called the customer service.

Go to **Cram101.com** for the Practice Tests for this Chapter.

New product development	New product development is the complete process of bringing a new product to market. There are two parallel aspects to this process : one involves product engineering ; the other marketing analysis.
Product development	In business and engineering, new product development is the complete process of bringing a new product to market. There are two parallel aspects to this process : one involves product engineering ; the other marketing analysis. Marketers see new product development as the first stage in product life cycle management, engineers as part of Product Lifecycle Management.
Integration	Economic integration refers to reducing barriers among countries to transactions and to movements of goods, capital, and labor, including harmonization of laws, regulations, and standards. Integrated markets theoretically function as a unified market.
Management	Management characterizes the process of leading and directing all or part of an organization, often a business, through the deployment and manipulation of resources. Early twentieth-century management writer Mary Parker Follett defined management as "the art of getting things done through people."
Journal	Book of original entry, in which transactions are recorded in a general ledger system, is referred to as a journal.
Technology	The body of knowledge and techniques that can be used to combine economic resources to produce goods and services is called technology.
Harvard Business Review	Harvard Business Review is a research-based magazine written for business practitioners, it claims a high ranking business readership and enjoys the reverence of academics, executives, and management consultants. It has been the frequent publishing home for well known scholars and management thinkers.
Core	A core is the set of feasible allocations in an economy that cannot be improved upon by subset of the set of the economy's consumers (a coalition). In construction, when the force in an element is within a certain center section, the core, the element will only be under compression.
Business Week	Business Week is a business magazine published by McGraw-Hill. It was first published in 1929 under the direction of Malcolm Muir, who was serving as president of the McGraw-Hill Publishing company at the time. It is considered to be the standard both in industry and among students.
Corporation	A legal entity chartered by a state or the Federal government that is distinct and separate from the individuals who own it is a corporation. This separation gives the corporation unique powers which other legal entities lack.
Production	The creation of finished goods and services using the factors of production: land, labor, capital, entrepreneurship, and knowledge.
Regulation	Regulation refers to restrictions state and federal laws place on business with regard to the conduct of its activities.
Personnel	A collective term for all of the employees of an organization. Personnel is also commonly used to refer to the personnel management function or the organizational unit responsible for administering personnel programs.
Policy	Similar to a script in that a policy can be a less than completely rational decision-making method. Involves the use of a pre-existing set of decision steps for any problem that presents itself.
Supply	Supply is the aggregate amount of any material good that can be called into being at a certain price point; it comprises one half of the equation of supply and demand. In classical

economic theory, a curve representing supply is one of the factors that produce price.

Supplier evaluation	Supplier evaluation refers to a tool used by many firms to differentiate and discriminate among suppliers. A supplier evaluation often involves report cards where potential suppliers are rated based on different criteria such as quality, technical capability, or ability to meet schedule demands.
Control system	A control system is a device or set of devices that manage the behavior of other devices. Some devices or systems are not controllable. A control system is an interconnection of components connected or related in such a manner as to command, direct, or regulate itself or another system.
Cost structure	The relative proportion of an organization's fixed, variable, and mixed costs is referred to as cost structure.
Compliance	A type of influence process where a receiver accepts the position advocated by a source to obtain favorable outcomes or to avoid punishment is the compliance.
Evaluation	The consumer's appraisal of the product or brand on important attributes is called evaluation.
Industry	A group of firms that produce identical or similar products is an industry. It is also used specifically to refer to an area of economic production focused on manufacturing which involves large amounts of capital investment before any profit can be realized, also called "heavy industry".
Assessment	Collecting information and providing feedback to employees about their behavior, communication style, or skills is an assessment.
Audit	An examination of the financial reports to ensure that they represent what they claim and conform with generally accepted accounting principles is referred to as audit.
Expense	In accounting, an expense represents an event in which an asset is used up or a liability is incurred. In terms of the accounting equation, expenses reduce owners' equity.
Board of directors	The group of individuals elected by the stockholders of a corporation to oversee its operations is a board of directors.
Option	A contract that gives the purchaser the option to buy or sell the underlying financial instrument at a specified price, called the exercise price or strike price, within a specific period of time.
Purchasing	Purchasing refers to the function in a firm that searches for quality material resources, finds the best suppliers, and negotiates the best price for goods and services.
Quality audit	Quality audit means a systematic, independent examination of a quality system. A quality audit is typically performed at defined intervals and ensures that the institution has clearly-defined internal quality monitoring procedures linked to effective action. The checking determines if the quality system complies with applicable regulations or standards The process involves assessing the standard operating procedures (SOP's) for compliance to the regulations, and also assessing the actual process and results against what is stated in the SOP.
Contract	A contract is a "promise" or an "agreement" that is enforced or recognized by the law. In the civil law, a contract is considered to be part of the general law of obligations.
Competitive bidding	A situation where two or more companies submit bids for a product, service, or project to a potential buyer is competitive bidding.
Bid	A bid price is a price offered by a buyer when he/she buys a good. In the context of stock trading on a stock exchange, the bid price is the highest price a buyer of a stock is willing

	to pay for a share of that given stock.
Service	Service refers to a "non tangible product" that is not embodied in a physical good and that typically effects some change in another product, person, or institution. Contrasts with good.
Anticipation	In finance, anticipation is where debts are paid off early, generally in order to pay less interest.
Buyer	A buyer refers to a role in the buying center with formal authority and responsibility to select the supplier and negotiate the terms of the contract.
Complexity	The technical sophistication of the product and hence the amount of understanding required to use it is referred to as complexity. It is the opposite of simplicity.
Single sourcing	Single sourcing is the origination of any design, set of concepts, or any article real or insubstantial from a single, well defined source, either a person or an organization.
Product design	Product Design is defined as the idea generation, concept development, testing and manufacturing or implementation of a physical object or service. It is possibly the evolution of former discipline name - Industrial Design.
Variable	A variable is something measured by a number; it is used to analyze what happens to other things when the size of that number changes.
Technological change	The introduction of new methods of production or new products intended to increase the productivity of existing inputs or to raise marginal products is a technological change.
Basket	A basket is an economic term for a group of several securities created for the purpose of simultaneous buying or selling. Baskets are frequently used for program trading.
Leverage	Leverage is using given resources in such a way that the potential positive or negative outcome is magnified. In finance, this generally refers to borrowing.
Information technology	Information technology refers to technology that helps companies change business by allowing them to use new methods.
Marketing	Promoting and selling products or services to customers, or prospective customers, is referred to as marketing.
Cabinet	The heads of the executive departments of a jurisdiction who report to and advise its chief executive; examples would include the president's cabinet, the governor's cabinet, and the mayor's cabinet.
Product line	A group of products that are physically similar or are intended for a similar market are called the product line.
Users	Users refer to people in the organization who actually use the product or service purchased by the buying center.
Argument	The discussion by counsel for the respective parties of their contentions on the law and the facts of the case being tried in order to aid the jury in arriving at a correct and just conclusion is called argument.
Market	A market is, as defined in economics, a social arrangement that allows buyers and sellers to discover information and carry out a voluntary exchange of goods or services.
Gain	In finance, gain is a profit or an increase in value of an investment such as a stock or bond. Gain is calculated by fair market value or the proceeds from the sale of the investment minus the sum of the purchase price and all costs associated with it.
Trade show	A type of exhibition or forum where manufacturers can display their products to current as

well as prospective buyers is referred to as trade show.

Advertisement	Advertisement is the promotion of goods, services, companies and ideas, usually by an identified sponsor. Marketers see advertising as part of an overall promotional strategy.
Wall Street Journal	Dow Jones & Company was founded in 1882 by reporters Charles Dow, Edward Jones and Charles Bergstresser. Jones converted the small Customers' Afternoon Letter into The Wall Street Journal, first published in 1889, and began delivery of the Dow Jones News Service via telegraph. The Journal featured the Jones 'Average', the first of several indexes of stock and bond prices on the New York Stock Exchange.
Appreciation	Appreciation refers to a rise in the value of a country's currency on the exchange market, relative either to a particular other currency or to a weighted average of other currencies. The currency is said to appreciate. Opposite of 'depreciation.' Appreciation can also refer to the increase in value of any asset.
Comprehensive	A comprehensive refers to a layout accurate in size, color, scheme, and other necessary details to show how a final ad will look. For presentation only, never for reproduction.
Business unit	The lowest level of the company which contains the set of functions that carry a product through its life span from concept through manufacture, distribution, sales and service is a business unit.
Direct marketing	Promotional element that uses direct communication with consumers to generate a response in the form of an order, a request for further information, or a visit to a retail outlet is direct marketing.
Consideration	Consideration in contract law, a basic requirement for an enforceable agreement under traditional contract principles, defined in this text as legal value, bargained for and given in exchange for an act or promise. In corporation law, cash or property contributed to a corporation in exchange for shares, or a promise to contribute such cash or property.
Financial analysis	Financial analysis is the analysis of the accounts and the economic prospects of a firm.
Financial risk	The risk related to the inability of the firm to meet its debt obligations as they come due is called financial risk.
Commodity	Could refer to any good, but in trade a commodity is usually a raw material or primary product that enters into international trade, such as metals or basic agricultural products.
Principal	In agency law, one under whose direction an agent acts and for whose benefit that agent acts is a principal.
Trend	Trend refers to the long-term movement of an economic variable, such as its average rate of increase or decrease over enough years to encompass several business cycles.
Financial ratio	A financial ratio is a ratio of two numbers of reported levels or flows of a company. It may be two financial flows categories divided by each other (profit margin, profit/revenue). It may be a level divided by a financial flow (price/earnings). It may be a flow divided by a level (return on equity or earnings/equity). The numerator or denominator may itself be a ratio (PEG ratio).
ISO 9000	ISO 9000 is a family of ISO standards for Quality Management Systems. It does not guarantee the quality of end products and services; rather, it certifies that consistent business processes are being applied.
Market share data	A comparative measure that determines relative positions of firms in the marketplace is called market share data.
Market share	That fraction of an industry's output accounted for by an individual firm or group of firms

	is called market share.
Interest	In finance and economics, interest is the price paid by a borrower for the use of a lender's money. In other words, interest is the amount of paid to "rent" money for a period of time.
Labor	People's physical and mental talents and efforts that are used to help produce goods and services are called labor.
Profit	Profit refers to the return to the resource entrepreneurial ability; total revenue minus total cost.
Incentive	An incentive is any factor (financial or non-financial) that provides a motive for a particular course of action, or counts as a reason for preferring one choice to the alternatives.
Negotiation	Negotiation is the process whereby interested parties resolve disputes, agree upon courses of action, bargain for individual or collective advantage, and/or attempt to craft outcomes which serve their mutual interests.
Research and development	The use of resources for the deliberate discovery of new information and ways of doing things, together with the application of that information in inventing new products or processes is referred to as research and development.
Competitiveness	Competitiveness usually refers to characteristics that permit a firm to compete effectively with other firms due to low cost or superior technology, perhaps internationally.
Brief	Brief refers to a statement of a party's case or legal arguments, usually prepared by an attorney. Also used to make legal arguments before appellate courts.
Turnover	Turnover in a financial context refers to the rate at which a provider of goods cycles through its average inventory. Turnover in a human resources context refers to the characteristic of a given company or industry, relative to rate at which an employer gains and loses staff.
Operation	A standardized method or technique that is performed repetitively, often on different materials resulting in different finished goods is called an operation.
Points	Loan origination fees that may be deductible as interest by a buyer of property. A seller of property who pays points reduces the selling price by the amount of the points paid for the buyer.
Strike	The withholding of labor services by an organized group of workers is referred to as a strike.
Continuous improvement	The constant effort to eliminate waste, reduce response time, simplify the design of both products and processes, and improve quality and customer service is referred to as continuous improvement.
Indirect labor	All costs of compensating employees who do not work directly on the firm's product but who are necessary for production to occur are referred to as indirect labor.
Overhead cost	An expenses of operating a business over and above the direct costs of producing a product is an overhead cost. They can include utilities (eg, electricity, telephone), advertizing and marketing, and any other costs not billed directly to the client or included in the price of the product.
Manufacturing	Production of goods primarily by the application of labor and capital to raw materials and other intermediate inputs, in contrast to agriculture, mining, forestry, fishing, and services a manufacturing.
Direct labor	The earnings of employees who work directly on the products being manufactured are direct

Go to **Cram101.com** for the Practice Tests for this Chapter.

	labor.
Total cost	The sum of fixed cost and variable cost is referred to as total cost.
Cost accounting	Cost accounting measures and reports financial and nonfinancial information relating to the cost of acquiring or consuming resources in an organization. It provides information for both management accounting and financial accounting.
Accounting	A system that collects and processes financial information about an organization and reports that information to decision makers is referred to as accounting.
Competitive advantage	A business is said to have a competitive advantage when its unique strengths, often based on cost, quality, time, and innovation, offer consumers a greater percieved value and there by diffetiating it from its competitors.
Pricing strategy	The process in which the price of a product can be determined and is decided upon is a pricing strategy.
Competitor	Other organizations in the same industry or type of business that provide a good or service to the same set of customers is referred to as a competitor.
Quality management	Quality management is a method for ensuring that all the activities necessary to design, develop and implement a product or service are effective and efficient with respect to the system and its performance.
Statistical process control	Statistical process control is a method for achieving quality control in manufacturing processes. It is a set of methods using statistical tools such as mean, variance and others, to detect whether the process observed is under control.
Quality improvement	Quality is inversely proportional to variability thus quality Improvement is the reduction of variability in products and processes.
Distribution	Distribution in economics, the manner in which total output and income is distributed among individuals or factors.
Motorola	The Six Sigma quality system was developed at Motorola even though it became most well known because of its use by General Electric. It was created by engineer Bill Smith, under the direction of Bob Galvin (son of founder Paul Galvin) when he was running the company.
Honeywell	Honeywell is a major American multinational corporation that produces electronic control systems and automation equipment. It is a major supplier of engineering services and avionics for NASA, Boeing and the United States Department of Defense.
Capital	Capital generally refers to financial wealth, especially that used to start or maintain a business. In classical economics, capital is one of four factors of production, the others being land and labor and entrepreneurship.
Ford	Ford is an American company that manufactures and sells automobiles worldwide. Ford introduced methods for large-scale manufacturing of cars, and large-scale management of an industrial workforce, especially elaborately engineered manufacturing sequences typified by the moving assembly lines.
Liability	A liability is a present obligation of the enterprise arizing from past events, the settlement of which is expected to result in an outflow from the enterprise of resources embodying economic benefits.
Public relations	Public relations refers to the management function that evaluates public attitudes, changes policies and procedures in response to the public's requests, and executes a program of action and information to earn public understanding and acceptance.
Administration	Administration refers to the management and direction of the affairs of governments and

	institutions; a collective term for all policymaking officials of a government; the execution and implementation of public policy.
Clean Air Act	A Clean Air Act describes one of a number of pieces of legislation relating to the reduction of smog and atmospheric pollution in general. The United States Congress passed the Clean Air Act in 1963, the Clean Air Act Amendment in 1966, the Clean Air Act Extension in 1970, and Clean Air Act Amendments in 1977 and 1990.
Composition	An out-of-court settlement in which creditors agree to accept a fractional settlement on their original claim is referred to as composition.
Screening	Screening in economics refers to a strategy of combating adverse selection, one of the potential decision-making complications in cases of asymmetric information.
Financial crisis	A loss of confidence in a country's currency or other financial assets causing international investors to withdraw their funds from the country is referred to as a financial crisis.
Material requirements planning	A dependent demand inventory planning and control system that schedules the precise amount of all materials required to support the production of desired end products is referred to as material requirements planning.
Vendor	A person who sells property to a vendee is a vendor. The words vendor and vendee are more commonly applied to the seller and purchaser of real estate, and the words seller and buyer are more commonly applied to the seller and purchaser of personal property.
Capacity planning	The determination and adjustment of the organization's ability to produce products and services to match customer demand is called capacity planning.
Asset	An item of property, such as land, capital, money, a share in ownership, or a claim on others for future payment, such as a bond or a bank deposit is an asset.
Asset management	Asset management is the method that a company uses to track fixed assets, for example factory equipment, desks and chairs, computers, even buildings. Although the exact details of the task varies widely from company to company, asset management often includes tracking the physical location of assets, managing demand for scarce resources, and accounting tasks such as amortization.
Cash flow	In finance, cash flow refers to the amounts of cash being received and spent by a business during a defined period of time, sometimes tied to a specific project. Most of the time they are being used to determine gaps in the liquid position of a company.
Credit	Credit refers to a recording as positive in the balance of payments, any transaction that gives rise to a payment into the country, such as an export, the sale of an asset, or borrowing from abroad.
Inventory	Tangible property held for sale in the normal course of business or used in producing goods or services for sale is an inventory.
Fixed asset	Fixed asset, also known as property, plant, and equipment (PP&E), is a term used in accountancy for assets and property which cannot easily be converted into cash. This can be compared with current assets such as cash or bank accounts, which are described as liquid assets. In most cases, only tangible assets are referred to as fixed.
Investment	Investment refers to spending for the production and accumulation of capital and additions to inventories. In a financial sense, buying an asset with the expectation of making a return.
Shareholder	A shareholder is an individual or company (including a corporation) that legally owns one or more shares of stock in a joined stock company.
Lender	Suppliers and financial institutions that lend money to companies is referred to as a lender.

Creditor	A person to whom a debt or legal obligation is owed, and who has the right to enforce payment of that debt or obligation is referred to as creditor.
Logistics	Those activities that focus on getting the right amount of the right products to the right place at the right time at the lowest possible cost is referred to as logistics.
Information system	An information system is a system whether automated or manual, that comprises people, machines, and/or methods organized to collect, process, transmit, and disseminate data that represent user information.
Commerce	Commerce is the exchange of something of value between two entities. It is the central mechanism from which capitalism is derived.
Electronic commerce	Electronic commerce or e-commerce, refers to any activity that uses some form of electronic communication in the inventory, exchange, advertisement, distribution, and payment of goods and services.
Ford Motor Company	Ford Motor Company introduced methods for large-scale manufacturing of cars, and large-scale management of an industrial workforce, especially elaborately engineered manufacturing sequences typified by the moving assembly lines. Henry Ford's combination of highly efficient factories, highly paid workers, and low prices revolutionized manufacturing and came to be known around the world as Fordism by 1914.
Exchange	The trade of things of value between buyer and seller so that each is better off after the trade is called the exchange.
Supply chain management	Supply chain management deals with the planning and execution issues involved in managing a supply chain. Supply chain management spans all movement and storage of raw materials, work-in-process inventory, and finished goods from point-of-origin to point-of-consumption.
Supply chain	Supply chain refers to the flow of goods, services, and information from the initial sources of materials and services to the delivery of products to consumers.
Innovation	Innovation refers to the first commercially successful introduction of a new product, the use of a new method of production, or the creation of a new form of business organization.
Chrysler	The Chrysler Corporation was an American automobile manufacturer that existed independently from 1925–1998. The company was formed by Walter Percy Chrysler on June 6, 1925, with the remaining assets of Maxwell Motor Company.
Extended enterprise	Extended Enterprise is a concept typically applied to a networked organization in which a dominant enterprise "extends" its boundaries to all or some of its suppliers. An extended enterprise can be seen as a particular case of a virtual enterprise and therefore a manifestation of a Collaborative Network.
DaimlerChrysler	In 2002, the merged company, DaimlerChrysler, appeared to run two independent product lines, with few signs of corporate integration. In 2003, however, it was alleged by the Detroit News that the "merger of equals" was, in fact, a takeover.
Enterprise	Enterprise refers to another name for a business organization. Other similar terms are business firm, sometimes simply business, sometimes simply firm, as well as company, and entity.
Partnership	In the common law, a partnership is a type of business entity in which partners share with each other the profits or losses of the business undertaking in which they have all invested.
Total quality management	The broad set of management and control processes designed to focus an entire organization and all of its employees on providing products or services that do the best possible job of satisfying the customer is called total quality management.
Scope	Scope of a project is the sum total of all projects products and their requirements or

Go to **Cram101.com** for the Practice Tests for this Chapter.

	features.
Factoring	In mathematics, factorization or factoring is the decomposition of an object into a product of other objects, or factors, which when multiplied together give the original.
Process control system	A computer system that monitors and controls ongoing physical processes, such as temperature or pressure changes is called process control system.
Performance requirement	Performance requirement refers to a requirement that an importer or exporter achieve some level of performance, in terms of exporting, domestic content, etc., in order to obtain an import or export license.
Alcoa	Alcoa (NYSE: AA) is the world's leading producer of alumina, primary and fabricated aluminum, with operations in 43 countries. (It is followed in this by a former subsidiary, Alcan, the second-leading producer.)
Authority	Authority in agency law, refers to an agent's ability to affect his principal's legal relations with third parties. Also used to refer to an actor's legal power or ability to do something. In addition, sometimes used to refer to a statute, case, or other legal source that justifies a particular result.
Committee	A long-lasting, sometimes permanent team in the organization structure created to deal with tasks that recur regularly is the committee.
Performance improvement	Performance improvement is the concept of measuring the output of a particular process or procedure then modifying the process or procedure in order to increase the output, increase efficiency, or increase the effectiveness of the process or procedure.
Matching	Matching refers to an accounting concept that establishes when expenses are recognized. Expenses are matched with the revenues they helped to generate and are recognized when those revenues are recognized.
Domestic	From or in one's own country. A domestic producer is one that produces inside the home country. A domestic price is the price inside the home country. Opposite of 'foreign' or 'world.'.
General Motors	General Motors is the world's largest automaker. Founded in 1908, today it employs about 327,000 people around the world. With global headquarters in Detroit, it manufactures its cars and trucks in 33 countries.
Countertrade	Countertrade is exchanging goods or services that are paid for, in whole or part, with other goods or services.
Boeing	Boeing is the world's largest aircraft manufacturer by revenue. Headquartered in Chicago, Illinois, Boeing is the second-largest defense contractor in the world. In 2005, the company was the world's largest civil aircraft manufacturer in terms of value.
Performance measurement	The process by which someone evaluates an employee's work behaviors by measurement and comparison with previously established standards, documents the results, and communicates the results to the employee is called performance measurement.
Continuous process	An uninterrupted production process in which long production runs turn out finished goods over time is called continuous process.
Inflation	An increase in the overall price level of an economy, usually as measured by the CPI or by the implicit price deflator is called inflation.
Frequency	Frequency refers to the speed of the up and down movements of a fluctuating economic variable; that is, the number of times per unit of time that the variable completes a cycle of up and down movement.

Honda	With more than 14 million internal combustion engines built each year, Honda is the largest engine-maker in the world. In 2004, the company began to produce diesel motors, which were both very quiet whilst not requiring particulate filters to pass pollution standards. It is arguable, however, that the foundation of their success is the motorcycle division.
Sourcing decisions	Whether a firm should make or buy component parts are sourcing decisions.
Performance report	A report showing the budgeted and actual amounts, and the variances between these amounts, of key financial results for a person or subunit is called a performance report.
Lockheed Martin	Lockheed Martin is the world's largest defense contractor (by defense revenue). As of 2005, 95% of revenues came from the U.S. Department of Defense, other U.S. federal government agencies, and foreign military customers.
Assembly line	An assembly line is a manufacturing process in which interchangeable parts are added to a product in a sequential manner to create a finished product.
Average cost	Average cost is equal to total cost divided by the number of goods produced (Quantity-Q). It is also equal to the sum of average variable costs (total variable costs divided by Q) plus average fixed costs (total fixed costs divided by Q).
Revenue	Revenue is a U.S. business term for the amount of money that a company receives from its activities, mostly from sales of products and/or services to customers.
Operational excellence	Operational excellence is a goal of conducting business in a manner that improves quality, obtains higher yields, faster throughput, and less waste.
Postal Service	The postal service was created in Philadelphia under Benjamin Franklin on July 26, 1775 by decree of the Second Continental Congress. Based on a clause in the United States Constitution empowering Congress "To establish Post Offices and post Roads."
Electronic mail	Electronic mail refers to electronic written communication between individuals using computers connected to the Internet.
Intranet	Intranet refers to a companywide network, closed to public access, that uses Internet-type technology. A set of communications links within one company that travel over the Internet but are closed to public access.
Specialist	A specialist is a trader who makes a market in one or several stocks and holds the limit order book for those stocks.
Stock	In financial terminology, stock is the capital raized by a corporation, through the issuance and sale of shares.
Invoice	The itemized bill for a transaction, stating the nature of the transaction and its cost. In international trade, the invoice price is often the preferred basis for levying an ad valorem tariff.
Warranty	An obligation of a company to replace defective goods or correct any deficiencies in performance or quality of a product is called a warranty.
Customer service	The ability of logistics management to satisfy users in terms of time, dependability, communication, and convenience is called the customer service.
Incremental cost	Additional total cost incurred for an activity is called incremental cost. A form of costing that classifies costs into their fixed and variable elements in order to calculate the extra cost of making and selling an additional batch of units.
Compatibility	Compatibility refers to used to describe a product characteristic, it means a good fit with other products used by the consumer or with the consumer's lifestyle. Used in a technical

	context, it means the ability of systems to work together.
Internal customer	An individuals or unit within the firm that receives services from other entities within the organization is an internal customer.
Foundation	A Foundation is a type of philanthropic organization set up by either individuals or institutions as a legal entity (either as a corporation or trust) with the purpose of distributing grants to support causes in line with the goals of the foundation.
Contribution	In business organization law, the cash or property contributed to a business by its owners is referred to as contribution.
Infraction	Infraction is an essentially minor violation of law where the penalty upon conviction only consists of monetary forfeiture. A violation of law which could include imprisonment is a crime. It is distinguished from a misdemeanor or a felony in that the penalty for an infraction cannot include any imprisonment.

Industry	A group of firms that produce identical or similar products is an industry. It is also used specifically to refer to an area of economic production focused on manufacturing which involves large amounts of capital investment before any profit can be realized, also called "heavy industry".
Purchasing	Purchasing refers to the function in a firm that searches for quality material resources, finds the best suppliers, and negotiates the best price for goods and services.
Operation	A standardized method or technique that is performed repetitively, often on different materials resulting in different finished goods is called an operation.
Journal	Book of original entry, in which transactions are recorded in a general ledger system, is referred to as a journal.
Operations research	Operations research is the use of mathematical models, statistics and algorithms to aid in decision-making. It is most often used to analyze complex real-world systems, typically with the goal of improving or optimizing performance.
Control system	A control system is a device or set of devices that manage the behavior of other devices. Some devices or systems are not controllable.A control system is an interconnection of components connected or related in such a manner as to command, direct, or regulate itself or another system.
Manufacturing	Production of goods primarily by the application of labor and capital to raw materials and other intermediate inputs, in contrast to agriculture, mining, forestry, fishing, and services a manufacturing.
Business Week	Business Week is a business magazine published by McGraw-Hill. It was first published in 1929 under the direction of Malcolm Muir, who was serving as president of the McGraw-Hill Publishing company at the time. It is considered to be the standard both in industry and among students.
Best practice	Best practice is a management idea which asserts that there is a technique, method, process, activity, incentive or reward that is more effective at delivering a particular outcome than any other technique, method, process, etc.
Buyer	A buyer refers to a role in the buying center with formal authority and responsibility to select the supplier and negotiate the terms of the contract.
Alcoa	Alcoa (NYSE: AA) is the world's leading producer of alumina, primary and fabricated aluminum, with operations in 43 countries. (It is followed in this by a former subsidiary, Alcan, the second-leading producer.)
Management	Management characterizes the process of leading and directing all or part of an organization, often a business, through the deployment and manipulation of resources. Early twentieth-century management writer Mary Parker Follett defined management as "the art of getting things done through people."
Materials management	Materials management refers to the activity that controls the transmission of physical materials through the value chain, from procurement through production and into distribution.
Evaluation	The consumer's appraisal of the product or brand on important attributes is called evaluation.
ISO 9000	ISO 9000 is a family of ISO standards for Quality Management Systems. It does not guarantee the quality of end products and services; rather, it certifies that consistent business processes are being applied.
Supply	Supply is the aggregate amount of any material good that can be called into being at a certain price point; it comprises one half of the equation of supply and demand. In classical

Go to **Cram101.com** for the Practice Tests for this Chapter.

economic theory, a curve representing supply is one of the factors that produce price.

Supplier evaluation	Supplier evaluation refers to a tool used by many firms to differentiate and discriminate among suppliers. A supplier evaluation often involves report cards where potential suppliers are rated based on different criteria such as quality, technical capability, or ability to meet schedule demands.
Malcolm Baldrige National Quality Award	Malcolm Baldrige national quality award refers to U.S. national quality award sponsored by the U.S. Department of Commerce and private industry. The program aims to reward quality in the business sector, health care, and education, and was inspired by the ideas of Total Quality Management.
Assessment	Collecting information and providing feedback to employees about their behavior, communication style, or skills is an assessment.
Option	A contract that gives the purchaser the option to buy or sell the underlying financial instrument at a specified price, called the exercise price or strike price, within a specific period of time.
Service	Service refers to a "non tangible product" that is not embodied in a physical good and that typically effects some change in another product, person, or institution. Contrasts with good.
Product design	Product Design is defined as the idea generation, concept development, testing and manufacturing or implementation of a physical object or service. It is possibly the evolution of former discipline name - Industrial Design.
Quality at the source	A method of process control whereby each worker is responsible for his or her own work and performs needed inspections at each stage of the process is referred to as the quality at the source.
Supply chain	Supply chain refers to the flow of goods, services, and information from the initial sources of materials and services to the delivery of products to consumers.
Market	A market is, as defined in economics, a social arrangement that allows buyers and sellers to discover information and carry out a voluntary exchange of goods or services.
Marketing	Promoting and selling products or services to customers, or prospective customers, is referred to as marketing.
Conformance	A dimension of quality that refers to the extent to which a product lies within an allowable range of deviation from its specification is called the conformance.
Users	Users refer to people in the organization who actually use the product or service purchased by the buying center.
Internal customer	An individuals or unit within the firm that receives services from other entities within the organization is an internal customer.
Raw material	Raw material refers to a good that has not been transformed by production; a primary product.
Eastman Kodak	Eastman Kodak Company is an American multinational public company producing photographic materials and equipment. Long known for its wide range of photographic film products, it has focused in recent years on three main businesses: digital photography, health imaging, and printing. This company remains the largest supplier of films in the world, both for the amateur and professional markets.
Competitor	Other organizations in the same industry or type of business that provide a good or service to the same set of customers is referred to as a competitor.
Performance	Performance improvement is the concept of measuring the output of a particular process or

improvement	procedure then modifying the process or procedure in order to increase the output, increase efficiency, or increase the effectiveness of the process or procedure.
Capital	Capital generally refers to financial wealth, especially that used to start or maintain a business. In classical economics, capital is one of four factors of production, the others being land and labor and entrepreneurship.
Durable good	A durable good is a good which does not quickly wear out, or more specifically, it yields services or utility over time rather than being completely used up when used once.
Technology	The body of knowledge and techniques that can be used to combine economic resources to produce goods and services is called technology.
Direct relationship	Direct relationship refers to the relationship between two variables that change in the same direction, for example, product price and quantity supplied.
Cost management	The approaches and activities of managers in short-run and long-run planning and control decisions that increase value for customers and lower costs of products and services are called cost management.
Firm	An organization that employs resources to produce a good or service for profit and owns and operates one or more plants is referred to as a firm.
Mistake	In contract law a mistake is incorrect understanding by one or more parties to a contract and may be used as grounds to invalidate the agreement. Common law has identified three different types of mistake in contract: unilateral mistake, mutual mistake, and common mistake.
Quality improvement	Quality is inversely proportional to variability thus quality Improvement is the reduction of variability in products and processes.
Total quality management	The broad set of management and control processes designed to focus an entire organization and all of its employees on providing products or services that do the best possible job of satisfying the customer is called total quality management.
Quality management	Quality management is a method for ensuring that all the activities necessary to design, develop and implement a product or service are effective and efficient with respect to the system and its performance.
Boeing	Boeing is the world's largest aircraft manufacturer by revenue. Headquartered in Chicago, Illinois, Boeing is the second-largest defense contractor in the world. In 2005, the company was the world's largest civil aircraft manufacturer in terms of value.
Profit	Profit refers to the return to the resource entrepreneurial ability; total revenue minus total cost.
Continental Airlines	Continental Airlines is an airline of the United States. Based in Houston, Texas, it is the 6th largest airline in the U.S. and the 8th largest in the world. Continental's tagline, since 1998, has been Work Hard, Fly Right.
Complaint	The pleading in a civil case in which the plaintiff states his claim and requests relief is called complaint. In the common law, it is a formal legal document that sets out the basic facts and legal reasons that the filing party (the plaintiffs) believes are sufficient to support a claim against another person, persons, entity or entities (the defendants) that entitles the plaintiff(s) to a remedy (either money damages or injunctive relief).
Competitiveness	Competitiveness usually refers to characteristics that permit a firm to compete effectively with other firms due to low cost or superior technology, perhaps internationally.
Global competition	Global competition exists when competitive conditions across national markets are linked strongly enough to form a true international market and when leading competitors compete head to head in many different countries.

Go to **Cram101.com** for the Practice Tests for this Chapter.

Instrument	Instrument refers to an economic variable that is controlled by policy makers and can be used to influence other variables, called targets. Examples are monetary and fiscal policies used to achieve external and internal balance.
Intel	Intel Corporation, founded in 1968 and based in Santa Clara, California, USA, is the world's largest semiconductor company. Intel is best known for its PC microprocessors, where it maintains roughly 80% market share.
Outsourcing	Outsourcing refers to a production activity that was previously done inside a firm or plant that is now conducted outside that firm or plant.
Product cost	Product cost refers to sum of the costs assigned to a product for a specific purpose. A concept used in applying the cost plus approach to product pricing in which only the costs of manufacturing the product are included in the cost amount to which the markup is added.
Administration	Administration refers to the management and direction of the affairs of governments and institutions; a collective term for all policymaking officials of a government; the execution and implementation of public policy.
Federal Aviation Administration	In 1967, a new U.S. Department of Transportation (DOT) combined major federal responsibilities for air and surface transport. The Federal Aviation Administration became one of several agencies within DOT. At the same time, a new National Transportation Safety Board took over the CAB's role of investigating aviation accidents.
Wall Street Journal	Dow Jones & Company was founded in 1882 by reporters Charles Dow, Edward Jones and Charles Bergstresser. Jones converted the small Customers' Afternoon Letter into The Wall Street Journal, first published in 1889, and began delivery of the Dow Jones News Service via telegraph. The Journal featured the Jones 'Average', the first of several indexes of stock and bond prices on the New York Stock Exchange.
Total cost	The sum of fixed cost and variable cost is referred to as total cost.
Proactive	To be proactive is to act before a situation becomes a source of confrontation or crisis. It is the opposite of "retroactive," which refers to actions taken after an event.
Continuous improvement	The constant effort to eliminate waste, reduce response time, simplify the design of both products and processes, and improve quality and customer service is referred to as continuous improvement.
Personnel	A collective term for all of the employees of an organization. Personnel is also commonly used to refer to the personnel management function or the organizational unit responsible for administering personnel programs.
Policy	Similar to a script in that a policy can be a less than completely rational decision-making method. Involves the use of a pre-existing set of decision steps for any problem that presents itself.
Performance target	A task established for an employee that provides the comparative basis for performance appraisal is a performance target.
Committee	A long-lasting, sometimes permanent team in the organization structure created to deal with tasks that recur regularly is the committee.
Production	The creation of finished goods and services using the factors of production: land, labor, capital, entrepreneurship, and knowledge.
Purchase order	A form on which items or services needed by a business firm are specified and then communicated to the vendor is a purchase order.
Confirmed	When the seller's bank agrees to assume liability on the letter of credit issued by the buyer's bank the transaction is confirmed. The term means that the credit is not only backed

up by the issuing foreign bank, but that payment is also guaranteed by the notifying American bank.

Brand	A name, symbol, or design that identifies the goods or services of one seller or group of sellers and distinguishes them from the goods and services of competitors is a brand.
Performance feedback	The process of providing employees with information regarding their performance effectiveness is referred to as performance feedback.
Budget	Budget refers to an account, usually for a year, of the planned expenditures and the expected receipts of an entity. For a government, the receipts are tax revenues.
Scope	Scope of a project is the sum total of all projects products and their requirements or features.
Information technology	Information technology refers to technology that helps companies change business by allowing them to use new methods.
Active management	Active management refers to a portfolio management strategy where the manager makes specific investments with the goal of outperforming a benchmark index. Ideally, the manager exploits market inefficiencies by selecting securities that are undervalued. Depending on the goals of the specific investment portfolio or mutual fund, active management may also strive to achieve a goal of less volatility or risk than the benchmark index instead of, or in addition to, greater long-term return.
Brief	Brief refers to a statement of a party's case or legal arguments, usually prepared by an attorney. Also used to make legal arguments before appellate courts.
Xerox	Xerox was founded in 1906 as "The Haloid Company" manufacturing photographic paper and equipment. The company came to prominence in 1959 with the introduction of the first plain paper photocopier using the process of xerography (electrophotography) developed by Chester Carlson, the Xerox 914.
Foundation	A Foundation is a type of philanthropic organization set up by either individuals or institutions as a legal entity (either as a corporation or trust) with the purpose of distributing grants to support causes in line with the goals of the foundation.
Trend	Trend refers to the long-term movement of an economic variable, such as its average rate of increase or decrease over enough years to encompass several business cycles.
Procurement	Procurement is the acquisition of goods or services at the best possible total cost of ownership, in the right quantity, at the right time, in the right place for the direct benefit or use of the governments, corporations, or individuals generally via, but not limited to a contract.
Performance measurement	The process by which someone evaluates an employee's work behaviors by measurement and comparison with previously established standards, documents the results, and communicates the results to the employee is called performance measurement.
Supply chain management	Supply chain management deals with the planning and execution issues involved in managing a supply chain. Supply chain management spans all movement and storage of raw materials, work-in-process inventory, and finished goods from point-of-origin to point-of-consumption.
Stretch target	A challenging goal or objective requiring significant effort to achieve is a stretch target.
Benchmarking	The continuous process of comparing the levels of performance in producing products and services and executing activities against the best levels of performance is benchmarking.
Motorola	The Six Sigma quality system was developed at Motorola even though it became most well known because of its use by General Electric. It was created by engineer Bill Smith, under the direction of Bob Galvin (son of founder Paul Galvin) when he was running the company.

Comprehensive	A comprehensive refers to a layout accurate in size, color, scheme, and other necessary details to show how a final ad will look. For presentation only, never for reproduction.
Incentive	An incentive is any factor (financial or non-financial) that provides a motive for a particular course of action, or counts as a reason for preferring one choice to the alternatives.
Chrysler	The Chrysler Corporation was an American automobile manufacturer that existed independently from 1925–1998. The company was formed by Walter Percy Chrysler on June 6, 1925, with the remaining assets of Maxwell Motor Company.
Shares	Shares refer to an equity security, representing a shareholder's ownership of a corporation. Shares are one of a finite number of equal portions in the capital of a company, entitling the owner to a proportion of distributed, non-reinvested profits known as dividends and to a portion of the value of the company in case of liquidation.
Contract	A contract is a "promise" or an "agreement" that is enforced or recognized by the law. In the civil law, a contract is considered to be part of the general law of obligations.
Inventory	Tangible property held for sale in the normal course of business or used in producing goods or services for sale is an inventory.
Fund	Independent accounting entity with a self-balancing set of accounts segregated for the purposes of carrying on specific activities is referred to as a fund.
Audit	An examination of the financial reports to ensure that they represent what they claim and conform with generally accepted accounting principles is referred to as audit.
Performance requirement	Performance requirement refers to a requirement that an importer or exporter achieve some level of performance, in terms of exporting, domestic content, etc., in order to obtain an import or export license.
QS 9000	A supplier development program developed by a Daimler Chrysler/Ford/General Motors supplier requirement task force is the QS 9000. The purpose of the QS 9000 is to provide a common standard and a set of procedures for the suppliers of the three companies.
Iso 9000 standards	International quality-control standards issued by the International Standards Organization are ISO 9000 standards. The standards do not specify a quality target level (99%, etc.), but stress the ability of a company to prove via third-party audit that they are complying with their defined procedures.
Ford	Ford is an American company that manufactures and sells automobiles worldwide. Ford introduced methods for large-scale manufacturing of cars, and large-scale management of an industrial workforce, especially elaborately engineered manufacturing sequences typified by the moving assembly lines.
Ford Motor Company	Ford Motor Company introduced methods for large-scale manufacturing of cars, and large-scale management of an industrial workforce, especially elaborately engineered manufacturing sequences typified by the moving assembly lines. Henry Ford's combination of highly efficient factories, highly paid workers, and low prices revolutionized manufacturing and came to be known around the world as Fordism by 1914.
Integration	Economic integration refers to reducing barriers among countries to transactions and to movements of goods, capital, and labor, including harmonization of laws, regulations, and standards. Integrated markets theoretically function as a unified market.
Honda	With more than 14 million internal combustion engines built each year, Honda is the largest engine-maker in the world. In 2004, the company began to produce diesel motors, which were both very quiet whilst not requiring particulate filters to pass pollution standards. It is arguable, however, that the foundation of their success is the motorcycle division.

Go to **Cram101.com** for the Practice Tests for this Chapter.

Product development	In business and engineering, new product development is the complete process of bringing a new product to market. There are two parallel aspects to this process : one involves product engineering ; the other marketing analysis. Marketers see new product development as the first stage in product life cycle management, engineers as part of Product Lifecycle Management.
John Deere	John Deere (February 7, 1804 - May 17, 1886) was an American blacksmith and manufacturer who founded one of the largest agricultural and construction equipment manufacturers in the world.
Union	A worker association that bargains with employers over wages and working conditions is called a union.
Variable	A variable is something measured by a number; it is used to analyze what happens to other things when the size of that number changes.
Quality assurance	Those activities associated with assuring the quality of a product or service is called quality assurance.
Customer satisfaction	Customer satisfaction is a business term which is used to capture the idea of measuring how satisfied an enterprise's customers are with the organization's efforts in a marketplace.
Interest	In finance and economics, interest is the price paid by a borrower for the use of a lender's money. In other words, interest is the amount of paid to "rent" money for a period of time.
Specialist	A specialist is a trader who makes a market in one or several stocks and holds the limit order book for those stocks.
Certification audits	Audits relating to registration are called certification audits.
Expense	In accounting, an expense represents an event in which an asset is used up or a liability is incurred. In terms of the accounting equation, expenses reduce owners' equity.
Commerce	Commerce is the exchange of something of value between two entities. It is the central mechanism from which capitalism is derived.
Diffusion	Diffusion is the process by which a new idea or new product is accepted by the market. The rate of diffusion is the speed that the new idea spreads from one consumer to the next.
Distribution	Distribution in economics, the manner in which total output and income is distributed among individuals or factors.
Assessor	An assessor is an expert who calculates the value of property. The value calculated by the assessor is then used as the basis for determining the amounts to be paid or assessed for tax or insurance purposes.
BellSouth	BellSouth is currently the only "Baby Bell" that does not operate pay telephones. By 2003, the payphone operation was discontinued because it had become too unprofitable, most likely due to the increased availability of cell phones. Cincinnati Bell has taken their place for payphones in northern BellSouth territory; independents have set in further south.
Honeywell	Honeywell is a major American multinational corporation that produces electronic control systems and automation equipment. It is a major supplier of engineering services and avionics for NASA, Boeing and the United States Department of Defense.
Quality audit	Quality audit means a systematic, independent examination of a quality system. A quality audit is typically performed at defined intervals and ensures that the institution has clearly-defined internal quality monitoring procedures linked to effective action. The checking determines if the quality system complies with applicable regulations or standards The process involves assessing the standard operating procedures (SOP's) for compliance to

Go to **Cram101.com** for the Practice Tests for this Chapter.

the regulations, and also assessing the actual process and results against what is stated in the SOP.

Process improvement	Process improvement is the activity of elevating the performance of a process, especially that of a business process with regard to its goal.
Continuous process	An uninterrupted production process in which long production runs turn out finished goods over time is called continuous process.
Strategic alliance	Strategic alliance refers to a long-term partnership between two or more companies established to help each company build competitive market advantages.
Partnership	In the common law, a partnership is a type of business entity in which partners share with each other the profits or losses of the business undertaking in which they have all invested.
Trial	An examination before a competent tribunal, according to the law of the land, of the facts or law put in issue in a cause, for the purpose of determining such issue is a trial. When the court hears and determines any issue of fact or law for the purpose of determining the rights of the parties, it may be considered a trial.
Trust	An arrangement in which shareholders of independent firms agree to give up their stock in exchange for trust certificates that entitle them to a share of the trust's common profits.
Juran	Juran is known as a business and industrial quality "guru," while making significant contributions to management theory, human resource management and consulting as well. He wrote several books, and is known worldwide as one of the most important 20th century thinkers in quality management.
Standardization	Standardization, in the context related to technologies and industries, is the process of establishing a technical standard among competing entities in a market, where this will bring benefits without hurting competition.
International Organization for Standardization	The International Organization for Standardization is an international standard-setting body composed of representatives from national standards bodies. Founded on February 23, 1947, the organization produces world-wide industrial and commercial standards.
Productivity	Productivity refers to the total output of goods and services in a given period of time divided by work hours.
Total quality control	A product-quality program in which the objective is complete elimination of product defects is called total quality control.
Quality control	The measurement of products and services against set standards is referred to as quality control.
American Management Association	American Management Association International is the world's largest membership-based management development and executive training organization. Their products include instructor led seminars, workshops, conferences, customized corporate programs, online learning, books, newsletters, research surveys and reports.

Go to **Cram101.com** for the Practice Tests for this Chapter.

Ford	Ford is an American company that manufactures and sells automobiles worldwide. Ford introduced methods for large-scale manufacturing of cars, and large-scale management of an industrial workforce, especially elaborately engineered manufacturing sequences typified by the moving assembly lines.
Production	The creation of finished goods and services using the factors of production: land, labor, capital, entrepreneurship, and knowledge.
Manufacturing	Production of goods primarily by the application of labor and capital to raw materials and other intermediate inputs, in contrast to agriculture, mining, forestry, fishing, and services a manufacturing.
Kaizen	Kaizen (Japanese for "change for the better" or "improvement") is an approach to productivity improvement originating in applications of the work of American experts such as Frederick Winslow Taylor, Frank Bunker Gilbreth, Walter Shewhart, and of the War Department's Training Within Industry program by Japanese manufacturers after World War II.
Performance improvement	Performance improvement is the concept of measuring the output of a particular process or procedure then modifying the process or procedure in order to increase the output, increase efficiency, or increase the effectiveness of the process or procedure.
Information system	An information system is a system whether automated or manual, that comprises people, machines, and/or methods organized to collect, process, transmit, and disseminate data that represent user information.
Managing director	Managing director is the term used for the chief executive of many limited companies in the United Kingdom, Commonwealth and some other English speaking countries. The title reflects their role as both a member of the Board of Directors but also as the senior manager.
Key Success Factor	A Key Success Factor is a factor in a given market that is a necessary condition for success.
Success factor	The term success factor refers to the characteristics necessary for high performance; knowledge, skills, abilities, behaviors.
Purchasing	Purchasing refers to the function in a firm that searches for quality material resources, finds the best suppliers, and negotiates the best price for goods and services.
Management	Management characterizes the process of leading and directing all or part of an organization, often a business, through the deployment and manipulation of resources. Early twentieth-century management writer Mary Parker Follett defined management as "the art of getting things done through people."
Supply	Supply is the aggregate amount of any material good that can be called into being at a certain price point; it comprises one half of the equation of supply and demand. In classical economic theory, a curve representing supply is one of the factors that produce price.
Quality assurance	Those activities associated with assuring the quality of a product or service is called quality assurance.
Market	A market is, as defined in economics, a social arrangement that allows buyers and sellers to discover information and carry out a voluntary exchange of goods or services.
Market share	That fraction of an industry's output accounted for by an individual firm or group of firms is called market share.
Competitor	Other organizations in the same industry or type of business that provide a good or service to the same set of customers is referred to as a competitor.
Foundation	A Foundation is a type of philanthropic organization set up by either individuals or institutions as a legal entity (either as a corporation or trust) with the purpose of

distributing grants to support causes in line with the goals of the foundation.

Rationalization	Rationalization in economics is an attempt to change a pre-existing ad-hoc workflow into one that is based on a set of published rules.
Continuous process	An uninterrupted production process in which long production runs turn out finished goods over time is called continuous process.
Performance management	The means through which managers ensure that employees' activities and outputs are congruent with the organization's goals is referred to as performance management.
Supplier evaluation	Supplier evaluation refers to a tool used by many firms to differentiate and discriminate among suppliers. A supplier evaluation often involves report cards where potential suppliers are rated based on different criteria such as quality, technical capability, or ability to meet schedule demands.
Evaluation	The consumer's appraisal of the product or brand on important attributes is called evaluation.
Operation	A standardized method or technique that is performed repetitively, often on different materials resulting in different finished goods is called an operation.
Total cost	The sum of fixed cost and variable cost is referred to as total cost.
Buyer	A buyer refers to a role in the buying center with formal authority and responsibility to select the supplier and negotiate the terms of the contract.
Technology	The body of knowledge and techniques that can be used to combine economic resources to produce goods and services is called technology.
Enterprise	Enterprise refers to another name for a business organization. Other similar terms are business firm, sometimes simply business, sometimes simply firm, as well as company, and entity.
Discount	The difference between the face value of a bond and its selling price, when a bond is sold for less than its face value it's referred to as a discount.
Continuous improvement	The constant effort to eliminate waste, reduce response time, simplify the design of both products and processes, and improve quality and customer service is referred to as continuous improvement.
Discount rate	Discount rate refers to the rate, per year, at which future values are diminished to make them comparable to values in the present. Can be either subjective or objective .
Outsourcing	Outsourcing refers to a production activity that was previously done inside a firm or plant that is now conducted outside that firm or plant.
Incentive	An incentive is any factor (financial or non-financial) that provides a motive for a particular course of action, or counts as a reason for preferring one choice to the alternatives.
Policy	Similar to a script in that a policy can be a less than completely rational decision-making method. Involves the use of a pre-existing set of decision steps for any problem that presents itself.
Consultant	A professional that provides expert advice in a particular field or area in which customers occassionaly require this type of knowledge is a consultant.
Supplier development program	Provided by firms to their suppliers, a supplier development program is a training and development program that will improve the speed, quality, and cost of product delivery.

Go to **Cram101.com** for the Practice Tests for this Chapter.

165

Gain	In finance, gain is a profit or an increase in value of an investment such as a stock or bond. Gain is calculated by fair market value or the proceeds from the sale of the investment minus the sum of the purchase price and all costs associated with it.
Product cost	Product cost refers to sum of the costs assigned to a product for a specific purpose. A concept used in applying the cost plus approach to product pricing in which only the costs of manufacturing the product are included in the cost amount to which the markup is added.
Service	Service refers to a "non tangible product" that is not embodied in a physical good and that typically effects some change in another product, person, or institution. Contrasts with good.
Honda	With more than 14 million internal combustion engines built each year, Honda is the largest engine-maker in the world. In 2004, the company began to produce diesel motors, which were both very quiet whilst not requiring particulate filters to pass pollution standards. It is arguable, however, that the foundation of their success is the motorcycle division.
Product development	In business and engineering, new product development is the complete process of bringing a new product to market. There are two parallel aspects to this process : one involves product engineering ; the other marketing analysis. Marketers see new product development as the first stage in product life cycle management, engineers as part of Product Lifecycle Management.
Argument	The discussion by counsel for the respective parties of their contentions on the law and the facts of the case being tried in order to aid the jury in arriving at a correct and just conclusion is called argument.
Single sourcing	Single sourcing is the origination of any design, set of concepts, or any article real or insubstantial from a single, well defined source, either a person or an organization.
Contract	A contract is a "promise" or an "agreement" that is enforced or recognized by the law. In the civil law, a contract is considered to be part of the general law of obligations.
Performance requirement	Performance requirement refers to a requirement that an importer or exporter achieve some level of performance, in terms of exporting, domestic content, etc., in order to obtain an import or export license.
Core	A core is the set of feasible allocations in an economy that cannot be improved upon by subset of the set of the economy's consumers (a coalition). In construction, when the force in an element is within a certain center section, the core, the element will only be under compression.
Revenue	Revenue is a U.S. business term for the amount of money that a company receives from its activities, mostly from sales of products and/or services to customers.
Investment	Investment refers to spending for the production and accumulation of capital and additions to inventories. In a financial sense, buying an asset with the expectation of making a return.
Economy	The income, expenditures, and resources that affect the cost of running a business and household are called an economy.
Economies of scale	In economics, returns to scale and economies of scale are related terms that describe what happens as the scale of production increases. They are different terms and not to be used interchangeably.
Procurement	Procurement is the acquisition of goods or services at the best possible total cost of ownership, in the right quantity, at the right time, in the right place for the direct benefit or use of the governments, corporations, or individuals generally via, but not limited to a contract.

Go to **Cram101.com** for the Practice Tests for this Chapter.

Keiretsu	Keiretsu is a set of companies with interlocking business relationships and shareholdings. It is a type of business group.
Nissan	Nissan is Japan's second largest car company after Toyota. Nissan is among the top three Asian rivals of the "big three" in the US.
Toyota	Toyota is a Japanese multinational corporation that manufactures automobiles, trucks and buses. Toyota is the world's second largest automaker by sales. Toyota also provides financial services through its subsidiary, Toyota Financial Services, and participates in other lines of business.
Corporation	A legal entity chartered by a state or the Federal government that is distinct and separate from the individuals who own it is a corporation. This separation gives the corporation unique powers which other legal entities lack.
Industry	A group of firms that produce identical or similar products is an industry. It is also used specifically to refer to an area of economic production focused on manufacturing which involves large amounts of capital investment before any profit can be realized, also called "heavy industry".
Restructuring	Restructuring is the corporate management term for the act of partially dismantling and reorganizing a company for the purpose of making it more efficient and therefore more profitable.
Commodity	Could refer to any good, but in trade a commodity is usually a raw material or primary product that enters into international trade, such as metals or basic agricultural products.
Union	A worker association that bargains with employers over wages and working conditions is called a union.
Strike	The withholding of labor services by an organized group of workers is referred to as a strike.
Partnership	In the common law, a partnership is a type of business entity in which partners share with each other the profits or losses of the business undertaking in which they have all invested.
Key Performance Indicator	A Key Performance Indicator is a financial and non-financial metric used to quantify objectives to reflect the strategic performance of an organization.
Distribution	Distribution in economics, the manner in which total output and income is distributed among individuals or factors.
Personnel	A collective term for all of the employees of an organization. Personnel is also commonly used to refer to the personnel management function or the organizational unit responsible for administering personnel programs.
Assessment	Collecting information and providing feedback to employees about their behavior, communication style, or skills is an assessment.
Interest	In finance and economics, interest is the price paid by a borrower for the use of a lender's money. In other words, interest is the amount of paid to "rent" money for a period of time.
Portfolio	In finance, a portfolio is a collection of investments held by an institution or a private individual. Holding but not always a portfolio is part of an investment and risk-limiting strategy called diversification. By owning several assets, certain types of risk (in particular specific risk) can be reduced.
Journal	Book of original entry, in which transactions are recorded in a general ledger system, is referred to as a journal.
Operations	A specialized area in management that converts or transforms resources into goods and

management	services is operations management.
Capital	Capital generally refers to financial wealth, especially that used to start or maintain a business. In classical economics, capital is one of four factors of production, the others being land and labor and entrepreneurship.
Performance measurement	The process by which someone evaluates an employee's work behaviors by measurement and comparison with previously established standards, documents the results, and communicates the results to the employee is called performance measurement.
Human resources	Human resources refers to the individuals within the firm, and to the portion of the firm's organization that deals with hiring, firing, training, and other personnel issues.
Committee	A long-lasting, sometimes permanent team in the organization structure created to deal with tasks that recur regularly is the committee.
Pareto analysis	Pareto analysis is a statistical technique in decision making used for selection of a limited number of tasks that produce significant overall effect.
Alignment	Term that refers to optimal coordination among disparate departments and divisions within a firm is referred to as alignment.
Supply chain	Supply chain refers to the flow of goods, services, and information from the initial sources of materials and services to the delivery of products to consumers.
Credibility	The extent to which a source is perceived as having knowledge, skill, or experience relevant to a communication topic and can be trusted to give an unbiased opinion or present objective information on the issue is called credibility.
Trust	An arrangement in which shareholders of independent firms agree to give up their stock in exchange for trust certificates that entitle them to a share of the trust's common profits.
Business case	The business case addresses, at a high level, the business need that a project seeks to resolve. It includes the reasons for the project, the expected business benefits, the options considered (with reasons for rejecting or carrying forward each option), the expected costs of the project, a gap analysis and the expected risks.
Changeover	Changeover in manufacturing is the process of converting a line or machine from running one product to another. Changeover times can last from a few minutes to as much as several weeks in the case of automobile manufacturers retooling for new models.
Specialist	A specialist is a trader who makes a market in one or several stocks and holds the limit order book for those stocks.
Value added	The value of output minus the value of all intermediate inputs, representing therefore the contribution of, and payments to, primary factors of production a value added.
Return on investment	Return on investment refers to the return a businessperson gets on the money he and other owners invest in the firm; for example, a business that earned $100 on a $1,000 investment would have a ROI of 10 percent: 100 divided by 1000.
Standardization	Standardization, in the context related to technologies and industries, is the process of establishing a technical standard among competing entities in a market, where this will bring benefits without hurting competition.
Time horizon	A time horizon is a fixed point of time in the future at which point certain processes will be evaluated or assumed to end. It is necessary in an accounting, finance or risk management regime to assign such a fixed horizon time so that alternatives can be evaluated for performance over the same period of time.
Innovation	Innovation refers to the first commercially successful introduction of a new product, the use

Go to **Cram101.com** for the Practice Tests for this Chapter.

of a new method of production, or the creation of a new form of business organization.

Product innovation	The development and sale of a new or improved product is a product innovation. Production of a new product on a commercial basis.
Firm	An organization that employs resources to produce a good or service for profit and owns and operates one or more plants is referred to as a firm.
Supply chain management	Supply chain management deals with the planning and execution issues involved in managing a supply chain. Supply chain management spans all movement and storage of raw materials, work-in-process inventory, and finished goods from point-of-origin to point-of-consumption.
Competitive Strategy	An outline of how a business intends to compete with other firms in the same industry is called competitive strategy.
Inputs	The inputs used by a firm or an economy are the labor, raw materials, electricity and other resources it uses to produce its outputs.
Profit	Profit refers to the return to the resource entrepreneurial ability; total revenue minus total cost.
Effective communication	When the intended meaning equals the perceived meaning it is called effective communication.
Organizational culture	The mindset of employees, including their shared beliefs, values, and goals is called the organizational culture.
Ombudsman	An ombudsman is an official, usually appointed by the government or by parliament, who is charged with representing the interests of the public by investigating and addressing complaints reported by individual citizens. An ombudsman need not be appointed by government; they may work for a corporation, a newspaper, an NGO, or even for the general public.
Negotiation	Negotiation is the process whereby interested parties resolve disputes, agree upon courses of action, bargain for individual or collective advantage, and/or attempt to craft outcomes which serve their mutual interests.
Motorola	The Six Sigma quality system was developed at Motorola even though it became most well known because of its use by General Electric. It was created by engineer Bill Smith, under the direction of Bob Galvin (son of founder Paul Galvin) when he was running the company.
Driving force	The key external pressure that will shape the future for an organization is a driving force. The driving force in an industry are the main underlying causes of changing industry and competitive conditions.
BMW	BMW is an independent German company and manufacturer of automobiles and motorcycles. BMW is the world's largest premium carmaker and is the parent company of the BMW MINI and Rolls-Royce car brands, and, formerly, Rover.
Inception	The date and time on which coverage under an insurance policy takes effect is inception. Also refers to the date at which a stock or mutual fund was first traded.
Senior management	Senior management is generally a team of individuals at the highest level of organizational management who have the day-to-day responsibilities of managing a corporation.
Verification	Verification refers to the final stage of the creative process where the validity or truthfulness of the insight is determined. The feedback portion of communication in which the receiver sends a message to the source indicating receipt of the message and the degree to which he or she understood the message.
Electronic data interchange	Electronic data interchange refers to the direct exchange between organizations of data via a computer-to-computer interface.

Competitiveness	Competitiveness usually refers to characteristics that permit a firm to compete effectively with other firms due to low cost or superior technology, perhaps internationally.
Warranty	An obligation of a company to replace defective goods or correct any deficiencies in performance or quality of a product is called a warranty.
Layout	Layout refers to the physical arrangement of the various parts of an advertisement including the headline, subheads, illustrations, body copy, and any identifying marks.
Productivity	Productivity refers to the total output of goods and services in a given period of time divided by work hours.
Collaboration	Collaboration occurs when the interaction between groups is very important to goal attainment and the goals are compatible. Wherein people work together —applying both to the work of individuals as well as larger collectives and societies.
Domestic	From or in one's own country. A domestic producer is one that produces inside the home country. A domestic price is the price inside the home country. Opposite of 'foreign' or 'world.'.
Competitive advantage	A business is said to have a competitive advantage when its unique strengths, often based on cost, quality, time, and innovation, offer consumers a greater percieved value and there by differtiating it from its competitors.
Mission statement	Mission statement refers to an outline of the fundamental purposes of an organization.
Relationship management	A method for developing long-term associations with customers is referred to as relationship management.
Inventory	Tangible property held for sale in the normal course of business or used in producing goods or services for sale is an inventory.
Equity	Equity is the name given to the set of legal principles, in countries following the English common law tradition, which supplement strict rules of law where their application would operate harshly, so as to achieve what is sometimes referred to as "natural justice."
Business plan	A detailed written statement that describes the nature of the business, the target market, the advantages the business will have in relation to competition, and the resources and qualifications of the owner is referred to as a business plan.
Cost structure	The relative proportion of an organization's fixed, variable, and mixed costs is referred to as cost structure.
Brand	A name, symbol, or design that identifies the goods or services of one seller or group of sellers and distinguishes them from the goods and services of competitors is a brand.
Points	Loan origination fees that may be deductible as interest by a buyer of property. A seller of property who pays points reduces the selling price by the amount of the points paid for the buyer.
Loyalty	Marketers tend to define customer loyalty as making repeat purchases. Some argue that it should be defined attitudinally as a strongly positive feeling about the brand.
Contribution	In business organization law, the cash or property contributed to a business by its owners is referred to as contribution.
Materials management	Materials management refers to the activity that controls the transmission of physical materials through the value chain, from procurement through production and into distribution.
Logistics	Those activities that focus on getting the right amount of the right products to the right place at the right time at the lowest possible cost is referred to as logistics.

Go to Cram101.com for the Practice Tests for this Chapter.

Logistics Management	Logistics management refers to the practice of organizing the cost-effective flow of raw materials, in-process inventory, finished goods, and related information from point of origin to point of consumption to satisfy customer requirements.
Total quality management	The broad set of management and control processes designed to focus an entire organization and all of its employees on providing products or services that do the best possible job of satisfying the customer is called total quality management.
Quality management	Quality management is a method for ensuring that all the activities necessary to design, develop and implement a product or service are effective and efficient with respect to the system and its performance.
Marketing	Promoting and selling products or services to customers, or prospective customers, is referred to as marketing.
Reverse marketing	The deliberate effort by organizational buyers to build relationships that shape suppliers' products, services, and capabilities to fit a buyer's needs and those of its customers is reverse marketing.
American Management Association	American Management Association International is the world's largest membership-based management development and executive training organization. Their products include instructor led seminars, workshops, conferences, customized corporate programs, online learning, books, newsletters, research surveys and reports.

Go to **Cram101.com** for the Practice Tests for this Chapter.

Technology	The body of knowledge and techniques that can be used to combine economic resources to produce goods and services is called technology.
Procurement	Procurement is the acquisition of goods or services at the best possible total cost of ownership, in the right quantity, at the right time, in the right place for the direct benefit or use of the governments, corporations, or individuals generally via, but not limited to a contract.
Gain	In finance, gain is a profit or an increase in value of an investment such as a stock or bond. Gain is calculated by fair market value or the proceeds from the sale of the investment minus the sum of the purchase price and all costs associated with it.
Leadership	Management merely consists of leadership applied to business situations; or in other words: management forms a sub-set of the broader process of leadership.
Logistics	Those activities that focus on getting the right amount of the right products to the right place at the right time at the lowest possible cost is referred to as logistics.
Supply	Supply is the aggregate amount of any material good that can be called into being at a certain price point; it comprises one half of the equation of supply and demand. In classical economic theory, a curve representing supply is one of the factors that produce price.
Globalization	The increasing world-wide integration of markets for goods, services and capital that attracted special attention in the late 1990s is called globalization.
Synergy	Corporate synergy occurs when corporations interact congruently. A corporate synergy refers to a financial benefit that a corporation expects to realize when it merges with or acquires another corporation.
Commodity	Could refer to any good, but in trade a commodity is usually a raw material or primary product that enters into international trade, such as metals or basic agricultural products.
Scope	Scope of a project is the sum total of all projects products and their requirements or features.
Purchasing	Purchasing refers to the function in a firm that searches for quality material resources, finds the best suppliers, and negotiates the best price for goods and services.
Contract	A contract is a "promise" or an "agreement" that is enforced or recognized by the law. In the civil law, a contract is considered to be part of the general law of obligations.
Decentralization	Decentralization is the process of redistributing decision-making closer to the point of service or action. This gives freedom to managers at lower levels of the organization to make decisions.
Committee	A long-lasting, sometimes permanent team in the organization structure created to deal with tasks that recur regularly is the committee.
Charter	Charter refers to an instrument or authority from the sovereign power bestowing the right or power to do business under the corporate form of organization. Also, the organic law of a city or town, and representing a portion of the statute law of the state.
Management	Management characterizes the process of leading and directing all or part of an organization, often a business, through the deployment and manipulation of resources. Early twentieth-century management writer Mary Parker Follett defined management as "the art of getting things done through people."
Market	A market is, as defined in economics, a social arrangement that allows buyers and sellers to discover information and carry out a voluntary exchange of goods or services.
Total cost	The sum of fixed cost and variable cost is referred to as total cost.

Go to **Cram101.com** for the Practice Tests for this Chapter.

International trade	The export of goods and services from a country and the import of goods and services into a country is referred to as the international trade.
Buyer	A buyer refers to a role in the buying center with formal authority and responsibility to select the supplier and negotiate the terms of the contract.
Variable	A variable is something measured by a number; it is used to analyze what happens to other things when the size of that number changes.
Regulation	Regulation refers to restrictions state and federal laws place on business with regard to the conduct of its activities.
Customs	Customs is an authority or agency in a country responsible for collecting customs duties and for controlling the flow of people, animals and goods (including personal effects and hazardous items) in and out of the country.
Firm	An organization that employs resources to produce a good or service for profit and owns and operates one or more plants is referred to as a firm.
Business unit	The lowest level of the company which contains the set of functions that carry a product through its life span from concept through manufacture, distribution, sales and service is a business unit.
Complexity	The technical sophistication of the product and hence the amount of understanding required to use it is referred to as complexity. It is the opposite of simplicity.
Production	The creation of finished goods and services using the factors of production: land, labor, capital, entrepreneurship, and knowledge.
Performance improvement	Performance improvement is the concept of measuring the output of a particular process or procedure then modifying the process or procedure in order to increase the output, increase efficiency, or increase the effectiveness of the process or procedure.
Embargo	Embargo refers to the prohibition of some category of trade. May apply to exports and/or imports, of particular products or of all trade, vis a vis the world or a particular country or countries.
Industry	A group of firms that produce identical or similar products is an industry. It is also used specifically to refer to an area of economic production focused on manufacturing which involves large amounts of capital investment before any profit can be realized, also called "heavy industry".
Domestic	From or in one's own country. A domestic producer is one that produces inside the home country. A domestic price is the price inside the home country. Opposite of 'foreign' or 'world.'.
Service	Service refers to a "non tangible product" that is not embodied in a physical good and that typically effects some change in another product, person, or institution. Contrasts with good.
Sony	Sony is a multinational corporation and one of the world's largest media conglomerates founded in Tokyo, Japan. One of its divisions Sony Electronics is one of the leading manufacturers of electronics, video, communications, and information technology products for the consumer and professional markets.
Countertrade	Countertrade is exchanging goods or services that are paid for, in whole or part, with other goods or services.
International Business	International business refers to any firm that engages in international trade or investment.

Go to **Cram101.com** for the Practice Tests for this Chapter.

Competitor	Other organizations in the same industry or type of business that provide a good or service to the same set of customers is referred to as a competitor.
Marketing	Promoting and selling products or services to customers, or prospective customers, is referred to as marketing.
Cost management	The approaches and activities of managers in short-run and long-run planning and control decisions that increase value for customers and lower costs of products and services are called cost management.
Distribution	Distribution in economics, the manner in which total output and income is distributed among individuals or factors.
Configuration	An organization's shape, which reflects the division of labor and the means of coordinating the divided tasks is configuration.
Assessment	Collecting information and providing feedback to employees about their behavior, communication style, or skills is an assessment.
Operation	A standardized method or technique that is performed repetitively, often on different materials resulting in different finished goods is called an operation.
Personnel	A collective term for all of the employees of an organization. Personnel is also commonly used to refer to the personnel management function or the organizational unit responsible for administering personnel programs.
Capital	Capital generally refers to financial wealth, especially that used to start or maintain a business. In classical economics, capital is one of four factors of production, the others being land and labor and entrepreneurship.
Supply chain management	Supply chain management deals with the planning and execution issues involved in managing a supply chain. Supply chain management spans all movement and storage of raw materials, work-in-process inventory, and finished goods from point-of-origin to point-of-consumption.
Supply chain	Supply chain refers to the flow of goods, services, and information from the initial sources of materials and services to the delivery of products to consumers.
Warranty	An obligation of a company to replace defective goods or correct any deficiencies in performance or quality of a product is called a warranty.
Senior management	Senior management is generally a team of individuals at the highest level of organizational management who have the day-to-day responsibilities of managing a corporation.
Deficit	The deficit is the amount by which expenditure exceed revenue.
Budget	Budget refers to an account, usually for a year, of the planned expenditures and the expected receipts of an entity. For a government, the receipts are tax revenues.
Budget deficit	A budget deficit occurs when an entity (often a government) spends more money than it takes
Competitiveness	Competitiveness usually refers to characteristics that permit a firm to compete effectively with other firms due to low cost or superior technology, perhaps internationally.
Exchange	The trade of things of value between buyer and seller so that each is better off after the trade is called the exchange.
Labor	People's physical and mental talents and efforts that are used to help produce goods and services are called labor.
Subsidy	Subsidy refers to government financial assistance to a domestic producer.
Profit	Profit refers to the return to the resource entrepreneurial ability; total revenue minus total cost.

Margin	A deposit by a buyer in stocks with a seller or a stockbroker, as security to cover fluctuations in the market in reference to stocks that the buyer has purchased but for which he has not paid is a margin. Commodities are also traded on margin.
Inputs	The inputs used by a firm or an economy are the labor, raw materials, electricity and other resources it uses to produce its outputs.
Profit margin	Profit margin is a measure of profitability. It is calculated using a formula and written as a percentage or a number. Profit margin = Net income before tax and interest / Revenue.
Exchange rate	Exchange rate refers to the price at which one country's currency trades for another, typically on the exchange market.
Productivity	Productivity refers to the total output of goods and services in a given period of time divided by work hours.
Relevant cost	A relevant cost refers to expected future costs that differ among alternative courses of action being considered. A cost that will be affected by taking a particular decision.
Market share	That fraction of an industry's output accounted for by an individual firm or group of firms is called market share.
Recession	A significant decline in economic activity. In the U.S., recession is approximately defined as two successive quarters of falling GDP, as judged by NBER.
Closing	The finalization of a real estate sales transaction that passes title to the property from the seller to the buyer is referred to as a closing. Closing is a sales term which refers to the process of making a sale. It refers to reaching the final step, which may be an exchange of money or acquiring a signature.
Global competition	Global competition exists when competitive conditions across national markets are linked strongly enough to form a true international market and when leading competitors compete head to head in many different countries.
Quick response	An inventory management system designed to reduce the retailer's lead-time, thereby lowering its inventory investment, improving customer service levels, and reducing logistics expense is referred to as quick response.
Inventory	Tangible property held for sale in the normal course of business or used in producing goods or services for sale is an inventory.
Insurance	Insurance refers to a system by which individuals can reduce their exposure to risk of large losses by spreading the risks among a large number of persons.
Invoice	The itemized bill for a transaction, stating the nature of the transaction and its cost. In international trade, the invoice price is often the preferred basis for levying an ad valorem tariff.
License	A license in the sphere of Intellectual Property Rights (IPR) is a document, contract or agreement giving permission or the 'right' to a legally-definable entity to do something (such as manufacture a product or to use a service), or to apply something (such as a trademark), with the objective of achieving commercial gain.
Credit	Credit refers to a recording as positive in the balance of payments, any transaction that gives rise to a payment into the country, such as an export, the sale of an asset, or borrowing from abroad.
Resistance to change	Resistance to change refers to an attitude or behavior that shows unwillingness to make or support a change.
World Trade	The World Trade Organization is an international, multilateral organization, which sets the

Organization	rules for the global trading system and resolves disputes between its member states, all of whom are signatories to its approximately 30 agreements.
Free trade	Free trade refers to a situation in which there are no artificial barriers to trade, such as tariffs and quotas. Usually used, often only implicitly, with frictionless trade, so that it implies that there are no barriers to trade of any kind.
Financial risk	The risk related to the inability of the firm to meet its debt obligations as they come due is called financial risk.
Negotiation	Negotiation is the process whereby interested parties resolve disputes, agree upon courses of action, bargain for individual or collective advantage, and/or attempt to craft outcomes which serve their mutual interests.
Agent	A person who makes economic decisions for another economic actor. A hired manager operates as an agent for a firm's owner.
Broker	In commerce, a broker is a party that mediates between a buyer and a seller. A broker who also acts as a seller or as a buyer becomes a principal party to the deal.
Evaluation	The consumer's appraisal of the product or brand on important attributes is called evaluation.
Product life cycle	Product life cycle refers to a series of phases in a product's sales and cash flows over time; these phases, in order of occurrence, are introductory, growth, maturity, and decline.
Intermediaries	Intermediaries specialize in information either to bring together two parties to a transaction or to buy in order to sell again.
Export	In economics, an export is any good or commodity, shipped or otherwise transported out of a country, province, town to another part of the world in a legitimate fashion, typically for use in trade or sale.
Exporter	A firm that sells its product in another country is an exporter.
Trade show	A type of exhibition or forum where manufacturers can display their products to current as well as prospective buyers is referred to as trade show.
Preshipment inspection	Preshipment inspection refers to certification of the value, quality, and/or identity of traded goods done in the exporting country by specialized agencies or firms on behalf of the importing country. Traditionally used as a means to prevent over- or under-invoicing, it is now being used also as a security measure.
Audit	An examination of the financial reports to ensure that they represent what they claim and conform with generally accepted accounting principles is referred to as audit.
Supplier evaluation	Supplier evaluation refers to a tool used by many firms to differentiate and discriminate among suppliers. A supplier evaluation often involves report cards where potential suppliers are rated based on different criteria such as quality, technical capability, or ability to meet schedule demands.
Quality audit	Quality audit means a systematic, independent examination of a quality system. A quality audit is typically performed at defined intervals and ensures that the institution has clearly-defined internal quality monitoring procedures linked to effective action. The checking determines if the quality system complies with applicable regulations or standards The process involves assessing the standard operating procedures (SOP's) for compliance to the regulations, and also assessing the actual process and results against what is stated in the SOP.
Mitsubishi	In a statement, the Mitsubishi says that forced labor is inconsistent with the company's values, and that the various lawsuits targeting Mitsubishi are misdirected. Instead, a

Go to **Cram101.com** for the Practice Tests for this Chapter.

	spokesman says the Mitsubishi of World War II is not the same Mitsubishi of today. The conglomerate also rejected a Chinese slave labor lawsuit demand by saying it bore no responsibility since it was national policy to employ Chinese laborers."
Option	A contract that gives the purchaser the option to buy or sell the underlying financial instrument at a specified price, called the exercise price or strike price, within a specific period of time.
Financial institution	A financial institution acts as an agent that provides financial services for its clients. Financial institutions generally fall under financial regulation from a government authority.
Commerce	Commerce is the exchange of something of value between two entities. It is the central mechanism from which capitalism is derived.
Specialist	A specialist is a trader who makes a market in one or several stocks and holds the limit order book for those stocks.
Ford	Ford is an American company that manufactures and sells automobiles worldwide. Ford introduced methods for large-scale manufacturing of cars, and large-scale management of an industrial workforce, especially elaborately engineered manufacturing sequences typified by the moving assembly lines.
Ford Motor Company	Ford Motor Company introduced methods for large-scale manufacturing of cars, and large-scale management of an industrial workforce, especially elaborately engineered manufacturing sequences typified by the moving assembly lines. Henry Ford's combination of highly efficient factories, highly paid workers, and low prices revolutionized manufacturing and came to be known around the world as Fordism by 1914.
Average total cost	Average total cost refers to a firm's total cost divided by output ; equal to average fixed cost plus average variable cost.
Manufacturing	Production of goods primarily by the application of labor and capital to raw materials and other intermediate inputs, in contrast to agriculture, mining, forestry, fishing, and services a manufacturing.
Warehouse	Warehouse refers to a location, often decentralized, that a firm uses to store, consolidate, age, or mix stock; house product-recall programs; or ease tax burdens.
Economics	The social science dealing with the use of scarce resources to obtain the maximum satisfaction of society's virtually unlimited economic wants is an economics.
Trial	An examination before a competent tribunal, according to the law of the land, of the facts or law put in issue in a cause, for the purpose of determining such issue is a trial. When the court hears and determines any issue of fact or law for the purpose of determining the rights of the parties, it may be considered a trial.
Market segments	Market segments refer to the groups that result from the process of market segmentation; these groups ideally have common needs and will respond similarly to a marketing action.
Product line	A group of products that are physically similar or are intended for a similar market are called the product line.
Organizational structure	Organizational structure is the way in which the interrelated groups of an organization are constructed. From a managerial point of view the main concerns are ensuring effective communication and coordination.
Differentiated product	A firm's product that is not identical to products of other firms in the same industry is a differentiated product.
Enabling	Enabling refers to giving workers the education and tools they need to assume their new decision-making powers.

Intervention	Intervention refers to an activity in which a government buys or sells its currency in the foreign exchange market in order to affect its currency's exchange rate.
Common cost	Any cost incurred by a utility providing more than one service, but which cannot be assigned solely to one or another function, as they relate to the utility's overall operations is a common cost.
Tariff	A tax imposed by a nation on an imported good is called a tariff.
Customs duty	A customs duty is a tariff or tax on the import or export of goods.
Authority	Authority in agency law, refers to an agent's ability to affect his principal's legal relations with third parties. Also used to refer to an actor's legal power or ability to do something. In addition, sometimes used to refer to a statute, case, or other legal source that justifies a particular result.
Customer service	The ability of logistics management to satisfy users in terms of time, dependability, communication, and convenience is called the customer service.
Escalation	Regarding the structure of tariffs. In the context of a trade war, escalation refers to the increase in tariffs that occurs as countries retaliate again and again.
Premium	Premium refers to the fee charged by an insurance company for an insurance policy. The rate of losses must be relatively predictable: In order to set the premium (prices) insurers must be able to estimate them accurately.
Marine insurance	Insurance that owners of vessels purchase to insure against loss or damage to the vessel and its cargo caused by perils at sea is referred to as the marine insurance.
Grant	Grant refers to an intergovernmental transfer of funds . Since the New Deal, state and local governments have become increasingly dependent upon federal grants for an almost infinite variety of programs.
Hedging	A technique for avoiding a risk by making a counteracting transaction is referred to as hedging.
Carrying costs	Carrying costs refers to costs that arise while holding an inventory of goods for sale.
Carrying cost	The cost to hold an asset, usually inventory is called a carrying cost. For inventory, a carrying cost includes such items as interest, warehousing costs, insurance, and material-handling expenses.
Property	Assets defined in the broadest legal sense. Property includes the unrealized receivables of a cash basis taxpayer, but not services rendered.
Interest	In finance and economics, interest is the price paid by a borrower for the use of a lender's money. In other words, interest is the amount of paid to "rent" money for a period of time.
Fund	Independent accounting entity with a self-balancing set of accounts segregated for the purposes of carrying on specific activities is referred to as a fund.
Interest rate	The rate of return on bonds, loans, or deposits. When one speaks of 'the' interest rate, it is usually in a model where there is only one.
Currency risk	Currency risk is a form of risk that arises from the change in price of one currency against another. Whenever investors or companies have assets or business operations across national borders, they face currency risk if their positions are not hedged.
Controller	Controller refers to the financial executive primarily responsible for management accounting and financial accounting. Also called chief accounting officer.
Risk sharing	The distribution of financial risk among parties furnishing a service is called risk sharing.

Risk aversion	Risk aversion is the reluctance of a person to accept a bargain with an uncertain payoff rather than another bargain with a more certain but possibly lower expected payoff.
Futures	Futures refer to contracts for the sale and future delivery of stocks or commodities, wherein either party may waive delivery, and receive or pay, as the case may be, the difference in market price at the time set for delivery.
Forward exchange	When two parties agree to exchange currency and execute a deal at some specific date in the future, we have forward exchange.
Currency exchange rate	The rate between two currencies that specifies how much one country's currency is worth expressed in terms of the other country's currency is the currency exchange rate.
Purchase order	A form on which items or services needed by a business firm are specified and then communicated to the vendor is a purchase order.
Hedge	Hedge refers to a process of offsetting risk. In the foreign exchange market, hedgers use the forward market to cover a transaction or open position and thereby reduce exchange risk. The term applies most commonly to trade.
Commodity exchange	Commodity exchange refers to a securities exchange that specializes in the buying and selling of precious metals and minerals and agricultural goods.
Speculative risk	A chance of either profit or loss is called speculative risk.
Speculation	The purchase or sale of an asset in hopes that its price will rise or fall respectively, in order to make a profit is called speculation.
Forward rate	Forward rate refers to the forward exchange rate, this is the exchange rate on a forward market transaction.
Favorable exchange rate	An exchange rate different from the market or official rate, provided by the government on a transaction as an indirect way of providing a subsidy is a favorable exchange rate.
Chrysler	The Chrysler Corporation was an American automobile manufacturer that existed independently from 1925–1998. The company was formed by Walter Percy Chrysler on June 6, 1925, with the remaining assets of Maxwell Motor Company.
Corporation	A legal entity chartered by a state or the Federal government that is distinct and separate from the individuals who own it is a corporation. This separation gives the corporation unique powers which other legal entities lack.
Barter	Barter is a type of trade where goods or services are exchanged for a certain amount of other goods or services; no money is involved in the transaction.
Administration	Administration refers to the management and direction of the affairs of governments and institutions; a collective term for all policymaking officials of a government; the execution and implementation of public policy.
Countertrading	The sale of goods or services that are paid for in whole or in part by the transfer of goods or services between seperate countries is called countertrading. Also referred to as bartering.
Manufactured good	A manufactured good refers to goods that have been processed in any way.
Foreign exchange	In finance, foreign exchange means currencies, such as U.S. Dollars and Euros. These are traded on foreign exchange markets.
Discount	The difference between the face value of a bond and its selling price, when a bond is sold for less than its face value it's referred to as a discount.

Preference	The act of a debtor in paying or securing one or more of his creditors in a manner more favorable to them than to other creditors or to the exclusion of such other creditors is a preference. In the absence of statute, a preference is perfectly good, but to be legal it must be bona fide, and not a mere subterfuge of the debtor to secure a future benefit to himself or to prevent the application of his property to his debts.
Internationa-ization	Internationalization refers to another term for fragmentation. Used by Grossman and Helpman.
Trend	Trend refers to the long-term movement of an economic variable, such as its average rate of increase or decrease over enough years to encompass several business cycles.
Ad hoc	Ad hoc is a Latin phrase which means "for this purpose." It generally signifies a solution that has been tailored to a specific purpose and is makeshift and non-general, such as a handcrafted network protocol or a specific-purpose equation, as opposed to general solutions.
Realization	Realization is the sale of assets when an entity is being liquidated.
Proactive	To be proactive is to act before a situation becomes a source of confrontation or crisis. It is the opposite of "retroactive," which refers to actions taken after an event.
Controlling	A management function that involves determining whether or not an organization is progressing toward its goals and objectives, and taking corrective action if it is not is called controlling.
Outbound	Communications originating inside an organization and destined for customers, prospects, or other people outside the organization are called outbound.
Finished goods	Completed products awaiting sale are called finished goods. An item considered a finished good in a supplying plant might be considered a component or raw material in a receiving plant.
Partnership agreement	A document that defines the specific terms of a partnership or business relationship, such as how much work each partner will do and how the profits are divided is a partnership agreement.
Partnership	In the common law, a partnership is a type of business entity in which partners share with each other the profits or losses of the business undertaking in which they have all invested.
Subsidiary	A company that is controlled by another company or corporation is a subsidiary.
Foreign subsidiary	A company owned in a foreign country by another company is referred to as foreign subsidiary.
Automation	Automation allows machines to do work previously accomplished by people.
Acquisition	A company's purchase of the property and obligations of another company is an acquisition.
Information system	An information system is a system whether automated or manual, that comprises people, machines, and/or methods organized to collect, process, transmit, and disseminate data that represent user information.
Integration	Economic integration refers to reducing barriers among countries to transactions and to movements of goods, capital, and labor, including harmonization of laws, regulations, and standards. Integrated markets theoretically function as a unified market.
Leverage	Leverage is using given resources in such a way that the potential positive or negative outcome is magnified. In finance, this generally refers to borrowing.
Raw material	Raw material refers to a good that has not been transformed by production; a primary product.
Enterprise	Enterprise refers to another name for a business organization. Other similar terms are

	business firm, sometimes simply business, sometimes simply firm, as well as company, and entity.
Gap	In December of 1995, Gap became the first major North American retailer to accept independent monitoring of the working conditions in a contract factory producing its garments. Gap is the largest specialty retailer in the United States.
Buying center	The group of people in an organization who participate in the buying process and share common goals, risks, and knowledge important to a purchase decision is referred to as buying center.
Liaison	An individual who serves as a bridge between groups, tying groups together and facilitating the communication flow needed to integrate group activities is a liaison.
Assignment	A transfer of property or some right or interest is referred to as assignment.
Core	A core is the set of feasible allocations in an economy that cannot be improved upon by subset of the set of the economy's consumers (a coalition). In construction, when the force in an element is within a certain center section, the core, the element will only be under compression.
Human resources	Human resources refers to the individuals within the firm, and to the portion of the firm's organization that deals with hiring, firing, training, and other personnel issues.
Management team	A management team is directly responsible for managing the day-to-day operations (and profitability) of a company.
Sourcing decisions	Whether a firm should make or buy component parts are sourcing decisions.
Core competency	A company's core competency are things that a firm can (alsosns) do well and that meet the following three conditions. 1. It provides customer benefits, 2. It is hard for competitors to imitate, and 3. it can be leveraged widely to many products and market. A core competency can take various forms, including technical/subject matter knowhow, a reliable process, and/or close relationships with customers and suppliers. It may also include product development or culture such as employee dedication. Modern business theories suggest that most activities that are not part of a company's core competency should be outsourced.
Vertical integration	Vertical integration refers to production of different stages of processing of a product within the same firm.
Outsourcing	Outsourcing refers to a production activity that was previously done inside a firm or plant that is now conducted outside that firm or plant.
Innovation	Innovation refers to the first commercially successful introduction of a new product, the use of a new method of production, or the creation of a new form of business organization.
Contract manufacturing	Contract manufacturing refers to a foreign country's production of private-label goods to which a domestic company then attaches its brand name or trademark; also called outsourcing.
Converse	Converse is an American shoe company which has been making shoes since the early 20th century. The company's main turning point came in 1917 when the Converse All-Star basketball shoe was introduced. This was a real innovation at the time, considering the sport was only 25 years old.
Long run	In economic models, the long run time frame assumes no fixed factors of production. Firms can enter or leave the marketplace, and the cost (and availability) of land, labor, raw materials, and capital goods can be assumed to vary.
Journal	Book of original entry, in which transactions are recorded in a general ledger system, is referred to as a journal.

Materials management	Materials management refers to the activity that controls the transmission of physical materials through the value chain, from procurement through production and into distribution.
Harvard Business Review	Harvard Business Review is a research-based magazine written for business practitioners, it claims a high ranking business readership and enjoys the reverence of academics, executives, and management consultants. It has been the frequent publishing home for well known scholars and management thinkers.
Business Week	Business Week is a business magazine published by McGraw-Hill. It was first published in 1929 under the direction of Malcolm Muir, who was serving as president of the McGraw-Hill Publishing company at the time. It is considered to be the standard both in industry and among students.

Discount	The difference between the face value of a bond and its selling price, when a bond is sold for less than its face value it's referred to as a discount.
Management	Management characterizes the process of leading and directing all or part of an organization, often a business, through the deployment and manipulation of resources. Early twentieth-century management writer Mary Parker Follett defined management as "the art of getting things done through people."
Market	A market is, as defined in economics, a social arrangement that allows buyers and sellers to discover information and carry out a voluntary exchange of goods or services.
Project management	Project management is the discipline of organizing and managing resources in such a way that these resources deliver all the work required to complete a project within defined scope, time, and cost constraints.
Quantity discount	A quantity discount is a price reduction given for a large order.
Competitor	Other organizations in the same industry or type of business that provide a good or service to the same set of customers is referred to as a competitor.
Project management software	Project management software is a term covering many types of software, including scheduling, resource allocation, collaboration software, communication and documentation systems, which are used to deal with the complexity of large projects.
Proactive	To be proactive is to act before a situation becomes a source of confrontation or crisis. It is the opposite of "retroactive," which refers to actions taken after an event.
Critical path	The sequence of tasks that limit how quickly a project can be completed is referred to as critical path.
Deliverable	A deliverable refers to a product created as a result of project work.
Consultant	A professional that provides expert advice in a particular field or area in which customers occassionaly require this type of knowledge is a consultant.
Respondent	Respondent refers to a term often used to describe the party charged in an administrative proceeding. The party adverse to the appellant in a case appealed to a higher court.
Personnel	A collective term for all of the employees of an organization. Personnel is also commonly used to refer to the personnel management function or the organizational unit responsible for administering personnel programs.
Product design	Product Design is defined as the idea generation, concept development, testing and manufacturing or implementation of a physical object or service. It is possibly the evolution of former discipline name - Industrial Design.
Budget	Budget refers to an account, usually for a year, of the planned expenditures and the expected receipts of an entity. For a government, the receipts are tax revenues.
Specialist	A specialist is a trader who makes a market in one or several stocks and holds the limit order book for those stocks.
Purchasing	Purchasing refers to the function in a firm that searches for quality material resources, finds the best suppliers, and negotiates the best price for goods and services.
Supply	Supply is the aggregate amount of any material good that can be called into being at a certain price point; it comprises one half of the equation of supply and demand. In classical economic theory, a curve representing supply is one of the factors that produce price.
Supply chain management	Supply chain management deals with the planning and execution issues involved in managing a supply chain. Supply chain management spans all movement and storage of raw materials, work-

	in-process inventory, and finished goods from point-of-origin to point-of-consumption.
Supply chain	Supply chain refers to the flow of goods, services, and information from the initial sources of materials and services to the delivery of products to consumers.
Users	Users refer to people in the organization who actually use the product or service purchased by the buying center.
Buyer	A buyer refers to a role in the buying center with formal authority and responsibility to select the supplier and negotiate the terms of the contract.
Bid	A bid price is a price offered by a buyer when he/she buys a good. In the context of stock trading on a stock exchange, the bid price is the highest price a buyer of a stock is willing to pay for a share of that given stock.
Quality improvement	Quality is inversely proportional to variability thus quality Improvement is the reduction of variability in products and processes.
Value analysis	Value analysis refers to a systematic appraisal of the design, quality, and performance of a product to reduce purchasing costs.
Learning curve	Learning curve is a function that measures how labor-hours per unit decline as units of production increase because workers are learning and becoming better at their jobs.
Marketing	Promoting and selling products or services to customers, or prospective customers, is referred to as marketing.
Marketing Plan	Marketing plan refers to a road map for the marketing activities of an organization for a specified future period of time, such as one year or five years.
Project manager	Project manager refers to a manager responsible for a temporary work project that involves the participation of other people from various functions and levels of the organization.
Controlling	A management function that involves determining whether or not an organization is progressing toward its goals and objectives, and taking corrective action if it is not is called controlling.
Customer satisfaction	Customer satisfaction is a business term which is used to capture the idea of measuring how satisfied an enterprise's customers are with the organization's efforts in a marketplace.
Internal customer	An individuals or unit within the firm that receives services from other entities within the organization is an internal customer.
Assignment	A transfer of property or some right or interest is referred to as assignment.
Cost management	The approaches and activities of managers in short-run and long-run planning and control decisions that increase value for customers and lower costs of products and services are called cost management.
Leadership	Management merely consists of leadership applied to business situations; or in other words: management forms a sub-set of the broader process of leadership.
Scope	Scope of a project is the sum total of all projects products and their requirements or features.
Correlation	A correlation is the measure of the extent to which two economic or statistical variables move together, normalized so that its values range from -1 to +1. It is defined as the covariance of the two variables divided by the square root of the product of their variances.
Project plan	A project plan lists the amount of time and the budget needed to complete the tasks involved in a project.
Firm	An organization that employs resources to produce a good or service for profit and owns and

operates one or more plants is referred to as a firm.

Accounting	A system that collects and processes financial information about an organization and reports that information to decision makers is referred to as accounting.
Change management	Change management is the process of developing a planned approach to change in an organization. Typically the objective is to maximize the collective benefits for all people involved in the change and minimize the risk of failure of implementing the change.
Technology	The body of knowledge and techniques that can be used to combine economic resources to produce goods and services is called technology.
Gantt chart	Bar graph showing production managers what projects are being worked on and what stage they are in at any given time is a gantt chart.
Program Evaluation and Review Technique	Program evaluation and review technique refers to a method for analyzing the tasks involved in completing a given project, estimating the time needed to complete each task, and identifying the minimum time needed to complete the total project.
Evaluation	The consumer's appraisal of the product or brand on important attributes is called evaluation.
Variance	Variance refers to a measure of how much an economic or statistical variable varies across values or observations. Its calculation is the same as that of the covariance, being the covariance of the variable with itself.
Variable	A variable is something measured by a number; it is used to analyze what happens to other things when the size of that number changes.
Distribution	Distribution in economics, the manner in which total output and income is distributed among individuals or factors.
Extension	Extension refers to an out-of-court settlement in which creditors agree to allow the firm more time to meet its financial obligations. A new repayment schedule will be developed, subject to the acceptance of creditors.
Commodity	Could refer to any good, but in trade a commodity is usually a raw material or primary product that enters into international trade, such as metals or basic agricultural products.
Information technology	Information technology refers to technology that helps companies change business by allowing them to use new methods.
Project objective	Project objective is a business benefit that an organization expects to achieve as a result of injecting project product(s) into itself or its environment.
Points	Loan origination fees that may be deductible as interest by a buyer of property. A seller of property who pays points reduces the selling price by the amount of the points paid for the buyer.
Control process	A process involving gathering processed data, analyzing processed data, and using this information to make adjustments to the process is a control process.
Interest	In finance and economics, interest is the price paid by a borrower for the use of a lender's money. In other words, interest is the amount of paid to "rent" money for a period of time.
Management control	That aspect of management concerned with the comparison of actual versus planned performance as well as the development and implementation of procedures to correct substandard performance is called management control.
Production	The creation of finished goods and services using the factors of production: land, labor, capital, entrepreneurship, and knowledge.

Contract	A contract is a "promise" or an "agreement" that is enforced or recognized by the law. In the civil law, a contract is considered to be part of the general law of obligations.
Labor	People's physical and mental talents and efforts that are used to help produce goods and services are called labor.
Direct labor	The earnings of employees who work directly on the products being manufactured are direct labor.
Factors of production	Economic resources: land, capital, labor, and entrepreneurial ability are called factors of production.
Experience curve	Experience curve refers to function that measures the decline in cost per unit in various value-chain functions such as manufacturing, marketing, distribution, and so on, as units produced increases.
Continuous improvement	The constant effort to eliminate waste, reduce response time, simplify the design of both products and processes, and improve quality and customer service is referred to as continuous improvement.
Vertical integration	Vertical integration refers to production of different stages of processing of a product within the same firm.
Integration	Economic integration refers to reducing barriers among countries to transactions and to movements of goods, capital, and labor, including harmonization of laws, regulations, and standards. Integrated markets theoretically function as a unified market.
Automation	Automation allows machines to do work previously accomplished by people.
Investment	Investment refers to spending for the production and accumulation of capital and additions to inventories. In a financial sense, buying an asset with the expectation of making a return.
Production efficiency	A situation in which the economy cannot produce more of one good without producing less of some other good is referred to as production efficiency.
Turnover	Turnover in a financial context refers to the rate at which a provider of goods cycles through its average inventory. Turnover in a human resources context refers to the characteristic of a given company or industry, relative to rate at which an employer gains and loses staff.
Negotiation	Negotiation is the process whereby interested parties resolve disputes, agree upon courses of action, bargain for individual or collective advantage, and/or attempt to craft outcomes which serve their mutual interests.
Analyst	Analyst refers to a person or tool with a primary function of information analysis, generally with a more limited, practical and short term set of goals than a researcher.
Profit	Profit refers to the return to the resource entrepreneurial ability; total revenue minus total cost.
Overhead cost	An expenses of operating a business over and above the direct costs of producing a product is an overhead cost. They can include utilities (eg, electricity, telephone), advertizing and marketing, and any other costs not billed directly to the client or included in the price of the product.
Total cost	The sum of fixed cost and variable cost is referred to as total cost.
Service	Service refers to a "non tangible product" that is not embodied in a physical good and that typically effects some change in another product, person, or institution. Contrasts with good.
Value	Systematic evaluation of all aspects of the value-chain business functions, with the

engineering	objective of reducing costs while satisfying customer needs is referred to as value engineering.
Tangible	Having a physical existence is referred to as the tangible. Personal property other than real estate, such as cars, boats, stocks, or other assets.
Holding	The holding is a court's determination of a matter of law based on the issue presented in the particular case. In other words: under this law, with these facts, this result.
Performance improvement	Performance improvement is the concept of measuring the output of a particular process or procedure then modifying the process or procedure in order to increase the output, increase efficiency, or increase the effectiveness of the process or procedure.
Performance attributes	Attributes having to do with the functioning of a product such as horsepower, signal-to-noise ratio, or decibel output are called performance attributes.
Standardization	Standardization, in the context related to technologies and industries, is the process of establishing a technical standard among competing entities in a market, where this will bring benefits without hurting competition.
Manufacturing	Production of goods primarily by the application of labor and capital to raw materials and other intermediate inputs, in contrast to agriculture, mining, forestry, fishing, and services a manufacturing.
Downturn	A decline in a stock market or economic cycle is a downturn.
Novation	A mutual agreement, between all parties concerned, for the discharge of a valid existing obligation by the substitution of a new valid obligation on the part of the debtor or another, or a like agreement for the discharge of a debtor to his creditor by the substitution of a new creditor is referred to as novation.
Expense	In accounting, an expense represents an event in which an asset is used up or a liability is incurred. In terms of the accounting equation, expenses reduce owners' equity.
Materials management	Materials management refers to the activity that controls the transmission of physical materials through the value chain, from procurement through production and into distribution.
Quality control	The measurement of products and services against set standards is referred to as quality control.
Consideration	Consideration in contract law, a basic requirement for an enforceable agreement under traditional contract principles, defined in this text as legal value, bargained for and given in exchange for an act or promise. In corporation law, cash or property contributed to a corporation in exchange for shares, or a promise to contribute such cash or property.
Speculation	The purchase or sale of an asset in hopes that its price will rise or fall respectively, in order to make a profit is called speculation.
Assessment	Collecting information and providing feedback to employees about their behavior, communication style, or skills is an assessment.
Gain	In finance, gain is a profit or an increase in value of an investment such as a stock or bond. Gain is calculated by fair market value or the proceeds from the sale of the investment minus the sum of the purchase price and all costs associated with it.
Incremental cost	Additional total cost incurred for an activity is called incremental cost. A form of costing that classifies costs into their fixed and variable elements in order to calculate the extra cost of making and selling an additional batch of units.
Unit cost	Unit cost refers to cost computed by dividing some amount of total costs by the related number of units. Also called average cost.

Go to **Cram101.com** for the Practice Tests for this Chapter.

Customer service	The ability of logistics management to satisfy users in terms of time, dependability, communication, and convenience is called the customer service.
Option	A contract that gives the purchaser the option to buy or sell the underlying financial instrument at a specified price, called the exercise price or strike price, within a specific period of time.
Short run	Short run refers to a period of time that permits an increase or decrease in current production volume with existing capacity, but one that is too short to permit enlargement of that capacity itself (eg, the building of new plants, training of additional workers, etc.).
Warehouse	Warehouse refers to a location, often decentralized, that a firm uses to store, consolidate, age, or mix stock; house product-recall programs; or ease tax burdens.
Accounts payable	A written record of all vendors to whom the business firm owes money is referred to as accounts payable.
Consolidation	The combination of two or more firms, generally of equal size and market power, to form an entirely new entity is a consolidation.
Leverage	Leverage is using given resources in such a way that the potential positive or negative outcome is magnified. In finance, this generally refers to borrowing.
Synergy	Corporate synergy occurs when corporations interact congruently. A corporate synergy refers to a financial benefit that a corporation expects to realize when it merges with or acquires another corporation.
Procurement	Procurement is the acquisition of goods or services at the best possible total cost of ownership, in the right quantity, at the right time, in the right place for the direct benefit or use of the governments, corporations, or individuals generally via, but not limited to a contract.
Business analyst	A business analyst is responsible for analyzing the business needs of their clients and stakeholders to help identify business problems and propose solutions.
Committee	A long-lasting, sometimes permanent team in the organization structure created to deal with tasks that recur regularly is the committee.
Balance	In banking and accountancy, the outstanding balance is the amount of money owned, (or due), that remains in a deposit account (or a loan account) at a given date, after all past remittances, payments and withdrawal have been accounted for. It can be positive (then, in the balance sheet of a firm, it is an asset) or negative (a liability).
Contribution	In business organization law, the cash or property contributed to a business by its owners is referred to as contribution.
Inputs	The inputs used by a firm or an economy are the labor, raw materials, electricity and other resources it uses to produce its outputs.
Competitiveness	Competitiveness usually refers to characteristics that permit a firm to compete effectively with other firms due to low cost or superior technology, perhaps internationally.

Go to **Cram101.com** for the Practice Tests for this Chapter.

Management	Management characterizes the process of leading and directing all or part of an organization, often a business, through the deployment and manipulation of resources. Early twentieth-century management writer Mary Parker Follett defined management as "the art of getting things done through people."
Cost management	The approaches and activities of managers in short-run and long-run planning and control decisions that increase value for customers and lower costs of products and services are called cost management.
Procurement	Procurement is the acquisition of goods or services at the best possible total cost of ownership, in the right quantity, at the right time, in the right place for the direct benefit or use of the governments, corporations, or individuals generally via, but not limited to a contract.
Purchasing	Purchasing refers to the function in a firm that searches for quality material resources, finds the best suppliers, and negotiates the best price for goods and services.
Operation	A standardized method or technique that is performed repetitively, often on different materials resulting in different finished goods is called an operation.
Policy	Similar to a script in that a policy can be a less than completely rational decision-making method. Involves the use of a pre-existing set of decision steps for any problem that presents itself.
Reengineering	The fundamental rethinking and redesign of business processes to achieve improvements in critical measures of performance, such as cost, quality, service, speed, and customer satisfaction is referred to as reengineering.
Outsourcing	Outsourcing refers to a production activity that was previously done inside a firm or plant that is now conducted outside that firm or plant.
Competitor	Other organizations in the same industry or type of business that provide a good or service to the same set of customers is referred to as a competitor.
Technology	The body of knowledge and techniques that can be used to combine economic resources to produce goods and services is called technology.
Revenue	Revenue is a U.S. business term for the amount of money that a company receives from its activities, mostly from sales of products and/or services to customers.
Commodity	Could refer to any good, but in trade a commodity is usually a raw material or primary product that enters into international trade, such as metals or basic agricultural products.
Production	The creation of finished goods and services using the factors of production: land, labor, capital, entrepreneurship, and knowledge.
Cost driver	Cost driver refers to a factor related to an activity that changes the volume or characteristics of that activity, and in doing so changes its costs. An activity can have more than one cost driver.
Warranty	An obligation of a company to replace defective goods or correct any deficiencies in performance or quality of a product is called a warranty.
Inventory	Tangible property held for sale in the normal course of business or used in producing goods or services for sale is an inventory.
Contract	A contract is a "promise" or an "agreement" that is enforced or recognized by the law. In the civil law, a contract is considered to be part of the general law of obligations.
Customer value	Customer value refers to the unique combination of benefits received by targeted buyers that includes quality, price, convenience, on-time delivery, and both before-sale and after-sale

	service.
Service	Service refers to a "non tangible product" that is not embodied in a physical good and that typically effects some change in another product, person, or institution. Contrasts with good.
Industry	A group of firms that produce identical or similar products is an industry. It is also used specifically to refer to an area of economic production focused on manufacturing which involves large amounts of capital investment before any profit can be realized, also called "heavy industry".
Evaluation	The consumer's appraisal of the product or brand on important attributes is called evaluation.
Market	A market is, as defined in economics, a social arrangement that allows buyers and sellers to discover information and carry out a voluntary exchange of goods or services.
Competitive market	A market in which no buyer or seller has market power is called a competitive market.
Specialist	A specialist is a trader who makes a market in one or several stocks and holds the limit order book for those stocks.
Supply	Supply is the aggregate amount of any material good that can be called into being at a certain price point; it comprises one half of the equation of supply and demand. In classical economic theory, a curve representing supply is one of the factors that produce price.
Supply chain	Supply chain refers to the flow of goods, services, and information from the initial sources of materials and services to the delivery of products to consumers.
Consideration	Consideration in contract law, a basic requirement for an enforceable agreement under traditional contract principles, defined in this text as legal value, bargained for and given in exchange for an act or promise. In corporation law, cash or property contributed to a corporation in exchange for shares, or a promise to contribute such cash or property.
Labor	People's physical and mental talents and efforts that are used to help produce goods and services are called labor.
Profit	Profit refers to the return to the resource entrepreneurial ability; total revenue minus total cost.
Administrative cost	An administrative cost is all executive, organizational, and clerical costs associated with the general management of an organization rather than with manufacturing, marketing, or selling
Value analysis	Value analysis refers to a systematic appraisal of the design, quality, and performance of a product to reduce purchasing costs.
Total cost	The sum of fixed cost and variable cost is referred to as total cost.
Financial statement	Financial statement refers to a summary of all the transactions that have occurred over a particular period.
Cost of goods sold	In accounting, the cost of goods sold describes the direct expenses incurred in producing a particular good for sale, including the actual cost of materials that comprise the good, and direct labor expense in putting the good in salable condition.
Fixed cost	The cost that a firm bears if it does not produce at all and that is independent of its output. The presence of a fixed cost tends to imply increasing returns to scale. Contrasts with variable cost.
Variable	A variable is something measured by a number; it is used to analyze what happens to other

	things when the size of that number changes.
Variable cost	The portion of a firm or industry's cost that changes with output, in contrast to fixed cost is referred to as variable cost.
Contribution	In business organization law, the cash or property contributed to a business by its owners is referred to as contribution.
Accounting	A system that collects and processes financial information about an organization and reports that information to decision makers is referred to as accounting.
Economy	The income, expenditures, and resources that affect the cost of running a business and household are called an economy.
Economies of scale	In economics, returns to scale and economies of scale are related terms that describe what happens as the scale of production increases. They are different terms and not to be used interchangeably.
Mixed cost	Mixed cost refers to a cost that has both fixed and variable elements.
Expense	In accounting, an expense represents an event in which an asset is used up or a liability is incurred. In terms of the accounting equation, expenses reduce owners' equity.
Semivariable costs	Semivariable costs refer to costs that are partially fixed but still change somewhat as volume changes.
Semivariable cost	A cost with both a fixed and a variable component is called semivariable cost.
Fixed expense	A fixed expense is an expense that remains constant as activity changes within the relevant range. Any costs not related directly to the production of your product or service.
Lease	A contract for the possession and use of land or other property, including goods, on one side, and a recompense of rent or other income on the other is the lease.
Operating expense	In throughput accounting, the cost accounting aspect of Theory of Constraints (TOC), operating expense is the money spent turning inventory into throughput. In TOC, operating expense is limited to costs that vary strictly with the quantity produced, like raw materials and purchased components.
Points	Loan origination fees that may be deductible as interest by a buyer of property. A seller of property who pays points reduces the selling price by the amount of the points paid for the buyer.
Total fixed costs	The total of all costs that do not change with output, even if output is zero is referred to as total fixed costs. Examples are rent, interest on loans, and insurance
Cost behavior	The relationship between cost and volume or activity is referred to as cost behavior.
Direct cost	A direct cost is a cost that can be identified specifically with a particular sponsored project, an instructional activity, or any other institutional activity, or that can be directly assigned to such activities relatively easily with a high degree of accuracy.
Indirect cost	Indirect cost refers to a cost that cannot be traced to a particular department.
Context	The effect of the background under which a message often takes on more and richer meaning is a context. Context is especially important in cross-cultural interactions because some cultures are said to be high context or low context.
Interest	In finance and economics, interest is the price paid by a borrower for the use of a lender's money. In other words, interest is the amount of paid to "rent" money for a period of time.
Product line	A group of products that are physically similar or are intended for a similar market are

called the product line.

Cost accounting	Cost accounting measures and reports financial and nonfinancial information relating to the cost of acquiring or consuming resources in an organization. It provides information for both management accounting and financial accounting.
Overhead cost	An expenses of operating a business over and above the direct costs of producing a product is an overhead cost. They can include utilities (eg, electricity, telephone), advertizing and marketing, and any other costs not billed directly to the client or included in the price of the product.
Supply chain management	Supply chain management deals with the planning and execution issues involved in managing a supply chain. Supply chain management spans all movement and storage of raw materials, work-in-process inventory, and finished goods from point-of-origin to point-of-consumption.
Inflation	An increase in the overall price level of an economy, usually as measured by the CPI or by the implicit price deflator is called inflation.
Target pricing	Manufacturer deliberately adjusting the composition and features of a product to achieve the target price to consumers is referred to as target pricing.
Quality function deployment	Quality function deployment involves developing a matrix that includes customer preferences and product attributes. A quality function deployment matrix allows a firm to quantitatively analyze the relationship between customer needs and design attributes.
Sourcing decisions	Whether a firm should make or buy component parts are sourcing decisions.
Product life cycle	Product life cycle refers to a series of phases in a product's sales and cash flows over time; these phases, in order of occurrence, are introductory, growth, maturity, and decline.
Product development	In business and engineering, new product development is the complete process of bringing a new product to market. There are two parallel aspects to this process : one involves product engineering ; the other marketing analysis. Marketers see new product development as the first stage in product life cycle management, engineers as part of Product Lifecycle Management.
Integration	Economic integration refers to reducing barriers among countries to transactions and to movements of goods, capital, and labor, including harmonization of laws, regulations, and standards. Integrated markets theoretically function as a unified market.
Trend	Trend refers to the long-term movement of an economic variable, such as its average rate of increase or decrease over enough years to encompass several business cycles.
Open market	In economics, the open market is the term used to refer to the environment in which bonds are bought and sold.
Market price	Market price is an economic concept with commonplace familiarity; it is the price that a good or service is offered at, or will fetch, in the marketplace; it is of interest mainly in the study of microeconomics.
Buyer	A buyer refers to a role in the buying center with formal authority and responsibility to select the supplier and negotiate the terms of the contract.
Appreciation	Appreciation refers to a rise in the value of a country's currency on the exchange market, relative either to a particular other currency or to a weighted average of other currencies. The currency is said to appreciate. Opposite of 'depreciation.' Appreciation can also refer to the increase in value of any asset.
Market structure	Market structure refers to the way that suppliers and demanders in an industry interact to determine price and quantity. Market structures range from perfect competition to monopoly.

Monopoly	A monopoly is defined as a persistent market situation where there is only one provider of a kind of product or service.
Perfect competition	An idealized market structure in which there are large numbers of both buyers and sellers, all of them small, so that they act as price takers. Perfect competition also assumes homogeneous products, free entry and exit, and complete information.
Monopolistic competition	Monopolistic competition refers to a market structure in which there are many sellers each producing a differentiated product.
Supply and demand	The partial equilibrium supply and demand economic model originally developed by Alfred Marshall attempts to describe, explain, and predict changes in the price and quantity of goods sold in competitive markets.
Long run	In economic models, the long run time frame assumes no fixed factors of production. Firms can enter or leave the marketplace, and the cost (and availability) of land, labor, raw materials, and capital goods can be assumed to vary.
Differentiated product	A firm's product that is not identical to products of other firms in the same industry is a differentiated product.
Pricing strategy	The process in which the price of a product can be determined and is decided upon is a pricing strategy.
Firm	An organization that employs resources to produce a good or service for profit and owns and operates one or more plants is referred to as a firm.
Price level	The overall level of prices in a country, as usually measured empirically by a price index, but often captured in theoretical models by a single variable is a price level.
International trade	The export of goods and services from a country and the import of goods and services into a country is referred to as the international trade.
Market power	The ability of a single economic actor to have a substantial influence on market prices is market power.
Pure monopoly	A market structure in which one firm sells a unique product, into which entry is blocked, in which the single firm has considerable control over product price, and in which non-price competition may or may not be found is called pure monopoly.
Utility	Utility refers to the want-satisfying power of a good or service; the satisfaction or pleasure a consumer obtains from the consumption of a good or service.
Natural monopoly	Natural monopoly refers to an industry in which economies of scale are so great that a single firm can produce the product at a lower average total cost than would be possible if more than one firm produced the product.
Barriers to entry	In economics and especially in the theory of competition, barriers to entry are obstacles in the path of a firm which wants to enter a given market.
Leverage	Leverage is using given resources in such a way that the potential positive or negative outcome is magnified. In finance, this generally refers to borrowing.
Producer price index	An index that measures prices at the wholesale level is referred to as producer price index.
Average product	The average product of a factor (i.e. labor, capital, etc.) in a firm or industry is its output divided by the amount of the factor employed. The total quantity of output divided the total quantity of some input.
Manufacturing	Production of goods primarily by the application of labor and capital to raw materials and other intermediate inputs, in contrast to agriculture, mining, forestry, fishing, and

Go to Cram101.com for the Practice Tests for this Chapter.

services a manufacturing.

Bureau of Labor Statistics	The Bureau of Labor Statistics is a unit of the United States Department of Labor, is the principal fact-finding agency for the U.S. government in the field of labor economics and statistics.
Price index	A measure of the average prices of a group of goods relative to a base year. A typical price index for a vector of quantities q and prices pb, pg in the base and given years respectively would be I = 100 Pgq / Pbq.
Escalation	Regarding the structure of tariffs. In the context of a trade war, escalation refers to the increase in tariffs that occurs as countries retaliate again and again.
Capital	Capital generally refers to financial wealth, especially that used to start or maintain a business. In classical economics, capital is one of four factors of production, the others being land and labor and entrepreneurship.
Margin	A deposit by a buyer in stocks with a seller or a stockbroker, as security to cover fluctuations in the market in reference to stocks that the buyer has purchased but for which he has not paid is a margin. Commodities are also traded on margin.
Profit margin	Profit margin is a measure of profitability. It is calculated using a formula and written as a percentage or a number. Profit margin = Net income before tax and interest / Revenue.
Deregulation	The lessening or complete removal of government regulations on an industry, especially concerning the price that firms are allowed to charge and leaving price to be determined by market forces a deregulation.
Investment	Investment refers to spending for the production and accumulation of capital and additions to inventories. In a financial sense, buying an asset with the expectation of making a return.
Internal rate of return	Internal rate of return refers to a discounted cash flow method for evaluating capital budgeting projects. The internal rate of return is a discount rate that makes the present value of the cash inflows equal to the present value of the cash outflows.
Cost of capital	Cost of capital refers to the percentage cost of funds used for acquiring resources for an organization, typically a weighted average of the firms cost of equity and cost of debt.
Rate of return	A rate of return is a comparison of the money earned (or lost) on an investment to the amount of money invested.
Interest rate	The rate of return on bonds, loans, or deposits. When one speaks of 'the' interest rate, it is usually in a model where there is only one.
Budget	Budget refers to an account, usually for a year, of the planned expenditures and the expected receipts of an entity. For a government, the receipts are tax revenues.
Cost structure	The relative proportion of an organization's fixed, variable, and mixed costs is referred to as cost structure.
Product manager	Product manager refers to a person who plans, implements, and controls the annual and long-range plans for the products for which he or she is responsible.
Penetration pricing	Setting a low initial price for a new product in order to penetrate the market deeply and gain a large and broad market share is referred to as penetration pricing.
Market penetration	A strategy of increasing sales of present products in their existing markets is called market penetration.
Appeal	Appeal refers to the act of asking an appellate court to overturn a decision after the trial court's final judgment has been entered.

Go to **Cram101.com** for the Practice Tests for this Chapter.

223

Dumping	Dumping refers to a practice of charging a very low price in a foreign market for such economic purposes as putting rival suppliers out of business.
Agent	A person who makes economic decisions for another economic actor. A hired manager operates as an agent for a firm's owner.
Users	Users refer to people in the organization who actually use the product or service purchased by the buying center.
Market share	That fraction of an industry's output accounted for by an individual firm or group of firms is called market share.
Social responsibility	Social responsibility is a doctrine that claims that an entity whether it is state, government, corporation, organization or individual has a responsibility to society.
Yield	The interest rate that equates a future value or an annuity to a given present value is a yield.
Single sourcing	Single sourcing is the origination of any design, set of concepts, or any article real or insubstantial from a single, well defined source, either a person or an organization.
Discount	The difference between the face value of a bond and its selling price, when a bond is sold for less than its face value it's referred to as a discount.
Quantity discounts	Quantity discounts refer to reductions in unit costs for a larger order.
Quantity discount	A quantity discount is a price reduction given for a large order.
Cash discount	Cash discount refers to a discount offered on merchandise sold to encourage prompt payment; offered by sellers of merchandise and represents sales discounts to the seller when they are used and purchase discounts to the purchaser of the merchandise.
Incentive	An incentive is any factor (financial or non-financial) that provides a motive for a particular course of action, or counts as a reason for preferring one choice to the alternatives.
Opportunity cost	The cost of something in terms of opportunity foregone. The opportunity cost to a country of producing a unit more of a good, such as for export or to replace an import, is the quantity of some other good that could have been produced instead.
Base year	The year used as the basis for comparison by a price index such as the CPI. The index for any year is the average of prices for that year compared to the base year; e.g., 110 means that prices are 10% higher than in the base year.
Correlation	A correlation is the measure of the extent to which two economic or statistical variables move together, normalized so that its values range from -1 to +1. It is defined as the covariance of the two variables divided by the square root of the product of their variances.
Rebate	Rebate refers to a sales promotion in which money is returned to the consumer based on proof of purchase.
Tying	Tying is the practice of making the sale of one good (the tying good) to the de facto or de jure customer conditional on the purchase of a second distinctive good.
Option	A contract that gives the purchaser the option to buy or sell the underlying financial instrument at a specified price, called the exercise price or strike price, within a specific period of time.
Driving force	The key external pressure that will shape the future for an organization is a driving force. The driving force in an industry are the main underlying causes of changing industry and

competitive conditions.

Business Week	Business Week is a business magazine published by McGraw-Hill. It was first published in 1929 under the direction of Malcolm Muir, who was serving as president of the McGraw-Hill Publishing company at the time. It is considered to be the standard both in industry and among students.
Personnel	A collective term for all of the employees of an organization. Personnel is also commonly used to refer to the personnel management function or the organizational unit responsible for administering personnel programs.
Drawback	Drawback refers to rebate of import duties when the imported good is re-exported or used as input to the production of an exported good.
Income statement	Income statement refers to a financial statement that presents the revenues and expenses and resulting net income or net loss of a company for a specific period of time.
Asset	An item of property, such as land, capital, money, a share in ownership, or a claim on others for future payment, such as a bond or a bank deposit is an asset.
Productive assets	Productive assets refers to assets used to operate the business; frequently called long-term assets. They are property such as land, livestock, and trees that produce income.
Labor force	In economics the labor force is the group of people who have a potential for being employed.
Productivity	Productivity refers to the total output of goods and services in a given period of time divided by work hours.
Tangible	Having a physical existence is referred to as the tangible. Personal property other than real estate, such as cars, boats, stocks, or other assets.
Average total cost	Average total cost refers to a firm's total cost divided by output ; equal to average fixed cost plus average variable cost.
Average fixed Cost	Average fixed cost refers to total fixed cost divided by the number of units of output; a per-unit measure of fixed costs.
Average variable cost	A firm's total variable cost divided by output is called average variable cost.
Total variable Cost	The total of all costs that vary with output in the short run is called total variable cost.
Competitive bidding	A situation where two or more companies submit bids for a product, service, or project to a potential buyer is competitive bidding.
Slope	The slope of a line in the plane containing the x and y axes is generally represented by the letter m, and is defined as the change in the y coordinate divided by the corresponding change in the x coordinate, between two distinct points on the line.
Strategic planning	The process of determining the major goals of the organization and the policies and strategies for obtaining and using resources to achieve those goals is called strategic planning.
Business unit	The lowest level of the company which contains the set of functions that carry a product through its life span from concept through manufacture, distribution, sales and service is a business unit.
Negotiation	Negotiation is the process whereby interested parties resolve disputes, agree upon courses of action, bargain for individual or collective advantage, and/or attempt to craft outcomes which serve their mutual interests.

Go to **Cram101.com** for the Practice Tests for this Chapter.
And, **NEVER** highlight a book again!

Direct relationship	Direct relationship refers to the relationship between two variables that change in the same direction, for example, product price and quantity supplied.
Preparation	Preparation refers to usually the first stage in the creative process. It includes education and formal training.
Average cost	Average cost is equal to total cost divided by the number of goods produced (Quantity-Q). It is also equal to the sum of average variable costs (total variable costs divided by Q) plus average fixed costs (total fixed costs divided by Q).
Quantitative factor	An outcome that is measured in numerical terms is referred to as a quantitative factor.
General Electric	In 1876, Thomas Alva Edison opened a new laboratory in Menlo Park, New Jersey. Out of the laboratory was to come perhaps the most famous invention of all—a successful development of the incandescent electric lamp. By 1890, Edison had organized his various businesses into the Edison General Electric Company.
Control system	A control system is a device or set of devices that manage the behavior of other devices. Some devices or systems are not controllable.A control system is an interconnection of components connected or related in such a manner as to command, direct, or regulate itself or another system.
Direct labor	The earnings of employees who work directly on the products being manufactured are direct labor.
Inverse relationship	The relationship between two variables that change in opposite directions, for example, product price and quantity demanded is an inverse relationship.
Complexity	The technical sophistication of the product and hence the amount of understanding required to use it is referred to as complexity. It is the opposite of simplicity.
Warehouse	Warehouse refers to a location, often decentralized, that a firm uses to store, consolidate, age, or mix stock; house product-recall programs; or ease tax burdens.
Data warehouse	A Data warehouse is a repository of integrated information, available for queries and analysis. Data and information are extracted from heterogeneous sources as they are generated.
Accounting method	Accounting method refers to the method under which income and expenses are determined for tax purposes. Important accounting methods include the cash basis and the accrual basis.
Enterprise resource planning	Computer-based production and operations system that links multiple firms into one integrated production unit is enterprise resource planning.
Enterprise	Enterprise refers to another name for a business organization. Other similar terms are business firm, sometimes simply business, sometimes simply firm, as well as company, and entity.
Quality assurance	Those activities associated with assuring the quality of a product or service is called quality assurance.
Scope	Scope of a project is the sum total of all projects products and their requirements or features.
Internal customer	An individuals or unit within the firm that receives services from other entities within the organization is an internal customer.
Comprehensive	A comprehensive refers to a layout accurate in size, color, scheme, and other necessary details to show how a final ad will look. For presentation only, never for reproduction.

229

Partnership	In the common law, a partnership is a type of business entity in which partners share with each other the profits or losses of the business undertaking in which they have all invested.
Performance improvement	Performance improvement is the concept of measuring the output of a particular process or procedure then modifying the process or procedure in order to increase the output, increase efficiency, or increase the effectiveness of the process or procedure.
Exchange	The trade of things of value between buyer and seller so that each is better off after the trade is called the exchange.
Marketing	Promoting and selling products or services to customers, or prospective customers, is referred to as marketing.
Target price	Target price refers to estimated price for a product or service that potential customers will
Product cost	Product cost refers to sum of the costs assigned to a product for a specific purpose. A concept used in applying the cost plus approach to product pricing in which only the costs of manufacturing the product are included in the cost amount to which the markup is added.
Target cost	The projected long-run product cost that will enable a firm to enter and remain in the market for the product and compete successfully with the firm's competitors is referred to as target cost.
Target costing	Target costing refers to designing a product so that it satisfies customers and meets the profit margins desired by the firm.
Honda	With more than 14 million internal combustion engines built each year, Honda is the largest engine-maker in the world. In 2004, the company began to produce diesel motors, which were both very quiet whilst not requiring particulate filters to pass pollution standards. It is arguable, however, that the foundation of their success is the motorcycle division.
Raw material	Raw material refers to a good that has not been transformed by production; a primary product.
Trust	An arrangement in which shareholders of independent firms agree to give up their stock in exchange for trust certificates that entitle them to a share of the trust's common profits.
Process improvement	Process improvement is the activity of elevating the performance of a process, especially that of a business process with regard to its goal.
Cooperative	A business owned and controlled by the people who use it, producers, consumers, or workers with similar needs who pool their resources for mutual gain is called cooperative.
Quality improvement	Quality is inversely proportional to variability thus quality Improvement is the reduction of variability in products and processes.
Warrant	A warrant is a security that entitles the holder to buy or sell a certain additional quantity of an underlying security at an agreed-upon price, at the holder's discretion.
Indirect labor	All costs of compensating employees who do not work directly on the firm's product but who are necessary for production to occur are referred to as indirect labor.
Labor productivity	In labor economics labor productivity is a measure of the efficiency of the labor force. It is usually measured as output per hour of all people. When comparing labor productivity one mostly looks at the change over time.
Cost curve	A cost curve is a graph of the costs of production as a function of total quantity produced. In a free market economy, productively efficient firms use these curves to find the optimal point of production, where they make the most profits.
Competitiveness	Competitiveness usually refers to characteristics that permit a firm to compete effectively with other firms due to low cost or superior technology, perhaps internationally.

Go to **Cram101.com** for the Practice Tests for this Chapter.

Total supply	Total supply refers to the supply schedule or the supply curve of all sellers of a good or service.
Inventory management	The planning, coordinating, and controlling activities related to the flow of inventory into, through, and out of an organization is referred to as inventory management.
Standardization	Standardization, in the context related to technologies and industries, is the process of establishing a technical standard among competing entities in a market, where this will bring benefits without hurting competition.
Competitive Strategy	An outline of how a business intends to compete with other firms in the same industry is called competitive strategy.
Keiretsu	Keiretsu is a set of companies with interlocking business relationships and shareholdings. It is a type of business group.
Competitive advantage	A business is said to have a competitive advantage when its unique strengths, often based on cost, quality, time, and innovation, offer consumers a greater percieved value and there by differtiating it from its competitors.
Acquisition	A company's purchase of the property and obligations of another company is an acquisition.
Liability	A liability is a present obligation of the enterprise arizing from past events, the settlement of which is expected to result in an outflow from the enterprise of resources embodying economic benefits.
Cash flow	In finance, cash flow refers to the amounts of cash being received and spent by a business during a defined period of time, sometimes tied to a specific project. Most of the time they are being used to determine gaps in the liquid position of a company.
Return on Assets	The Return on Assets percentage shows how profitable a company's assets are in generating revenue.

Pricing strategy	The process in which the price of a product can be determined and is decided upon is a pricing strategy.
Managerial Accounting	Managerial accounting is the branch of accounting that uses both past and future data in providing information that management uses in conducting daily operations in planning future operations, and in developing overall business strategies.
Business Week	Business Week is a business magazine published by McGraw-Hill. It was first published in 1929 under the direction of Malcolm Muir, who was serving as president of the McGraw-Hill Publishing company at the time. It is considered to be the standard both in industry and among students.
Accounting	A system that collects and processes financial information about an organization and reports that information to decision makers is referred to as accounting.
Contract	A contract is a "promise" or an "agreement" that is enforced or recognized by the law. In the civil law, a contract is considered to be part of the general law of obligations.
Purchasing	Purchasing refers to the function in a firm that searches for quality material resources, finds the best suppliers, and negotiates the best price for goods and services.
Tactic	A short-term immediate decision that, in its totality, leads to the achievement of strategic goals is called a tactic.
Negotiation	Negotiation is the process whereby interested parties resolve disputes, agree upon courses of action, bargain for individual or collective advantage, and/or attempt to craft outcomes which serve their mutual interests.
Buyer	A buyer refers to a role in the buying center with formal authority and responsibility to select the supplier and negotiate the terms of the contract.
Concession	A concession is a business operated under a contract or license associated with a degree of exclusivity in exploiting a business within a certain geographical area. For example, sports arenas or public parks may have concession stands; and public services such as water supply may be operated as concessions.
Management	Management characterizes the process of leading and directing all or part of an organization, often a business, through the deployment and manipulation of resources. Early twentieth-century management writer Mary Parker Follett defined management as "the art of getting things done through people."
Compromise	Compromise occurs when the interaction is moderately important to meeting goals and the goals are neither completely compatible nor completely incompatible.
Interest	In finance and economics, interest is the price paid by a borrower for the use of a lender's money. In other words, interest is the amount of paid to "rent" money for a period of time.
Senior executive	Senior executive means a chief executive officer, chief operating officer, chief financial officer and anyone in charge of a principal business unit or function.
Operation	A standardized method or technique that is performed repetitively, often on different materials resulting in different finished goods is called an operation.
Equity	Equity is the name given to the set of legal principles, in countries following the English common law tradition, which supplement strict rules of law where their application would operate harshly, so as to achieve what is sometimes referred to as "natural justice."
Realization	Realization is the sale of assets when an entity is being liquidated.
Supply	Supply is the aggregate amount of any material good that can be called into being at a certain price point; it comprises one half of the equation of supply and demand. In classical

Go to **Cram101.com** for the Practice Tests for this Chapter.

	economic theory, a curve representing supply is one of the factors that produce price.
Competitive bidding	A situation where two or more companies submit bids for a product, service, or project to a potential buyer is competitive bidding.
Incentive	An incentive is any factor (financial or non-financial) that provides a motive for a particular course of action, or counts as a reason for preferring one choice to the alternatives.
Capital	Capital generally refers to financial wealth, especially that used to start or maintain a business. In classical economics, capital is one of four factors of production, the others being land and labor and entrepreneurship.
Cost management	The approaches and activities of managers in short-run and long-run planning and control decisions that increase value for customers and lower costs of products and services are called cost management.
Consideration	Consideration in contract law, a basic requirement for an enforceable agreement under traditional contract principles, defined in this text as legal value, bargained for and given in exchange for an act or promise. In corporation law, cash or property contributed to a corporation in exchange for shares, or a promise to contribute such cash or property.
Partnership	In the common law, a partnership is a type of business entity in which partners share with each other the profits or losses of the business undertaking in which they have all invested.
Product design	Product Design is defined as the idea generation, concept development, testing and manufacturing or implementation of a physical object or service. It is possibly the evolution of former discipline name - Industrial Design.
Preparation	Preparation refers to usually the first stage in the creative process. It includes education and formal training.
Users	Users refer to people in the organization who actually use the product or service purchased by the buying center.
Service	Service refers to a "non tangible product" that is not embodied in a physical good and that typically effects some change in another product, person, or institution. Contrasts with good.
Exchange	The trade of things of value between buyer and seller so that each is better off after the trade is called the exchange.
Action plan	Action plan refers to a written document that includes the steps the trainee and manager will take to ensure that training transfers to the job.
Option	A contract that gives the purchaser the option to buy or sell the underlying financial instrument at a specified price, called the exercise price or strike price, within a specific period of time.
Performance feedback	The process of providing employees with information regarding their performance effectiveness is referred to as performance feedback.
Argument	The discussion by counsel for the respective parties of their contentions on the law and the facts of the case being tried in order to aid the jury in arriving at a correct and just conclusion is called argument.
Competitor	Other organizations in the same industry or type of business that provide a good or service to the same set of customers is referred to as a competitor.
Assessment	Collecting information and providing feedback to employees about their behavior, communication style, or skills is an assessment.

Production	The creation of finished goods and services using the factors of production: land, labor, capital, entrepreneurship, and knowledge.
Cost structure	The relative proportion of an organization's fixed, variable, and mixed costs is referred to as cost structure.
Labor	People's physical and mental talents and efforts that are used to help produce goods and services are called labor.
Yield	The interest rate that equates a future value or an annuity to a given present value is a yield.
Personnel	A collective term for all of the employees of an organization. Personnel is also commonly used to refer to the personnel management function or the organizational unit responsible for administering personnel programs.
Manufacturing	Production of goods primarily by the application of labor and capital to raw materials and other intermediate inputs, in contrast to agriculture, mining, forestry, fishing, and services a manufacturing.
Target price	Target price refers to estimated price for a product or service that potential customers will
Points	Loan origination fees that may be deductible as interest by a buyer of property. A seller of property who pays points reduces the selling price by the amount of the points paid for the buyer.
Strategic planning	The process of determining the major goals of the organization and the policies and strategies for obtaining and using resources to achieve those goals is called strategic planning.
Brief	Brief refers to a statement of a party's case or legal arguments, usually prepared by an attorney. Also used to make legal arguments before appellate courts.
Firm	An organization that employs resources to produce a good or service for profit and owns and operates one or more plants is referred to as a firm.
Coercive power	Coercive power refers to the extent to which a person has the ability to punish or physically or psychologically harm someone else.
Retaliation	The use of an increased trade barrier in response to another country increasing its trade barrier, either as a way of undoing the adverse effects of the latter's action or of punishing it is retaliation.
Recovery	Characterized by rizing output, falling unemployment, rizing profits, and increasing economic activity following a decline is a recovery.
Market	A market is, as defined in economics, a social arrangement that allows buyers and sellers to discover information and carry out a voluntary exchange of goods or services.
Legitimate power	Legitimate power refers to power that is granted by virtue of one's position in the organization.
Expert power	The extent to which a person controls information that is valuable to someone else is referred to as expert power.
Specialist	A specialist is a trader who makes a market in one or several stocks and holds the limit order book for those stocks.
Referent power	Referent power is individual power based on a high level of identification with, admiration of, or respect for the powerholder.
Holder	A person in possession of a document of title or an instrument payable or indorsed to him,

Go to **Cram101.com** for the Practice Tests for this Chapter.

his order, or to bearer is a holder.

General Electric	In 1876, Thomas Alva Edison opened a new laboratory in Menlo Park, New Jersey. Out of the laboratory was to come perhaps the most famous invention of all—a successful development of the incandescent electric lamp. By 1890, Edison had organized his various businesses into the Edison General Electric Company.
Frequency	Frequency refers to the speed of the up and down movements of a fluctuating economic variable; that is, the number of times per unit of time that the variable completes a cycle of up and down movement.
In kind	Referring to a payment made with goods instead of money is an in kind. An expression relating to the insurer's right in many Property contracts to replace damaged objects with new or equivalent (in kind) material, rather than to pay a cash benefit.
Reciprocity	An industrial buying practice in which two organizations agree to purchase each other's products and services is called reciprocity.
Authority	Authority in agency law, refers to an agent's ability to affect his principal's legal relations with third parties. Also used to refer to an actor's legal power or ability to do something. In addition, sometimes used to refer to a statute, case, or other legal source that justifies a particular result.
Scarcity	Scarcity is defined as not having sufficient resources to produce enough to fulfill unlimited subjective wants. Alternatively, scarcity implies that not all of society's goals can be attained at the same time, so that trade-offs one good against others are made.
Trust	An arrangement in which shareholders of independent firms agree to give up their stock in exchange for trust certificates that entitle them to a share of the trust's common profits.
Trial	An examination before a competent tribunal, according to the law of the land, of the facts or law put in issue in a cause, for the purpose of determining such issue is a trial. When the court hears and determines any issue of fact or law for the purpose of determining the rights of the parties, it may be considered a trial.
Stock	In financial terminology, stock is the capital raized by a corporation, through the issuance and sale of shares.
Mistake	In contract law a mistake is incorrect understanding by one or more parties to a contract and may be used as grounds to invalidate the agreement. Common law has identified three different types of mistake in contract: unilateral mistake, mutual mistake, and common mistake.
Closing	The finalization of a real estate sales transaction that passes title to the property from the seller to the buyer is referred to as a closing. Closing is a sales term which refers to the process of making a sale. It refers to reaching the final step, which may be an exchange of money or acquiring a signature.
Attachment	Attachment in general, the process of taking a person's property under an appropriate judicial order by an appropriate officer of the court. Used for a variety of purposes, including the acquisition of jurisdiction over the property seized and the securing of property that may be used to satisfy a debt.
Expense	In accounting, an expense represents an event in which an asset is used up or a liability is incurred. In terms of the accounting equation, expenses reduce owners' equity.
Integrative bargaining	The part of the labor-management negotiation process that seeks solutions beneficial to both sides is called integrative bargaining.
Cooperative	A business owned and controlled by the people who use it, producers, consumers, or workers with similar needs who pool their resources for mutual gain is called cooperative.

Go to **Cram101.com** for the Practice Tests for this Chapter.

Go to **Cram101.com** for the Practice Tests for this Chapter.
And, **NEVER** highlight a book again!

Technology	The body of knowledge and techniques that can be used to combine economic resources to produce goods and services is called technology.
Purchase order	A form on which items or services needed by a business firm are specified and then communicated to the vendor is a purchase order.
Profit	Profit refers to the return to the resource entrepreneurial ability; total revenue minus total cost.
Transactions cost	Any cost associated with bringing buyers and sellers together is referred to as transactions cost.
Variable	A variable is something measured by a number; it is used to analyze what happens to other things when the size of that number changes.
Customs	Customs is an authority or agency in a country responsible for collecting customs duties and for controlling the flow of people, animals and goods (including personal effects and hazardous items) in and out of the country.
Complexity	The technical sophistication of the product and hence the amount of understanding required to use it is referred to as complexity. It is the opposite of simplicity.
Chrysler	The Chrysler Corporation was an American automobile manufacturer that existed independently from 1925–1998. The company was formed by Walter Percy Chrysler on June 6, 1925, with the remaining assets of Maxwell Motor Company.
Merger	Merger refers to the combination of two firms into a single firm.
Analogy	Analogy is either the cognitive process of transferring information from a particular subject to another particular subject (the target), or a linguistic expression corresponding to such a process. In a narrower sense, analogy is an inference or an argument from a particular to another particular, as opposed to deduction, induction, and abduction, where at least one of the premises or the conclusion is general.
Competitiveness	Competitiveness usually refers to characteristics that permit a firm to compete effectively with other firms due to low cost or superior technology, perhaps internationally.
Channel	Channel, in communications (sometimes called communications channel), refers to the medium used to convey information from a sender (or transmitter) to a receiver.
Communication channel	The pathways through which messages are communicated are called a communication channel.
Net assets	Net assets refers to portion of the assets remaining after the creditors' claims have been satisfied; also called equity or residual interest.
Asset	An item of property, such as land, capital, money, a share in ownership, or a claim on others for future payment, such as a bond or a bank deposit is an asset.
Bethlehem Steel	During its life, Bethlehem Steel was one of the largest shipbuilding companies in the world and was one of the most powerful symbols of American manufacturing leadership. It was the second largest steel producer in the United States, but following its 2001 bankruptcy, the company was dissolved and the remaining assets sold to International Steel Group in 2003.
Corporation	A legal entity chartered by a state or the Federal government that is distinct and separate from the individuals who own it is a corporation. This separation gives the corporation unique powers which other legal entities lack.
Property	Assets defined in the broadest legal sense. Property includes the unrealized receivables of a cash basis taxpayer, but not services rendered.
Subsidiary	A company that is controlled by another company or corporation is a subsidiary.

Go to **Cram101.com** for the Practice Tests for this Chapter.

243

Inventory	Tangible property held for sale in the normal course of business or used in producing goods or services for sale is an inventory.
Liability	A liability is a present obligation of the enterprise arizing from past events, the settlement of which is expected to result in an outflow from the enterprise of resources embodying economic benefits.
Accounts receivable	Accounts receivable is one of a series of accounting transactions dealing with the billing of customers which owe money to a person, company or organization for goods and services that have been provided to the customer. This is typically done in a one person organization by writing an invoice and mailing or delivering it to each customer.
Current liability	Current liability refers to a debt that can reasonably be expected to be paid from existing current assets or through the creation of other current liabilities, within one year or the operating cycle, whichever is longer.
Accounts payable	A written record of all vendors to whom the business firm owes money is referred to as accounts payable.
Earnings before interest and taxes	Income from operations before subtracting interest expense and income taxes is an earnings before interest and taxes.
Profit center	Responsibility center where the manager is accountable for revenues and costs is referred to as a profit center.
Return on Assets	The Return on Assets percentage shows how profitable a company's assets are in generating revenue.
Parent company	Parent company refers to the entity that has a controlling influence over another company. It may have its own operations, or it may have been set up solely for the purpose of owning the Subject Company.
Consignment	Consignment refers to a bailment for sale. The consignee does not undertake the absolute obligation to sell or pay for the goods.
Warehouse	Warehouse refers to a location, often decentralized, that a firm uses to store, consolidate, age, or mix stock; house product-recall programs; or ease tax burdens.
Cash flow	In finance, cash flow refers to the amounts of cash being received and spent by a business during a defined period of time, sometimes tied to a specific project. Most of the time they are being used to determine gaps in the liquid position of a company.
Investment	Investment refers to spending for the production and accumulation of capital and additions to inventories. In a financial sense, buying an asset with the expectation of making a return.
Inventory investment	Spending by firms on additional holdings of raw materials, parts, and finished goods is called inventory investment.
Downsizing	The process of eliminating managerial and non-managerial positions are called downsizing.
Critical success factor	Critical Success Factor is a business term for an element which is necessary for an organization or project to achieve its mission.
Success factor	The term success factor refers to the characteristics necessary for high performance; knowledge, skills, abilities, behaviors.
Industry	A group of firms that produce identical or similar products is an industry. It is also used specifically to refer to an area of economic production focused on manufacturing which involves large amounts of capital investment before any profit can be realized, also called "heavy industry".

Lease	A contract for the possession and use of land or other property, including goods, on one side, and a recompense of rent or other income on the other is the lease.
Invoice	The itemized bill for a transaction, stating the nature of the transaction and its cost. In international trade, the invoice price is often the preferred basis for levying an ad valorem tariff.
Inventory management	The planning, coordinating, and controlling activities related to the flow of inventory into, through, and out of an organization is referred to as inventory management.
Carrying costs	Carrying costs refers to costs that arise while holding an inventory of goods for sale.
Carrying cost	The cost to hold an asset, usually inventory is called a carrying cost. For inventory, a carrying cost includes such items as interest, warehousing costs, insurance, and material-handling expenses.
Fixed price	Fixed price is a phrase used to mean that no bargaining is allowed over the price of a good or, less commonly, a service.
Raw material	Raw material refers to a good that has not been transformed by production; a primary product.
Commodity	Could refer to any good, but in trade a commodity is usually a raw material or primary product that enters into international trade, such as metals or basic agricultural products.
Tying	Tying is the practice of making the sale of one good (the tying good) to the de facto or de jure customer conditional on the purchase of a second distinctive good.
Procurement	Procurement is the acquisition of goods or services at the best possible total cost of ownership, in the right quantity, at the right time, in the right place for the direct benefit or use of the governments, corporations, or individuals generally via, but not limited to a contract.
Prentice Hall	Prentice Hall is a leading educational publisher. It is an imprint of the Pearson Education Company, based in New Jersey, USA.
International Business	International business refers to any firm that engages in international trade or investment.

Technology	The body of knowledge and techniques that can be used to combine economic resources to produce goods and services is called technology.
Contract	A contract is a "promise" or an "agreement" that is enforced or recognized by the law. In the civil law, a contract is considered to be part of the general law of obligations.
Personnel	A collective term for all of the employees of an organization. Personnel is also commonly used to refer to the personnel management function or the organizational unit responsible for administering personnel programs.
Negotiation	Negotiation is the process whereby interested parties resolve disputes, agree upon courses of action, bargain for individual or collective advantage, and/or attempt to craft outcomes which serve their mutual interests.
Interest	In finance and economics, interest is the price paid by a borrower for the use of a lender's money. In other words, interest is the amount of paid to "rent" money for a period of time.
Purchasing	Purchasing refers to the function in a firm that searches for quality material resources, finds the best suppliers, and negotiates the best price for goods and services.
Hearing	A hearing is a proceeding before a court or other decision-making body or officer. A hearing is generally distinguished from a trial in that it is usually shorter and often less formal.
License	A license in the sphere of Intellectual Property Rights (IPR) is a document, contract or agreement giving permission or the 'right' to a legally-definable entity to do something (such as manufacture a product or to use a service), or to apply something (such as a trademark), with the objective of achieving commercial gain.
Competitor	Other organizations in the same industry or type of business that provide a good or service to the same set of customers is referred to as a competitor.
Electronic signature	Uses digital signature technology to make the person's signature part of a document in such a way that any alteration can be detected are referred to as electronic signature.
Information system	An information system is a system whether automated or manual, that comprises people, machines, and/or methods organized to collect, process, transmit, and disseminate data that represent user information.
Service	Service refers to a "non tangible product" that is not embodied in a physical good and that typically effects some change in another product, person, or institution. Contrasts with good.
Market	A market is, as defined in economics, a social arrangement that allows buyers and sellers to discover information and carry out a voluntary exchange of goods or services.
Market price	Market price is an economic concept with commonplace familiarity; it is the price that a good or service is offered at, or will fetch, in the marketplace; it is of interest mainly in the study of microeconomics.
Labor	People's physical and mental talents and efforts that are used to help produce goods and services are called labor.
Profit	Profit refers to the return to the resource entrepreneurial ability; total revenue minus total cost.
Raw material	Raw material refers to a good that has not been transformed by production; a primary product.
Firm	An organization that employs resources to produce a good or service for profit and owns and operates one or more plants is referred to as a firm.
Escalation	Regarding the structure of tariffs. In the context of a trade war, escalation refers to the increase in tariffs that occurs as countries retaliate again and again.

Go to **Cram101.com** for the Practice Tests for this Chapter.

Fixed price	Fixed price is a phrase used to mean that no bargaining is allowed over the price of a good or, less commonly, a service.
Producer price index	An index that measures prices at the wholesale level is referred to as producer price index.
Price index	A measure of the average prices of a group of goods relative to a base year. A typical price index for a vector of quantities q and prices pb, pg in the base and given years respectively would be I = 100 Pgq / Pbq.
Production	The creation of finished goods and services using the factors of production: land, labor, capital, entrepreneurship, and knowledge.
Incentive	An incentive is any factor (financial or non-financial) that provides a motive for a particular course of action, or counts as a reason for preferring one choice to the alternatives.
Production efficiency	A situation in which the economy cannot produce more of one good without producing less of some other good is referred to as production efficiency.
Contingency fee	Agent's compenzation that consists of a percentage of the amount the agent secured for the principal in a business transaction is a contingency fee.
Management	Management characterizes the process of leading and directing all or part of an organization, often a business, through the deployment and manipulation of resources. Early twentieth-century management writer Mary Parker Follett defined management as "the art of getting things done through people."
Audit	An examination of the financial reports to ensure that they represent what they claim and conform with generally accepted accounting principles is referred to as audit.
Cost management	The approaches and activities of managers in short-run and long-run planning and control decisions that increase value for customers and lower costs of products and services are called cost management.
Internal audit	An internal audit is an independent appraisal of operations, conducted under the direction of management, to assess the effectiveness of internal administrative and accounting controls and help ensure conformance with managerial policies.
Financial risk	The risk related to the inability of the firm to meet its debt obligations as they come due is called financial risk.
Raytheon	Since nearly all of Raytheon's revenues are obtained from defense contracts, there is necessarily a tight cooperation between Raytheon and the U.S. Department of Defense. This, along with heavy lobbying, has led to perennial charges of influence peddling. Raytheon contributed nearly a million dollars to various defense-related political campaigns in 2004, spending much more than that on lobbying expenses. And there are many tight ties between the company and all levels of government.
Corporation	A legal entity chartered by a state or the Federal government that is distinct and separate from the individuals who own it is a corporation. This separation gives the corporation unique powers which other legal entities lack.
Operation	A standardized method or technique that is performed repetitively, often on different materials resulting in different finished goods is called an operation.
Target cost	The projected long-run product cost that will enable a firm to enter and remain in the market for the product and compete successfully with the firm's competitors is referred to as target cost.
Expense	In accounting, an expense represents an event in which an asset is used up or a liability is

incurred. In terms of the accounting equation, expenses reduce owners' equity.

Productivity	Productivity refers to the total output of goods and services in a given period of time divided by work hours.
Factor market	Any place where factors of production, resources, are bought and sold is referred to as factor market.
Economic risk	The likelihood that events, including economic mismanagement, will cause drastic changes in a country's business environment that adversely affects the profit and other goals of a particular business enterprise is referred to as economic risk.
Buyer	A buyer refers to a role in the buying center with formal authority and responsibility to select the supplier and negotiate the terms of the contract.
Trust	An arrangement in which shareholders of independent firms agree to give up their stock in exchange for trust certificates that entitle them to a share of the trust's common profits.
Continuous improvement	The constant effort to eliminate waste, reduce response time, simplify the design of both products and processes, and improve quality and customer service is referred to as continuous improvement.
Contracting party	Contracting party refers to a country that has signed the GATT.
Strategic alliance	Strategic alliance refers to a long-term partnership between two or more companies established to help each company build competitive market advantages.
Partnership	In the common law, a partnership is a type of business entity in which partners share with each other the profits or losses of the business undertaking in which they have all invested.
Covenant	A covenant is a signed written agreement between two or more parties. Also referred to as a contract.
Time horizon	A time horizon is a fixed point of time in the future at which point certain processes will be evaluated or assumed to end. It is necessary in an accounting, finance or risk management regime to assign such a fixed horizon time so that alternatives can be evaluated for performance over the same period of time.
Risk sharing	The distribution of financial risk among parties furnishing a service is called risk sharing.
Termination	The ending of a corporation that occurs only after the winding-up of the corporation's affairs, the liquidation of its assets, and the distribution of the proceeds to the claimants are referred to as a termination.
Industry	A group of firms that produce identical or similar products is an industry. It is also used specifically to refer to an area of economic production focused on manufacturing which involves large amounts of capital investment before any profit can be realized, also called "heavy industry".
Copyright	The legal right to the proceeds from and control over the use of a created product, such a written work, audio, video, film, or software is a copyright. This right generally extends over the life of the author plus fifty years.
Patent	The legal right to the proceeds from and control over the use of an invented product or process, granted for a fixed period of time, usually 20 years. Patent is one form of intellectual property that is subject of the TRIPS agreement.
Competitive advantage	A business is said to have a competitive advantage when its unique strengths, often based on cost, quality, time, and innovation, offer consumers a greater percieved value and there by differtiating it from its competitors.

Tying	Tying is the practice of making the sale of one good (the tying good) to the de facto or de jure customer conditional on the purchase of a second distinctive good.
Product life cycle	Product life cycle refers to a series of phases in a product's sales and cash flows over time; these phases, in order of occurrence, are introductory, growth, maturity, and decline.
Introductory stage	The first stage of the product life cycle in which sales grow slowly and profit is minimal is the introductory stage.
Exchange	The trade of things of value between buyer and seller so that each is better off after the trade is called the exchange.
Leverage	Leverage is using given resources in such a way that the potential positive or negative outcome is magnified. In finance, this generally refers to borrowing.
Performance improvement	Performance improvement is the concept of measuring the output of a particular process or procedure then modifying the process or procedure in order to increase the output, increase efficiency, or increase the effectiveness of the process or procedure.
Learning curve	Learning curve is a function that measures how labor-hours per unit decline as units of production increase because workers are learning and becoming better at their jobs.
Cost structure	The relative proportion of an organization's fixed, variable, and mixed costs is referred to as cost structure.
Bid	A bid price is a price offered by a buyer when he/she buys a good. In the context of stock trading on a stock exchange, the bid price is the highest price a buyer of a stock is willing to pay for a share of that given stock.
Information technology	Information technology refers to technology that helps companies change business by allowing them to use new methods.
Analyst	Analyst refers to a person or tool with a primary function of information analysis, generally with a more limited, practical and short term set of goals than a researcher.
Merrill Lynch	Merrill Lynch through its subsidiaries and affiliates, provides capital markets services, investment banking and advisory services, wealth management, asset management, insurance, banking and related products and services on a global basis. It is best known for its Global Private Client services and its strong sales force.
Outsourcing	Outsourcing refers to a production activity that was previously done inside a firm or plant that is now conducted outside that firm or plant.
Subcontractor	A subcontractor is an individual or in many cases a business that signs a contract to perform part or all of the obligations of another's contract. A subcontractor is hired by a general or prime contractor to perform a specific task as part of the overall project.
Cost overrun	Cost overrun is defined as excess of actual cost over budget. Cost overrun is typically calculated in one of two ways. Either as a percentage, namely actual cost minus budgeted cost, in percent of budgeted cost. Or as a ratio, viz. actual cost divided by budgeted cost.
Users	Users refer to people in the organization who actually use the product or service purchased by the buying center.
Customer satisfaction	Customer satisfaction is a business term which is used to capture the idea of measuring how satisfied an enterprise's customers are with the organization's efforts in a marketplace.
Budget	Budget refers to an account, usually for a year, of the planned expenditures and the expected receipts of an entity. For a government, the receipts are tax revenues.
General Accounting	According to the General Accounting Office current mission statement, the agency exists to support the Congress in meeting its Constitutional responsibilities and to help improve the

Go to **Cram101.com** for the Practice Tests for this Chapter.
And, **NEVER** highlight a book again!

Office	performance and ensure the accountability of the federal government for the American people.
Acquisition	A company's purchase of the property and obligations of another company is an acquisition.
Accounting	A system that collects and processes financial information about an organization and reports that information to decision makers is referred to as accounting.
Appropriation	A privacy tort that consists of using a person's name or likeness for commercial gain without the person's permission is an appropriation.
Enabling	Enabling refers to giving workers the education and tools they need to assume their new decision-making powers.
Commodity	Could refer to any good, but in trade a commodity is usually a raw material or primary product that enters into international trade, such as metals or basic agricultural products.
Total cost	The sum of fixed cost and variable cost is referred to as total cost.
Discount	The difference between the face value of a bond and its selling price, when a bond is sold for less than its face value it's referred to as a discount.
Turnover	Turnover in a financial context refers to the rate at which a provider of goods cycles through its average inventory. Turnover in a human resources context refers to the characteristic of a given company or industry, relative to rate at which an employer gains and loses staff.
Performance measurement	The process by which someone evaluates an employee's work behaviors by measurement and comparison with previously established standards, documents the results, and communicates the results to the employee is called performance measurement.
Benchmarking	The continuous process of comparing the levels of performance in producing products and services and executing activities against the best levels of performance is benchmarking.
Regulation	Regulation refers to restrictions state and federal laws place on business with regard to the conduct of its activities.
Consideration	Consideration in contract law, a basic requirement for an enforceable agreement under traditional contract principles, defined in this text as legal value, bargained for and given in exchange for an act or promise. In corporation law, cash or property contributed to a corporation in exchange for shares, or a promise to contribute such cash or property.
Business opportunity	A business opportunity involves the sale or lease of any product, service, equipment, etc. that will enable the purchaser-licensee to begin a business
Adjustment mechanism	The theoretical process by which a market moves from disequilibrium toward equilibrium is the adjustment mechanism.
Excess profit	Profit of a firm over and above what provides its owners with a normal return to capital is called excess profit.
Gain	In finance, gain is a profit or an increase in value of an investment such as a stock or bond. Gain is calculated by fair market value or the proceeds from the sale of the investment minus the sum of the purchase price and all costs associated with it.
Escape clause	The portion of a legal text that permits departure from ts provisions in the event of specified adverse circumstances is the escape clause.
Conflict resolution	Conflict resolution is the process of resolving a dispute or a conflict. Successful conflict resolution occurs by providing each side's needs, and adequately addressing their interests so that they are each satisfied with the outcome. Conflict resolution aims to end conflicts before they start or lead to physical fighting.

Evaluation	The consumer's appraisal of the product or brand on important attributes is called evaluation.
Turnkey	A turnkey is a project in which a separate entity is responsible for setting up a plant or equipment (e.g. trains/infrastructure) and putting it into operations.
Level of service	The degree of service provided to the customer by self, limited, and full-service retailers is referred to as the level of service.
Modular approach	A manufacturing company uses outside suppliers to provide the large components of the product, which are then assembled into a final product by a few workers is called a modular approach.
Data processing	Data processing refers to a name for business technology in the 1970s; included technology that supported an existing business and was primarily used to improve the flow of financial information.
Conversion	Conversion refers to any distinct act of dominion wrongfully exerted over another's personal property in denial of or inconsistent with his rights therein. That tort committed by a person who deals with chattels not belonging to him in a manner that is inconsistent with the ownership of the lawful owner.
Federal government	Federal government refers to the government of the United States, as distinct from the state and local governments.
Authority	Authority in agency law, refers to an agent's ability to affect his principal's legal relations with third parties. Also used to refer to an actor's legal power or ability to do something. In addition, sometimes used to refer to a statute, case, or other legal source that justifies a particular result.
Commerce	Commerce is the exchange of something of value between two entities. It is the central mechanism from which capitalism is derived.
Policy	Similar to a script in that a policy can be a less than completely rational decision-making method. Involves the use of a pre-existing set of decision steps for any problem that presents itself.
Aid	Assistance provided by countries and by international institutions such as the World Bank to developing countries in the form of monetary grants, loans at low interest rates, in kind, or a combination of these is called aid. Aid can also refer to assistance of any type rendered to benefit some group or individual.
Business development	Business development emcompasses a number of techniques designed to grow an economic enterprise. Such techniques include, but are not limited to, assessments of marketing opportunities and target markets, intelligence gathering on customers and competitors, generating leads for possible sales, followup sales activity, and formal proposal writing.
Executive order	A legal rule issued by a chief executive usually pursuant to a delegation of power from the legislature is called executive order.
Enterprise	Enterprise refers to another name for a business organization. Other similar terms are business firm, sometimes simply business, sometimes simply firm, as well as company, and entity.
Public law	Public law is the law governing the relationship between individuals (citizens, companies) and the state. Constitutional law, administrative law and criminal law are sub-divisions of public law.
Subcontract	A subcontract is a contract that assigns part of an existing contract to a different party.
Core	A core is the set of feasible allocations in an economy that cannot be improved upon by

Go to **Cram101.com** for the Practice Tests for this Chapter.

	subset of the set of the economy's consumers (a coalition). In construction, when the force in an element is within a certain center section, the core, the element will only be under compression.
Capital	Capital generally refers to financial wealth, especially that used to start or maintain a business. In classical economics, capital is one of four factors of production, the others being land and labor and entrepreneurship.
Supply	Supply is the aggregate amount of any material good that can be called into being at a certain price point; it comprises one half of the equation of supply and demand. In classical economic theory, a curve representing supply is one of the factors that produce price.
Supplier Diversity	Supplier Diversity is a business program that encourages the use of previously underutilized minority owned vendors as suppliers. It is not directly correlated with supply chain diversification, although utilizing more vendors may enhance supply chain diversification.
Consumer good	Products and services that are ultimately consumed rather than used in the production of another good are a consumer good.
Consultant	A professional that provides expert advice in a particular field or area in which customers occassionaly require this type of knowledge is a consultant.
Property	Assets defined in the broadest legal sense. Property includes the unrealized receivables of a cash basis taxpayer, but not services rendered.
Agent	A person who makes economic decisions for another economic actor. A hired manager operates as an agent for a firm's owner.
Intellectual property	In law, intellectual property is an umbrella term for various legal entitlements which attach to certain types of information, ideas, or other intangibles in their expressed form. The holder of this legal entitlement is generally entitled to exercise various exclusive rights in relation to its subject matter.
Independent contractor	Independent contractor refers to a self-employed person as distinguished from one who is employed as an employee.
Option	A contract that gives the purchaser the option to buy or sell the underlying financial instrument at a specified price, called the exercise price or strike price, within a specific period of time.
Balance	In banking and accountancy, the outstanding balance is the amount of money owned, (or due), that remains in a deposit account (or a loan account) at a given date, after all past remittances, payments and withdrawal have been accounted for. It can be positive (then, in the balance sheet of a firm, it is an asset) or negative (a liability).
Litigation	The process of bringing, maintaining, and defending a lawsuit is litigation.
Liability	A liability is a present obligation of the enterprise arizing from past events, the settlement of which is expected to result in an outflow from the enterprise of resources embodying economic benefits.
Principal	In agency law, one under whose direction an agent acts and for whose benefit that agent acts is a principal.
Public relations	Public relations refers to the management function that evaluates public attitudes, changes policies and procedures in response to the public's requests, and executes a program of action and information to earn public understanding and acceptance.
Distribution	Distribution in economics, the manner in which total output and income is distributed among individuals or factors.

Indirect cost	Indirect cost refers to a cost that cannot be traced to a particular department.
Cost allocation	Cost allocation refers to the process of assigning costs in a cost pool to the appropriate cost objects.
Recovery	Characterized by rizing output, falling unemployment, rizing profits, and increasing economic activity following a decline is a recovery.
Overhead cost	An expenses of operating a business over and above the direct costs of producing a product is an overhead cost. They can include utilities (eg, electricity, telephone), advertizing and marketing, and any other costs not billed directly to the client or included in the price of the product.
Insurance	Insurance refers to a system by which individuals can reduce their exposure to risk of large losses by spreading the risks among a large number of persons.
Premium	Premium refers to the fee charged by an insurance company for an insurance policy. The rate of losses must be relatively predictable: In order to set the premium (prices) insurers must be able to estimate them accurately.
Supervisor	A Supervisor is an employee of an organization with some of the powers and responsibilities of management, occupying a role between true manager and a regular employee. A Supervisor position is typically the first step towards being promoted into a management role.
Standard cost	A carefully determined cost of a unit of output is standard cost. Takes into account the cost of material, labor, or overheads expected to be paid during a given accounting period.
Business unit	The lowest level of the company which contains the set of functions that carry a product through its life span from concept through manufacture, distribution, sales and service is a business unit.
Purchase order	A form on which items or services needed by a business firm are specified and then communicated to the vendor is a purchase order.
Marketing	Promoting and selling products or services to customers, or prospective customers, is referred to as marketing.
Trend	Trend refers to the long-term movement of an economic variable, such as its average rate of increase or decrease over enough years to encompass several business cycles.
Electronic commerce	Electronic commerce or e-commerce, refers to any activity that uses some form of electronic communication in the inventory, exchange, advertisement, distribution, and payment of goods and services.
Grainger	Grainger is a Fortune 400 industrial supply company founded in 1927 in Chicago, Illinois. Grainger provides their clients the products they need to keep their facilities running. Revenue is generally comprized of business to business sales, not consumer sales.
Credit	Credit refers to a recording as positive in the balance of payments, any transaction that gives rise to a payment into the country, such as an export, the sale of an asset, or borrowing from abroad.
Precedent	A previously decided court decision that is recognized as authority for the disposition of future decisions is a precedent.
Warranty	An obligation of a company to replace defective goods or correct any deficiencies in performance or quality of a product is called a warranty.
Attachment	Attachment in general, the process of taking a person's property under an appropriate judicial order by an appropriate officer of the court. Used for a variety of purposes, including the acquisition of jurisdiction over the property seized and the securing of

property that may be used to satisfy a debt.

Legal system	Legal system refers to system of rules that regulate behavior and the processes by which the laws of a country are enforced and through which redress of grievances is obtained.
Jurisprudence	Jurisprudence is the theory and philosophy of law. Students of jurisprudence aim to understand the fundamental nature of law, and to analyze its purpose, structure, and application. Jurisprudential scholars (sometimes confusingly referred to as "jurists") hope to obtain a deeper understanding of the law, the kind of power that it exercises, and its role in human societies.
Administrative agency	Administrative agency refers to a unit of government charged with the administration of particular laws. In the United States, those most important for administering laws related to international trade are the ITC and ITA.
Private sector	The households and business firms of the economy are referred to as private sector.
Arbitration	Arbitration is a form of mediation or conciliation, where the mediating party is given power by the disputant parties to settle the dispute by making a finding. In practice arbitration is generally used as a substitute for judicial systems, particularly when the judicial processes are viewed as too slow, expensive or biased. Arbitration is also used by communities which lack formal law, as a substitute for formal law.
Mediation	Mediation consists of a process of alternative dispute resolution in which a (generally) neutral third party using appropriate techniques, assists two or more parties to help them negotiate an agreement, with concrete effects, on a matter of common interest.
Intervention	Intervention refers to an activity in which a government buys or sells its currency in the foreign exchange market in order to affect its currency's exchange rate.
Compromise	Compromise occurs when the interaction is moderately important to meeting goals and the goals are neither completely compatible nor completely incompatible.
Minitrial	An alternative dispute-resolution method in which lawyers for each side present an abbreviated version of the case for their side at a proceeding referred by a neutral adviser, but settlement authority usually resides with senior executives of the disputing corporations is called a minitrial.
Trial	An examination before a competent tribunal, according to the law of the land, of the facts or law put in issue in a cause, for the purpose of determining such issue is a trial. When the court hears and determines any issue of fact or law for the purpose of determining the rights of the parties, it may be considered a trial.
Verdict	Usually, the decision made by a jury and reported to the judge on the matters or questions submitted to it at trial is a verdict. In some situations, however, the judge may be the party issuing a verdict.
Channel	Channel, in communications (sometimes called communications channel), refers to the medium used to convey information from a sender (or transmitter) to a receiver.
Arbitrate	To submit some disputed matter to selected persons and to accept their decision or award as a substitute for the decision of a judicial tribunal is called the arbitrate.
Direct relationship	Direct relationship refers to the relationship between two variables that change in the same direction, for example, product price and quantity supplied.
Publicity	Publicity refers to any information about an individual, product, or organization that's distributed to the public through the media and that's not paid for or controlled by the seller.
Trade secret	Trade secret refers to a secret formula, pattern, process, program, device, method,

Go to Cram101.com for the Practice Tests for this Chapter.

	technique, or compilation of information that is used in its owner's business and affords that owner a competitive advantage. Trade secrets are protected by state law.
Credibility	The extent to which a source is perceived as having knowledge, skill, or experience relevant to a communication topic and can be trusted to give an unbiased opinion or present objective information on the issue is called credibility.
Intel	Intel Corporation, founded in 1968 and based in Santa Clara, California, USA, is the world's largest semiconductor company. Intel is best known for its PC microprocessors, where it maintains roughly 80% market share.
Revenue	Revenue is a U.S. business term for the amount of money that a company receives from its activities, mostly from sales of products and/or services to customers.
Proprietary	Proprietary indicates that a party, or proprietor, exercises private ownership, control or use over an item of property, usually to the exclusion of other parties. Where a party, holds or claims proprietary interests in relation to certain types of property (eg. a creative literary work, or software), that property may also be the subject of intellectual property law (eg. copyright or patents).
Core competency	A company's core competency are things that a firm can (alsosns) do well and that meet the following three conditions. 1. It provides customer benefits, 2. It is hard for competitors to imitate, and 3. it can be leveraged widely to many products and market. A core competency can take various forms, including technical/subject matter knowhow, a reliable process, and/or close relationships with customers and suppliers. It may also include product development or culture such as employee dedication. Modern business theories suggest that most activities that are not part of a company's core competency should be outsourced.
Integration	Economic integration refers to reducing barriers among countries to transactions and to movements of goods, capital, and labor, including harmonization of laws, regulations, and standards. Integrated markets theoretically function as a unified market.
Holding	The holding is a court's determination of a matter of law based on the issue presented in the particular case. In other words: under this law, with these facts, this result.
Business strategy	Business strategy, which refers to the aggregated operational strategies of single business firm or that of an SBU in a diversified corporation refers to the way in which a firm competes in its chosen arenas.
Gap	In December of 1995, Gap became the first major North American retailer to accept independent monitoring of the working conditions in a contract factory producing its garments. Gap is the largest specialty retailer in the United States.
Preventive maintenance	Maintaining scheduled upkeep and improvement to equipment so equipment can actually improve with age is called the preventive maintenance.
Gap analysis	A measurement of the sensitivity of bank profits to changes in interest rates, calculated by subtracting the amount of rate-sensitive liabilities from the amount of rate-sensitive assets is referred to as gap analysis.
Labor market	Any arrangement that brings buyers and sellers of labor services together to agree on conditions of work and pay is called a labor market.
Scope	Scope of a project is the sum total of all projects products and their requirements or features.
Cost behavior	The relationship between cost and volume or activity is referred to as cost behavior.
Mentor	An experienced employee who supervises, coaches, and guides lower-level employees by introducing them to the right people and generally being their organizational sponsor is a

Go to **Cram101.com** for the Practice Tests for this Chapter.

Go to **Cram101.com** for the Practice Tests for this Chapter.
And, **NEVER** highlight a book again!

	mentor.
Staffing	Staffing refers to a management function that includes hiring, motivating, and retaining the best people available to accomplish the company's objectives.
Administration	Administration refers to the management and direction of the affairs of governments and institutions; a collective term for all policymaking officials of a government; the execution and implementation of public policy.
Manufacturing	Production of goods primarily by the application of labor and capital to raw materials and other intermediate inputs, in contrast to agriculture, mining, forestry, fishing, and services a manufacturing.
Journal	Book of original entry, in which transactions are recorded in a general ledger system, is referred to as a journal.
Materials management	Materials management refers to the activity that controls the transmission of physical materials through the value chain, from procurement through production and into distribution.
Alternative dispute resolution	A general name applied to the many nonjudicial means of settling private disputes is referred to as alternative dispute resolution.
Public administration	Whatever governments do, for good or ill, is referred to as public administration. It is public administration's political context that makes it public, that distinguishes it from private or business administration.
Compliance	A type of influence process where a receiver accepts the position advocated by a source to obtain favorable outcomes or to avoid punishment is the compliance.
Operations management	A specialized area in management that converts or transforms resources into goods and services is operations management.
Business Week	Business Week is a business magazine published by McGraw-Hill. It was first published in 1929 under the direction of Malcolm Muir, who was serving as president of the McGraw-Hill Publishing company at the time. It is considered to be the standard both in industry and among students.
Downsizing	The process of eliminating managerial and non-managerial positions are called downsizing.

Conflict resolution	Conflict resolution is the process of resolving a dispute or a conflict. Successful conflict resolution occurs by providing each side's needs, and adequately addressing their interests so that they are each satisfied with the outcome. Conflict resolution aims to end conflicts before they start or lead to physical fighting.
Business law	Business law is the body of law which governs business and commerce and is often considered to be a branch of civil law and deals both with issues of private law and public law. It regulates corporate contracts, hiring practices, and the manufacture and sales of consumer goods.
Legal system	Legal system refers to system of rules that regulate behavior and the processes by which the laws of a country are enforced and through which redress of grievances is obtained.
Arbitration	Arbitration is a form of mediation or conciliation, where the mediating party is given power by the disputant parties to settle the dispute by making a finding. In practice arbitration is generally used as a substitute for judicial systems, particularly when the judicial processes are viewed as too slow, expensive or biased. Arbitration is also used by communities which lack formal law, as a substitute for formal law.
Technology	The body of knowledge and techniques that can be used to combine economic resources to produce goods and services is called technology.
Operation	A standardized method or technique that is performed repetitively, often on different materials resulting in different finished goods is called an operation.
Napster	Napster is an online music service which was originally a file sharing service created by Shawn Fanning. Napster was the first widely-used peer-to-peer (or P2P) music sharing service, and it made a major impact on how people, especially university students, used the Internet.
Swap	In finance a swap is a derivative, where two counterparties exchange one stream of cash flows against another stream. These streams are called the legs of the swap. The cash flows are calculated over a notional principal amount. Swaps are often used to hedge certain risks, for instance interest rate risk. Another use is speculation.
Venture capitalists	Venture capitalists refer to individuals or companies that invest in new businesses in exchange for partial ownership of those businesses.
Holding	The holding is a court's determination of a matter of law based on the issue presented in the particular case. In other words: under this law, with these facts, this result.
License	A license in the sphere of Intellectual Property Rights (IPR) is a document, contract or agreement giving permission or the 'right' to a legally-definable entity to do something (such as manufacture a product or to use a service), or to apply something (such as a trademark), with the objective of achieving commercial gain.
Leverage	Leverage is using given resources in such a way that the potential positive or negative outcome is magnified. In finance, this generally refers to borrowing.
Appeal	Appeal refers to the act of asking an appellate court to overturn a decision after the trial court's final judgment has been entered.
Management	Management characterizes the process of leading and directing all or part of an organization, often a business, through the deployment and manipulation of resources. Early twentieth-century management writer Mary Parker Follett defined management as "the art of getting things done through people."
Injunction	Injunction refers to a court order directing a person or organization not to perform a certain act because the act would do irreparable damage to some other person or persons; a restraining order.

Go to Cram101.com for the Practice Tests for this Chapter.

Cost management	The approaches and activities of managers in short-run and long-run planning and control decisions that increase value for customers and lower costs of products and services are called cost management.
Industry	A group of firms that produce identical or similar products is an industry. It is also used specifically to refer to an area of economic production focused on manufacturing which involves large amounts of capital investment before any profit can be realized, also called "heavy industry".
Service	Service refers to a "non tangible product" that is not embodied in a physical good and that typically effects some change in another product, person, or institution. Contrasts with good.
Purchasing	Purchasing refers to the function in a firm that searches for quality material resources, finds the best suppliers, and negotiates the best price for goods and services.
Journal	Book of original entry, in which transactions are recorded in a general ledger system, is referred to as a journal.
Wall Street Journal	Dow Jones & Company was founded in 1882 by reporters Charles Dow, Edward Jones and Charles Bergstresser. Jones converted the small Customers' Afternoon Letter into The Wall Street Journal, first published in 1889, and began delivery of the Dow Jones News Service via telegraph. The Journal featured the Jones 'Average', the first of several indexes of stock and bond prices on the New York Stock Exchange.
Contract	A contract is a "promise" or an "agreement" that is enforced or recognized by the law. In the civil law, a contract is considered to be part of the general law of obligations.
Offer and acceptance	Offer and acceptance analysis is a traditional approach in contract law used to determine whether an agreement exists between two parties. An offer is an indication by one person to another of their willingness to contract on certain terms without further negotiations. A contract is then formed if there is express or implied agreement.
Supply	Supply is the aggregate amount of any material good that can be called into being at a certain price point; it comprises one half of the equation of supply and demand. In classical economic theory, a curve representing supply is one of the factors that produce price.
Supply chain	Supply chain refers to the flow of goods, services, and information from the initial sources of materials and services to the delivery of products to consumers.
Foundation	A Foundation is a type of philanthropic organization set up by either individuals or institutions as a legal entity (either as a corporation or trust) with the purpose of distributing grants to support causes in line with the goals of the foundation.
Agency law	Agency law refers to the large body of common law that governs agency; a mixture of contract law and tort law.
Agent	A person who makes economic decisions for another economic actor. A hired manager operates as an agent for a firm's owner.
Property	Assets defined in the broadest legal sense. Property includes the unrealized receivables of a cash basis taxpayer, but not services rendered.
Patent	The legal right to the proceeds from and control over the use of an invented product or process, granted for a fixed period of time, usually 20 years. Patent is one form of intellectual property that is subject of the TRIPS agreement.
Intellectual property	In law, intellectual property is an umbrella term for various legal entitlements which attach to certain types of information, ideas, or other intangibles in their expressed form. The holder of this legal entitlement is generally entitled to exercise various exclusive

Go to **Cram101.com** for the Practice Tests for this Chapter.

	rights in relation to its subject matter.
Contract law	Set of laws that specify what constitutes a legally enforceable agreement is called contract
Authority	Authority in agency law, refers to an agent's ability to affect his principal's legal relations with third parties. Also used to refer to an actor's legal power or ability to do something. In addition, sometimes used to refer to a statute, case, or other legal source that justifies a particular result.
Principal	In agency law, one under whose direction an agent acts and for whose benefit that agent acts is a principal.
Firm	An organization that employs resources to produce a good or service for profit and owns and operates one or more plants is referred to as a firm.
Scope	Scope of a project is the sum total of all projects products and their requirements or features.
Interest	In finance and economics, interest is the price paid by a borrower for the use of a lender's money. In other words, interest is the amount of paid to "rent" money for a period of time.
Liability	A liability is a present obligation of the enterprise arizing from past events, the settlement of which is expected to result in an outflow from the enterprise of resources embodying economic benefits.
Actual authority	Actual authority includes expressed authority as well as implied authority, or that authority customarily given to an agent in an industry, trade, or profession is called actual authority.
Apparent authority	Apparent authority is a term used in the law of agency to describe a situation in which a principal leads a third party to believe that an agent has authority to bind the principal, even where the agent lacks the actual authority to bind the principal.
Procurement	Procurement is the acquisition of goods or services at the best possible total cost of ownership, in the right quantity, at the right time, in the right place for the direct benefit or use of the governments, corporations, or individuals generally via, but not limited to a contract.
Commerce	Commerce is the exchange of something of value between two entities. It is the central mechanism from which capitalism is derived.
Electronic signature	Uses digital signature technology to make the person's signature part of a document in such a way that any alteration can be detected are referred to as electronic signature.
Electronic commerce	Electronic commerce or e-commerce, refers to any activity that uses some form of electronic communication in the inventory, exchange, advertisement, distribution, and payment of goods and services.
Channel	Channel, in communications (sometimes called communications channel), refers to the medium used to convey information from a sender (or transmitter) to a receiver.
Customer service	The ability of logistics management to satisfy users in terms of time, dependability, communication, and convenience is called the customer service.
Security	Security refers to a claim on the borrower future income that is sold by the borrower to the lender. A security is a type of transferable interest representing financial value.
Mortgage	Mortgage refers to a note payable issued for property, such as a house, usually repaid in equal installments consisting of part principle and part interest, over a specified period.
Buyer	A buyer refers to a role in the buying center with formal authority and responsibility to select the supplier and negotiate the terms of the contract.

Go to Cram101.com for the Practice Tests for this Chapter.

Policy	Similar to a script in that a policy can be a less than completely rational decision-making method. Involves the use of a pre-existing set of decision steps for any problem that presents itself.
Litigation	The process of bringing, maintaining, and defending a lawsuit is litigation.
Bankruptcy	Bankruptcy is a legally declared inability or impairment of ability of an individual or organization to pay their creditors.
Bribery	When one person gives another person money, property, favors, or anything else of value for a favor in return, we have bribery. Often referred to as a payoff or 'kickback.'
Developing country	Developing country refers to a country whose per capita income is low by world standards. Same as LDC. As usually used, it does not necessarily connote that the country's income is rising.
Variable	A variable is something measured by a number; it is used to analyze what happens to other things when the size of that number changes.
Organizational environment	Organizational environment refers to everything outside an organization. It includes all elements, people, other organizations, economic factors, objects, and events that lie outside the boundaries of the organization.
Regulation	Regulation refers to restrictions state and federal laws place on business with regard to the conduct of its activities.
Market	A market is, as defined in economics, a social arrangement that allows buyers and sellers to discover information and carry out a voluntary exchange of goods or services.
Federal trade commission	The commission of five members established by the Federal Trade Commission Act of 1914 to investigate unfair competitive practices of firms, to hold hearings on the complaints of such practices, and to issue cease-and-desist orders when firms were found guilty of unfair practices.
Market opportunities	Market opportunities refer to areas where a company believes there are favorable demand trends, needs, and/or wants that are not being satisfied, and where it can compete effectively.
Competitive market	A market in which no buyer or seller has market power is called a competitive market.
Buying power	The dollar amount available to purchase securities on margin is buying power. The amount is calculated by adding the cash held in the brokerage accounts and the amount that could be spent if securities were fully margined to their limit. If an investor uses their buying power, they are purchasing securities on credit.
Consideration	Consideration in contract law, a basic requirement for an enforceable agreement under traditional contract principles, defined in this text as legal value, bargained for and given in exchange for an act or promise. In corporation law, cash or property contributed to a corporation in exchange for shares, or a promise to contribute such cash or property.
Statute	A statute is a formal, written law of a country or state, written and enacted by its legislative authority, perhaps to then be ratified by the highest executive in the government, and finally published.
Trade diversion	Trade diversion refers to trade that occurs between members of a preferential trading arrangement that replaces what would have been imports from a country outside the PTA.
Fringe benefit	Benefits such as sick-leave pay, vacation pay, pension plans, and health plans that represent additional compenzation to employees beyond base wages is a fringe benefit.

Infraction	Infraction is an essentially minor violation of law where the penalty upon conviction only consists of monetary forfeiture. A violation of law which could include imprisonment is a crime. It is distinguished from a misdemeanor or a felony in that the penalty for an infraction cannot include any imprisonment.
Appreciation	Appreciation refers to a rise in the value of a country's currency on the exchange market, relative either to a particular other currency or to a weighted average of other currencies. The currency is said to appreciate. Opposite of 'depreciation.' Appreciation can also refer to the increase in value of any asset.
Misrepresent-tion	The assertion of a fact that is not in accord with the truth is misrepresentation. A contract can be rescinded on the ground of misrepresentation when the assertion relates to a material fact or is made fraudulently and the other party actually and justifiably relies on the assertion.
Fraud	Tax fraud falls into two categories: civil and criminal. Under civil fraud, the IRS may impose as a penalty of an amount equal to as much as 75 percent of the underpayment.
Concession	A concession is a business operated under a contract or license associated with a degree of exclusivity in exploiting a business within a certain geographical area. For example, sports arenas or public parks may have concession stands; and public services such as water supply may be operated as concessions.
Bid	A bid price is a price offered by a buyer when he/she buys a good. In the context of stock trading on a stock exchange, the bid price is the highest price a buyer of a stock is willing to pay for a share of that given stock.
Deception	According to the Federal Trade Commission, a misrepresentation, omission, or practice that is likely to mislead the consumer acting reasonably in the circumstances to the consumer's detriment is referred to as deception.
Stock	In financial terminology, stock is the capital raized by a corporation, through the issuance and sale of shares.
Fund	Independent accounting entity with a self-balancing set of accounts segregated for the purposes of carrying on specific activities is referred to as a fund.
Mutual fund	A mutual fund is a form of collective investment that pools money from many investors and invests the money in stocks, bonds, short-term money market instruments, and/or other securities. In a mutual fund, the fund manager trades the fund's underlying securities, realizing capital gains or loss, and collects the dividend or interest income.
Code of ethics	A formal statement of ethical principles and rules of conduct is a code of ethics. Some may have the force of law; these are often promulgated by the (quasi-)governmental agency responsible for licensing a profession. Violations of these codes may be subject to administrative (e.g., loss of license), civil or penal remedies.
Standards of conduct	Standards of conduct refers to a compendium of ethical norms promulgated by an organization to guide the behavior of its members. Many government agencies have formal codes of conduct for their employees.
Loyalty	Marketers tend to define customer loyalty as making repeat purchases. Some argue that it should be defined attitudinally as a strongly positive feeling about the brand.
Prejudice	Prejudice is, as the name implies, the process of "pre-judging" something. It implies coming to a judgment on a subject before learning where the preponderance of evidence actually lies, or forming a judgment without direct experience.
Accord	An agreement whereby the parties agree to accept something different in satisfaction of the original contract is an accord.

Go to **Cram101.com** for the Practice Tests for this Chapter.

Standing	Standing refers to the legal requirement that anyone seeking to challenge a particular action in court must demonstrate that such action substantially affects his legitimate interests before he will be entitled to bring suit.
Marketing	Promoting and selling products or services to customers, or prospective customers, is referred to as marketing.
Trend	Trend refers to the long-term movement of an economic variable, such as its average rate of increase or decrease over enough years to encompass several business cycles.
Personnel	A collective term for all of the employees of an organization. Personnel is also commonly used to refer to the personnel management function or the organizational unit responsible for administering personnel programs.
Ethics training	Training programs to help employees deal with ethical questions and values are called ethics training.
Commodity	Could refer to any good, but in trade a commodity is usually a raw material or primary product that enters into international trade, such as metals or basic agricultural products.
Uniform Commercial Code	Uniform commercial code refers to a comprehensive commercial law adopted by every state in the United States; it covers sales laws and other commercial laws.
Administrative law	Any rule that directly or indirectly affects an administrative agency is called administrative law.
Legislative branch	The part of the government that consists of Congress and has the power to adopt laws is called the legislative branch.
Executive branch	The executive branch is the part of government charged with implementing or enforcing the laws. Consists of the President and Vice President.
Judicial branch	Judicial branch refers to the part of the government that consists of the Supreme Court and other federal courts.
Common law	The legal system that is based on the judgement and decree of courts rather than legislative action is called common law.
Federal government	Federal government refers to the government of the United States, as distinct from the state and local governments.
Objection	In the trial of a case the formal remonstrance made by counsel to something that has been said or done, in order to obtain the court's ruling thereon is an objection.
Confirmed	When the seller's bank agrees to assume liability on the letter of credit issued by the buyer's bank the transaction is confirmed. The term means that the credit is not only backed up by the issuing foreign bank, but that payment is also guaranteed by the notifying American bank.
Purchase order	A form on which items or services needed by a business firm are specified and then communicated to the vendor is a purchase order.
Jurisprudence	Jurisprudence is the theory and philosophy of law. Students of jurisprudence aim to understand the fundamental nature of law, and to analyze its purpose, structure, and application. Jurisprudential scholars (sometimes confusingly referred to as "jurists") hope to obtain a deeper understanding of the law, the kind of power that it exercises, and its role in human societies.
Warranty	An obligation of a company to replace defective goods or correct any deficiencies in performance or quality of a product is called a warranty.
Express warranty	An express warranty is a written guarantee from the manufacturer or distributor that

Go to **Cram101.com** for the Practice Tests for this Chapter.

	specifies the conditions under which the product can be returned,replaced,or repaired.
Implied warranty	A warranty created by operation of law is called implied warranty.
Warranty of merchantability	The warranty of merchantability is implied, unless expressly disclaimed by name, or the sale is identified with the phrase "as is" or "with all faults." To be "merchantable", the goods must reasonably conform to an ordinary buyer's expectations, i.e., they are what they say they are.
Merchant	Under the Uniform Commercial Code, one who regularly deals in goods of the kind sold in the contract at issue, or holds himself out as having special knowledge or skill relevant to such goods, or who makes the sale through an agent who regularly deals in such goods or claims such knowledge or skill is referred to as merchant.
Implied warranty of merchantability	Unless properly disclosed, a warranty that is implied that sold or leased goods are fit for the ordinary purpose for which they are sold or leased, and other assurances are called implied warranty of merchantability.
Lien	In its most extensive meaning, it is a charge on property for the payment or discharge of a debt or duty is referred to as lien.
Warrant	A warrant is a security that entitles the holder to buy or sell a certain additional quantity of an underlying security at an agreed-upon price, at the holder's discretion.
Security interest	A security interest is a property interest created by agreement or by operation of law over assets to secure the performance of an obligation (usually but not always the payment of a debt) which gives the beneficiary of the security interest certain preferential rights in relation to the assets.
Warranty of title	The warranty of title implies that the seller of goods has the right to sell them (e.g., they are not stolen, or patent infringements, or already sold to someone else). This theoretically saves a seller from having to "pay twice" for a product, if it is confiscated by the rightful owner, but only if the seller can be found and makes restitution.
Patent infringement	Patent infringement refers to unauthorized use of another's patent. A patent holder may recover damages and other remedies against a patent infringer.
Indemnification	Right of a partner to be reimbursed for expenditures incurred on behalf of the partnership is referred to as indemnification.
Domestic	From or in one's own country. A domestic producer is one that produces inside the home country. A domestic price is the price inside the home country. Opposite of 'foreign' or 'world.'.
Bill of lading	Bill of lading refers to the receipt given by a transportation company to an exporter when the former accepts goods for transport. It includes the contract specifying what transport service will be provided and the limits of liability.
Credit	Credit refers to a recording as positive in the balance of payments, any transaction that gives rise to a payment into the country, such as an export, the sale of an asset, or borrowing from abroad.
Price discrimination	Price discrimination refers to the sale by a firm to buyers at two different prices. When this occurs internationally and the lower price is charged for export, it is regarded as dumping.
Interstate commerce commission	A federal regulatory group created by Congress in 1887 to oversee and correct abuses in the railroad industry is an interstate commerce commission.
Warehouse	Warehouse refers to a location, often decentralized, that a firm uses to store, consolidate,

Go to Cram101.com for the Practice Tests for this Chapter.

age, or mix stock; house product-recall programs; or ease tax burdens.

Insurance	Insurance refers to a system by which individuals can reduce their exposure to risk of large losses by spreading the risks among a large number of persons.
Default	In finance, default occurs when a debtor has not met its legal obligations according to the debt contract, e.g. it has not made a scheduled payment, or violated a covenant (condition) of the debt contract.
Expense	In accounting, an expense represents an event in which an asset is used up or a liability is incurred. In terms of the accounting equation, expenses reduce owners' equity.
Breach of contract	When one party fails to follow the terms of a contract, we have breach of contract.
Inventory	Tangible property held for sale in the normal course of business or used in producing goods or services for sale is an inventory.
Specific performance	A contract remedy whereby the defendant is ordered to perform according to the terms of his contract is referred to as specific performance.
Breach of warranty	A breach of warranty occurs when the promise is broken, i.e., a product is defective or not as should be expected by a reasonable buyer.
Commercial law	The law that relates to the rights of property and persons engaged in trade or commerce and regulates corporate contracts, hiring practices, and the manufacture and sales of consumer goods is called commercial law.
Exchange	The trade of things of value between buyer and seller so that each is better off after the trade is called the exchange.
Writ	Writ refers to a commandment of a court given for the purpose of compelling certain action from the defendant, and usually executed by a sheriff or other judicial officer.
Negotiation	Negotiation is the process whereby interested parties resolve disputes, agree upon courses of action, bargain for individual or collective advantage, and/or attempt to craft outcomes which serve their mutual interests.
Coercion	Economic coercion is when an agent puts economic pressure onto the victim. The most common example of this is cutting off the supply to an essential resource, such as water.
Contracting party	Contracting party refers to a country that has signed the GATT.
Contract A	Contract A is a concept applied in Canadian contract law (a Common Law system country) which has recently been applied by courts regarding the fairness and equal treatment of bidders in a contract tendering process. Essentially this concept formalises previously applied precedents and strengthens the protection afforded to Contractors in the tendering process.
Anticipatory breach	A contracting party's indication before the time for performance that he cannot or will not perform the contract is an anticipatory breach.
Production	The creation of finished goods and services using the factors of production: land, labor, capital, entrepreneurship, and knowledge.
Damages	The sum of money recoverable by a plaintiff who has received a judgment in a civil case is called damages.
Anticipation	In finance, anticipation is where debts are paid off early, generally in order to pay less interest.
Tender	An unconditional offer of payment, consisting in the actual production in money or legal

Go to **Cram101.com** for the Practice Tests for this Chapter.

tender of a sum not less than the amount due.

Complaint	The pleading in a civil case in which the plaintiff states his claim and requests relief is called complaint. In the common law, it is a formal legal document that sets out the basic facts and legal reasons that the filing party (the plaintiffs) believes are sufficient to support a claim against another person, persons, entity or entities (the defendants) that entitles the plaintiff(s) to a remedy (either money damages or injunctive relief).
Precedent	A previously decided court decision that is recognized as authority for the disposition of future decisions is a precedent.
Liquidated	Damages made certain by the prior agreement of the parties are called liquidated.
Liquidated damages	The stipulation by the parties to a contract of the sum of money to be recovered by the aggrieved party in the event of a breach of the contract by the other party are referred to as liquidated damages.
Termination	The ending of a corporation that occurs only after the winding-up of the corporation's affairs, the liquidation of its assets, and the distribution of the proceeds to the claimants are referred to as a termination.
Punitive	Damages designed to punish flagrant wrongdoers and to deter them and others from engaging in similar conduct in the future are called punitive.
Punitive damages	Damages received or paid by the taxpayer can be classified as compensatory damages or as punitive damages. Punitive damages are those awarded to punish the defendant for gross negligence or the intentional infliction of harm. Such damages are includible.
Plaintiff	A plaintiff is the party who initiates a lawsuit (also known as an action) before a court. By doing so, the plaintiff seeks a legal remedy, and if successful, the court will issue judgment in favour of the plaintiff and make the appropriate court order.
Restitution	A remedy whereby one is able to obtain the return of that which he has given the other party, or an amount of money equivalent to that which he has given the other party is referred to as restitution.
Gain	In finance, gain is a profit or an increase in value of an investment such as a stock or bond. Gain is calculated by fair market value or the proceeds from the sale of the investment minus the sum of the purchase price and all costs associated with it.
Wholesale	According to the United Nations Statistics Division Wholesale is the resale of new and used goods to retailers, to industrial, commercial, institutional or professional users, or to other wholesalers, or involves acting as an agent or broker in buying merchandise for, or selling merchandise, to such persons or companies.
Valid contract	Valid contract refers to a contract that meets all of the essential elements to establish a contract; a contract that is enforceable by at least one of the parties.
Profit	Profit refers to the return to the resource entrepreneurial ability; total revenue minus total cost.
Custody	The bare control or care of a thing as distinguished from the possession of it is called custody.
Consequential	Damages that do not flow directly and immediately from an act but rather flow from the results of the act are consequential.
Mistake	In contract law a mistake is incorrect understanding by one or more parties to a contract and may be used as grounds to invalidate the agreement. Common law has identified three different types of mistake in contract: unilateral mistake, mutual mistake, and common mistake.

Go to Cram101.com for the Practice Tests for this Chapter.

Best efforts	Best efforts refer to a distribution in which the investment banker agrees to work for a commission rather than actually underwriting the issue for resale. It is a procedure that is used by smaller investment bankers with relatively unknown companies. The investment banker is not directly taking the risk for distribution.
International law	Law that governs affairs between nations and that regulates transactions between individuals and businesses of different countries is an international law.
Negligence	The omission to do something that a reasonable person, guided by those considerations that ordinarily regulate human affairs, would do, or doing something that a prudent and reasonable person would not do is negligence.
Copyright	The legal right to the proceeds from and control over the use of a created product, such a written work, audio, video, film, or software is a copyright. This right generally extends over the life of the author plus fifty years.
Trade secret	Trade secret refers to a secret formula, pattern, process, program, device, method, technique, or compilation of information that is used in its owner's business and affords that owner a competitive advantage. Trade secrets are protected by state law.
Variance	Variance refers to a measure of how much an economic or statistical variable varies across values or observations. Its calculation is the same as that of the covariance, being the covariance of the variable with itself.
Disclosure	Disclosure means the giving out of information, either voluntarily or to be in compliance with legal regulations or workplace rules.
Monopoly	A monopoly is defined as a persistent market situation where there is only one provider of a kind of product or service.
Distribution	Distribution in economics, the manner in which total output and income is distributed among individuals or factors.
Proprietary	Proprietary indicates that a party, or proprietor, exercises private ownership, control or use over an item of property, usually to the exclusion of other parties. Where a party, holds or claims proprietary interests in relation to certain types of property (eg. a creative literary work, or software), that property may also be the subject of intellectual property law (eg. copyright or patents).
Possession	Possession refers to respecting real property, exclusive dominion and control such as owners of like property usually exercise over it. Manual control of personal property either as owner or as one having a qualified right in it.
Boycott	To protest by refusing to purchase from someone, or otherwise do business with them. In international trade, a boycott most often takes the form of refusal to import a country's goods.
Export	In economics, an export is any good or commodity, shipped or otherwise transported out of a country, province, town to another part of the world in a legitimate fashion, typically for use in trade or sale.
Administration	Administration refers to the management and direction of the affairs of governments and institutions; a collective term for all policymaking officials of a government; the execution and implementation of public policy.
Exporting	Selling products to another country is called exporting.
Customs	Customs is an authority or agency in a country responsible for collecting customs duties and for controlling the flow of people, animals and goods (including personal effects and hazardous items) in and out of the country.

Go to Cram101.com for the Practice Tests for this Chapter.

Broker	In commerce, a broker is a party that mediates between a buyer and a seller. A broker who also acts as a seller or as a buyer becomes a principal party to the deal.
Collusion	Collusion refers to cooperation among firms to raise price and otherwise increase their profits.
Price fixing	Price fixing refers to the conspiring by two or more firms to set the price of their products; an illegal practice under the Sherman Act.
Antitrust	Government intervention to alter market structure or prevent abuse of market power is called antitrust.
Sherman Antitrust Act	The Sherman Antitrust Act, formally known as the Act of July 2, 1890 was the first United States federal government action to limit monopolies.
Restraint of trade	Contracts in restraint of trade are contracts which have the effect of restricting a person's freedom to conduct business in a specified or unspecified location for a specified or unspecified length of time.
Federal trade commission act	The federal act of 1914 that established the Federal Trade Commission is referred to as Federal Trade Commission Act.
Unfair competition	Antitrust or competition laws, legislate against trade practices that undermine competitiveness or are considered to be unfair competition. The term antitrust derives from the U.S. law that was originally formulated to combat business trusts - now commonly known as cartels.
Lockheed Martin	Lockheed Martin is the world's largest defense contractor (by defense revenue). As of 2005, 95% of revenues came from the U.S. Department of Defense, other U.S. federal government agencies, and foreign military customers.
Business ethics	The study of what makes up good and bad conduct as related to business activities and values is business ethics.
Corporation	A legal entity chartered by a state or the Federal government that is distinct and separate from the individuals who own it is a corporation. This separation gives the corporation unique powers which other legal entities lack.
Audit	An examination of the financial reports to ensure that they represent what they claim and conform with generally accepted accounting principles is referred to as audit.
Sexual harassment	Unwelcome sexual advances, requests for sexual favors, and other conduct of a sexual nature is called sexual harassment.
Insider trading	Insider trading is the trading of a corporation's stock or other securities (e.g. Bonds or stock options) by corporate insiders such as officers, directors, or holders of more than ten percent of the firm's shares.
Merger	Merger refers to the combination of two firms into a single firm.
Labor	People's physical and mental talents and efforts that are used to help produce goods and services are called labor.
Compliance	A type of influence process where a receiver accepts the position advocated by a source to obtain favorable outcomes or to avoid punishment is the compliance.
Advertising	Advertising refers to paid, nonpersonal communication through various media by organizations and individuals who are in some way identified in the advertising message.
American Bar Association	The American Bar Association is a voluntary bar association of lawyers and law students, which is not specific to any jurisdiction in the United States. The most important activities are the setting of academic standards for law schools, and the formulation of model legal

Go to Cram101.com for the Practice Tests for this Chapter.

codes.

Committee
A long-lasting, sometimes permanent team in the organization structure created to deal with tasks that recur regularly is the committee.

Materials management
Materials management refers to the activity that controls the transmission of physical materials through the value chain, from procurement through production and into distribution.

Lease
A contract for the possession and use of land or other property, including goods, on one side, and a recompense of rent or other income on the other is the lease.

293

Discount	The difference between the face value of a bond and its selling price, when a bond is sold for less than its face value it's referred to as a discount.
Purchasing	Purchasing refers to the function in a firm that searches for quality material resources, finds the best suppliers, and negotiates the best price for goods and services.
Production	The creation of finished goods and services using the factors of production: land, labor, capital, entrepreneurship, and knowledge.
Investment	Investment refers to spending for the production and accumulation of capital and additions to inventories. In a financial sense, buying an asset with the expectation of making a return.
Inventory	Tangible property held for sale in the normal course of business or used in producing goods or services for sale is an inventory.
Yield	The interest rate that equates a future value or an annuity to a given present value is a yield.
Stock	In financial terminology, stock is the capital raized by a corporation, through the issuance and sale of shares.
Hedge	Hedge refers to a process of offsetting risk. In the foreign exchange market, hedgers use the forward market to cover a transaction or open position and thereby reduce exchange risk. The term applies most commonly to trade.
Buyer	A buyer refers to a role in the buying center with formal authority and responsibility to select the supplier and negotiate the terms of the contract.
Service	Service refers to a "non tangible product" that is not embodied in a physical good and that typically effects some change in another product, person, or institution. Contrasts with good.
Supply	Supply is the aggregate amount of any material good that can be called into being at a certain price point; it comprises one half of the equation of supply and demand. In classical economic theory, a curve representing supply is one of the factors that produce price.
Inventory investment	Spending by firms on additional holdings of raw materials, parts, and finished goods is called inventory investment.
Quantity discounts	Quantity discounts refer to reductions in unit costs for a larger order.
Quantity discount	A quantity discount is a price reduction given for a large order.
Customer service	The ability of logistics management to satisfy users in terms of time, dependability, communication, and convenience is called the customer service.
Manufacturing	Production of goods primarily by the application of labor and capital to raw materials and other intermediate inputs, in contrast to agriculture, mining, forestry, fishing, and services a manufacturing.
Distribution	Distribution in economics, the manner in which total output and income is distributed among individuals or factors.
Supply chain	Supply chain refers to the flow of goods, services, and information from the initial sources of materials and services to the delivery of products to consumers.
Safety stock	Safety stock is additional inventory planned to buffer against the variability in supply and demand plans, that could otherwise result in inventory shortages.
Controlling	A management function that involves determining whether or not an organization is progressing

	toward its goals and objectives, and taking corrective action if it is not is called controlling.
Operation	A standardized method or technique that is performed repetitively, often on different materials resulting in different finished goods is called an operation.
Operations technology	The combination of resources, knowledge, and techniques that creates a product or service output for an organization is operations technology.
Business operations	Business operations are those activities involved in the running of a business for the purpose of producing value for the stakeholders. The outcome of business operations is the harvesting of value from assets owned by a business.
Technology	The body of knowledge and techniques that can be used to combine economic resources to produce goods and services is called technology.
Points	Loan origination fees that may be deductible as interest by a buyer of property. A seller of property who pays points reduces the selling price by the amount of the points paid for the buyer.
Chief executive officer	A chief executive officer is the highest-ranking corporate officer or executive officer of a corporation, or agency. In closely held corporations, it is general business culture that the office chief executive officer is also the chairman of the board.
Management	Management characterizes the process of leading and directing all or part of an organization, often a business, through the deployment and manipulation of resources. Early twentieth-century management writer Mary Parker Follett defined management as "the art of getting things done through people."
Portfolio	In finance, a portfolio is a collection of investments held by an institution or a private individual. Holding but not always a portfolio is part of an investment and risk-limiting strategy called diversification. By owning several assets, certain types of risk (in particular specific risk) can be reduced.
Change management	Change management is the process of developing a planned approach to change in an organization. Typically the objective is to maximize the collective benefits for all people involved in the change and minimize the risk of failure of implementing the change.
Business process	Business process refers to the individual activities of an enterprise. Processes can be viewed at a high level, for example, 'marketing,' or at the level of detailed subprocesses, for example, 'customer retention.'.
Capital	Capital generally refers to financial wealth, especially that used to start or maintain a business. In classical economics, capital is one of four factors of production, the others being land and labor and entrepreneurship.
Margin	A deposit by a buyer in stocks with a seller or a stockbroker, as security to cover fluctuations in the market in reference to stocks that the buyer has purchased but for which he has not paid is a margin. Commodities are also traded on margin.
Working capital	The dollar difference between total current assets and total current liabilities is called working capital.
Operating income	Total revenues from operation minus cost of goods sold and operating costs are called operating income.
Promotion	Promotion refers to all the techniques sellers use to motivate people to buy products or services. An attempt by marketers to inform people about products and to persuade them to participate in an exchange.
Warehouse	Warehouse refers to a location, often decentralized, that a firm uses to store, consolidate,

Go to Cram101.com for the Practice Tests for this Chapter.

age, or mix stock; house product-recall programs; or ease tax burdens.

Inventory management	The planning, coordinating, and controlling activities related to the flow of inventory into, through, and out of an organization is referred to as inventory management.
Category management	An organizational system whereby managers have responsibility for the marketing programs for a particular category or line of products is a category management.
Reengineering	The fundamental rethinking and redesign of business processes to achieve improvements in critical measures of performance, such as cost, quality, service, speed, and customer satisfaction is referred to as reengineering.
Merchandising	Merchandising refers to the business of acquiring finished goods for resale, either in a wholesale or a retail operation.
Information technology	Information technology refers to technology that helps companies change business by allowing them to use new methods.
Senior management	Senior management is generally a team of individuals at the highest level of organizational management who have the day-to-day responsibilities of managing a corporation.
Comprehensive	A comprehensive refers to a layout accurate in size, color, scheme, and other necessary details to show how a final ad will look. For presentation only, never for reproduction.
Business case	The business case addresses, at a high level, the business need that a project seeks to resolve. It includes the reasons for the project, the expected business benefits, the options considered (with reasons for rejecting or carrying forward each option), the expected costs of the project, a gap analysis and the expected risks.
Market	A market is, as defined in economics, a social arrangement that allows buyers and sellers to discover information and carry out a voluntary exchange of goods or services.
Productivity	Productivity refers to the total output of goods and services in a given period of time divided by work hours.
Bottom line	The bottom line is net income on the last line of a income statement.
Profit	Profit refers to the return to the resource entrepreneurial ability; total revenue minus total cost.
Carrying costs	Carrying costs refers to costs that arise while holding an inventory of goods for sale.
Carrying cost	The cost to hold an asset, usually inventory is called a carrying cost. For inventory, a carrying cost includes such items as interest, warehousing costs, insurance, and material-handling expenses.
Market share	That fraction of an industry's output accounted for by an individual firm or group of firms is called market share.
Firm	An organization that employs resources to produce a good or service for profit and owns and operates one or more plants is referred to as a firm.
Policy	Similar to a script in that a policy can be a less than completely rational decision-making method. Involves the use of a pre-existing set of decision steps for any problem that presents itself.
Raw material	Raw material refers to a good that has not been transformed by production; a primary product.
Inputs	The inputs used by a firm or an economy are the labor, raw materials, electricity and other resources it uses to produce its outputs.
Anticipation	In finance, anticipation is where debts are paid off early, generally in order to pay less interest.

Finished goods	Completed products awaiting sale are called finished goods. An item considered a finished good in a supplying plant might be considered a component or raw material in a receiving plant.
Industry	A group of firms that produce identical or similar products is an industry. It is also used specifically to refer to an area of economic production focused on manufacturing which involves large amounts of capital investment before any profit can be realized, also called "heavy industry".
Trend	Trend refers to the long-term movement of an economic variable, such as its average rate of increase or decrease over enough years to encompass several business cycles.
Performance improvement	Performance improvement is the concept of measuring the output of a particular process or procedure then modifying the process or procedure in order to increase the output, increase efficiency, or increase the effectiveness of the process or procedure.
Supply chain management	Supply chain management deals with the planning and execution issues involved in managing a supply chain. Supply chain management spans all movement and storage of raw materials, work-in-process inventory, and finished goods from point-of-origin to point-of-consumption.
Inventory turns	In business management, inventory turns measures the number of times capital invested in goods to be sold turns over in a year.
Profit margin	Profit margin is a measure of profitability. It is calculated using a formula and written as a percentage or a number. Profit margin = Net income before tax and interest / Revenue.
Consultant	A professional that provides expert advice in a particular field or area in which customers occassionaly require this type of knowledge is a consultant.
Holding	The holding is a court's determination of a matter of law based on the issue presented in the particular case. In other words: under this law, with these facts, this result.
Optimum	Optimum refers to the best. Usually refers to a most preferred choice by consumers subject to a budget constraint or a profit maximizing choice by firms or industry subject to a technological constraint.
Possession	Possession refers to respecting real property, exclusive dominion and control such as owners of like property usually exercise over it. Manual control of personal property either as owner or as one having a qualified right in it.
Balance	In banking and accountancy, the outstanding balance is the amount of money owned, (or due), that remains in a deposit account (or a loan account) at a given date, after all past remittances, payments and withdrawal have been accounted for. It can be positive (then, in the balance sheet of a firm, it is an asset) or negative (a liability).
Competitive advantage	A business is said to have a competitive advantage when its unique strengths, often based on cost, quality, time, and innovation, offer consumers a greater percieved value and there by diffetiating it from its competitors.
Channel	Channel, in communications (sometimes called communications channel), refers to the medium used to convey information from a sender (or transmitter) to a receiver.
Distribution channel	A distribution channel is a chain of intermediaries, each passing a product down the chain to the next organization, before it finally reaches the consumer or end-user.
In transit	A state in which goods are in the possession of a bailee or carrier and not in the hands of the buyer, seller, lessee, or lessor is referred to as in transit.
Fund	Independent accounting entity with a self-balancing set of accounts segregated for the purposes of carrying on specific activities is referred to as a fund.

Go to **Cram101.com** for the Practice Tests for this Chapter.

Unit cost	Unit cost refers to cost computed by dividing some amount of total costs by the related number of units. Also called average cost.
Labor	People's physical and mental talents and efforts that are used to help produce goods and services are called labor.
Ordering costs	Costs of preparing, issuing, and paying purchase orders, plus receiving and inspecting the items included in the orders are ordering costs.
Setup cost	A setup cost is any cost necessary to prepare for production and to purchase inventory.
Cost of capital	Cost of capital refers to the percentage cost of funds used for acquiring resources for an organization, typically a weighted average of the firms cost of equity and cost of debt.
Opportunity cost	The cost of something in terms of opportunity foregone. The opportunity cost to a country of producing a unit more of a good, such as for export or to replace an import, is the quantity of some other good that could have been produced instead.
Variable	A variable is something measured by a number; it is used to analyze what happens to other things when the size of that number changes.
Insurance	Insurance refers to a system by which individuals can reduce their exposure to risk of large losses by spreading the risks among a large number of persons.
Cycle count	A cycle count is an inventory management procedure where a small subset of inventory is counted on any given day.
Short run	Short run refers to a period of time that permits an increase or decrease in current production volume with existing capacity, but one that is too short to permit enlargement of that capacity itself (eg, the building of new plants, training of additional workers, etc.).
Fixed cost	The cost that a firm bears if it does not produce at all and that is independent of its output. The presence of a fixed cost tends to imply increasing returns to scale. Contrasts with variable cost.
Total cost	The sum of fixed cost and variable cost is referred to as total cost.
Cost of poor quality	The costs incurred by producing products or services of poor quality is the cost of poor quality. These costs usually include the cost of inspection, rework, duplicate work, scrapping rejects, replacements and refunds, complaints, and loss of customers and reputation.
Cost accounting	Cost accounting measures and reports financial and nonfinancial information relating to the cost of acquiring or consuming resources in an organization. It provides information for both management accounting and financial accounting.
Accounting	A system that collects and processes financial information about an organization and reports that information to decision makers is referred to as accounting.
Aid	Assistance provided by countries and by international institutions such as the World Bank to developing countries in the form of monetary grants, loans at low interest rates, in kind, or a combination of these is called aid. Aid can also refer to assistance of any type rendered to benefit some group or individual.
Asset	An item of property, such as land, capital, money, a share in ownership, or a claim on others for future payment, such as a bond or a bank deposit is an asset.
Financial manager	Managers who make recommendations to top executives regarding strategies for improving the financial strength of a firm are referred to as a financial manager.
Financial perspective	Financial perspective is one of the four standard perspectives used with the Balanced Scorecard. Financial perspective measures inform an organization whether strategy execution,

which is detailed through measures in the other three perspectives, is leading to improved bottom line results.

Balance sheet	A statement of the assets, liabilities, and net worth of a firm or individual at some given time often at the end of its "fiscal year," is referred to as a balance sheet.
Return on investment	Return on investment refers to the return a businessperson gets on the money he and other owners invest in the firm; for example, a business that earned $100 on a $1,000 investment would have a ROI of 10 percent: 100 divided by 1000.
Performance measurement	The process by which someone evaluates an employee's work behaviors by measurement and comparison with previously established standards, documents the results, and communicates the results to the employee is called performance measurement.
Evaluation	The consumer's appraisal of the product or brand on important attributes is called evaluation.
Cost driver	Cost driver refers to a factor related to an activity that changes the volume or characteristics of that activity, and in doing so changes its costs. An activity can have more than one cost driver.
Competitor	Other organizations in the same industry or type of business that provide a good or service to the same set of customers is referred to as a competitor.
Information system	An information system is a system whether automated or manual, that comprises people, machines, and/or methods organized to collect, process, transmit, and disseminate data that represent user information.
Control system	A control system is a device or set of devices that manage the behavior of other devices. Some devices or systems are not controllable. A control system is an interconnection of components connected or related in such a manner as to command, direct, or regulate itself or another system.
Hedging	A technique for avoiding a risk by making a counteracting transaction is referred to as hedging.
Strike	The withholding of labor services by an organized group of workers is referred to as a strike.
Commodity	Could refer to any good, but in trade a commodity is usually a raw material or primary product that enters into international trade, such as metals or basic agricultural products.
Exporter	A firm that sells its product in another country is an exporter.
Adoption	In corporation law, a corporation's acceptance of a pre-incorporation contract by action of its board of directors, by which the corporation becomes liable on the contract, is referred to as adoption.
Mitsubishi	In a statement, the Mitsubishi says that forced labor is inconsistent with the company's values, and that the various lawsuits targeting Mitsubishi are misdirected. Instead, a spokesman says the Mitsubishi of World War II is not the same Mitsubishi of today. The conglomerate also rejected a Chinese slave labor lawsuit demand by saying it bore no responsibility since it was national policy to employ Chinese laborers."
Ford	Ford is an American company that manufactures and sells automobiles worldwide. Ford introduced methods for large-scale manufacturing of cars, and large-scale management of an industrial workforce, especially elaborately engineered manufacturing sequences typified by the moving assembly lines.
Corporation	A legal entity chartered by a state or the Federal government that is distinct and separate from the individuals who own it is a corporation. This separation gives the corporation

Go to **Cram101.com** for the Practice Tests for this Chapter.

unique powers which other legal entities lack.

Economics	The social science dealing with the use of scarce resources to obtain the maximum satisfaction of society's virtually unlimited economic wants is an economics.
Journal	Book of original entry, in which transactions are recorded in a general ledger system, is referred to as a journal.
Logistics	Those activities that focus on getting the right amount of the right products to the right place at the right time at the lowest possible cost is referred to as logistics.
Customs	Customs is an authority or agency in a country responsible for collecting customs duties and for controlling the flow of people, animals and goods (including personal effects and hazardous items) in and out of the country.
Domestic	From or in one's own country. A domestic producer is one that produces inside the home country. A domestic price is the price inside the home country. Opposite of 'foreign' or 'world.'.
Consideration	Consideration in contract law, a basic requirement for an enforceable agreement under traditional contract principles, defined in this text as legal value, bargained for and given in exchange for an act or promise. In corporation law, cash or property contributed to a corporation in exchange for shares, or a promise to contribute such cash or property.
Goodyear	Goodyear was founded in 1898 by German immigrants Charles and Frank Seiberling. Today it is the third largest tire and rubber company in the world.
Analyst	Analyst refers to a person or tool with a primary function of information analysis, generally with a more limited, practical and short term set of goals than a researcher.
Lean manufacturing	The production of goods using less of everything compared to mass production is called lean manufacturing.
Economy	The income, expenditures, and resources that affect the cost of running a business and household are called an economy.
Overtime	Overtime is the amount of time someone works beyond normal working hours.
Business Week	Business Week is a business magazine published by McGraw-Hill. It was first published in 1929 under the direction of Malcolm Muir, who was serving as president of the McGraw-Hill Publishing company at the time. It is considered to be the standard both in industry and among students.
Personnel	A collective term for all of the employees of an organization. Personnel is also commonly used to refer to the personnel management function or the organizational unit responsible for administering personnel programs.
Cooperative	A business owned and controlled by the people who use it, producers, consumers, or workers with similar needs who pool their resources for mutual gain is called cooperative.
Trust	An arrangement in which shareholders of independent firms agree to give up their stock in exchange for trust certificates that entitle them to a share of the trust's common profits.
Product development	In business and engineering, new product development is the complete process of bringing a new product to market. There are two parallel aspects to this process : one involves product engineering ; the other marketing analysis. Marketers see new product development as the first stage in product life cycle management, engineers as part of Product Lifecycle Management.
Contract	A contract is a "promise" or an "agreement" that is enforced or recognized by the law. In the civil law, a contract is considered to be part of the general law of obligations.

Go to **Cram101.com** for the Practice Tests for this Chapter.

Innovation	Innovation refers to the first commercially successful introduction of a new product, the use of a new method of production, or the creation of a new form of business organization.
Configuration	An organization's shape, which reflects the division of labor and the means of coordinating the divided tasks is configuration.
Changeover	Changeover in manufacturing is the process of converting a line or machine from running one product to another. Changeover times can last from a few minutes to as much as several weeks in the case of automobile manufacturers retooling for new models.
Analogy	Analogy is either the cognitive process of transferring information from a particular subject to another particular subject (the target), or a linguistic expression corresponding to such a process. In a narrower sense, analogy is an inference or an argument from a particular to another particular, as opposed to deduction, induction, and abduction, where at least one of the premises or the conclusion is general.
Time and motion study	A time and motion study would be used to reduce the number of motions in performing a task in order to increase productivity. The best known experiment involved bricklaying.
Nonverbal communication	The many additional ways that communication is accomplished beyond the oral or written word is referred to as nonverbal communication.
Bottleneck	An operation where the work to be performed approaches or exceeds the capacity available to do it is a bottleneck.
Layout	Layout refers to the physical arrangement of the various parts of an advertisement including the headline, subheads, illustrations, body copy, and any identifying marks.
Facility layout	The physical arrangement of resources in the production process is called facility layout.
Quality assurance	Those activities associated with assuring the quality of a product or service is called quality assurance.
Product mix	The combination of product lines offered by a manufacturer is referred to as product mix.
Volatility	Volatility refers to the extent to which an economic variable, such as a price or an exchange rate, moves up and down over time.
Cash flow	In finance, cash flow refers to the amounts of cash being received and spent by a business during a defined period of time, sometimes tied to a specific project. Most of the time they are being used to determine gaps in the liquid position of a company.
Turnover	Turnover in a financial context refers to the rate at which a provider of goods cycles through its average inventory. Turnover in a human resources context refers to the characteristic of a given company or industry, relative to rate at which an employer gains and loses staff.
Grainger	Grainger is a Fortune 400 industrial supply company founded in 1927 in Chicago, Illinois. Grainger provides their clients the products they need to keep their facilities running. Revenue is generally comprized of business to business sales, not consumer sales.
Materials management	Materials management refers to the activity that controls the transmission of physical materials through the value chain, from procurement through production and into distribution.
Procurement	Procurement is the acquisition of goods or services at the best possible total cost of ownership, in the right quantity, at the right time, in the right place for the direct benefit or use of the governments, corporations, or individuals generally via, but not limited to a contract.
Product cost	Product cost refers to sum of the costs assigned to a product for a specific purpose. A concept used in applying the cost plus approach to product pricing in which only the costs of

manufacturing the product are included in the cost amount to which the markup is added.

Process improvement	Process improvement is the activity of elevating the performance of a process, especially that of a business process with regard to its goal.
Buying power	The dollar amount available to purchase securities on margin is buying power. The amount is calculated by adding the cash held in the brokerage accounts and the amount that could be spent if securities were fully margined to their limit. If an investor uses their buying power, they are purchasing securities on credit.
Enterprise	Enterprise refers to another name for a business organization. Other similar terms are business firm, sometimes simply business, sometimes simply firm, as well as company, and entity.
Inventory control	Inventory control, in the field of loss prevention, are systems designed to introduce technical barriers to shoplifting.
Marketing	Promoting and selling products or services to customers, or prospective customers, is referred to as marketing.
Sales forecast	Sales forecast refers to the maximum total sales of a product that a firm expects to sell during a specified time period under specified environmental conditions and its own marketing efforts.
Product design	Product Design is defined as the idea generation, concept development, testing and manufacturing or implementation of a physical object or service. It is possibly the evolution of former discipline name - Industrial Design.
Premium	Premium refers to the fee charged by an insurance company for an insurance policy. The rate of losses must be relatively predictable: In order to set the premium (prices) insurers must be able to estimate them accurately.
Partnership	In the common law, a partnership is a type of business entity in which partners share with each other the profits or losses of the business undertaking in which they have all invested.
Exchange	The trade of things of value between buyer and seller so that each is better off after the trade is called the exchange.
Nuisance	Nuisance refers to that which endangers life or health, gives offense to the senses, violates the laws of decency, or obstructs the reasonable and comfortable use of property.
Material requirements planning	A dependent demand inventory planning and control system that schedules the precise amount of all materials required to support the production of desired end products is referred to as material requirements planning.
Product line	A group of products that are physically similar or are intended for a similar market are called the product line.
Electronic data interchange	Electronic data interchange refers to the direct exchange between organizations of data via a computer-to-computer interface.
Point of Sale	Point of sale can mean a retail shop, a checkout counter in a shop, or a variable location where a transaction occurs.
Planning horizon	The length of time it takes to conceive, develop, and complete a project and to recover the cost of the project on a discounted cash flow basis is referred to as planning horizon.
Total supply	Total supply refers to the supply schedule or the supply curve of all sellers of a good or service.
Interest	In finance and economics, interest is the price paid by a borrower for the use of a lender's money. In other words, interest is the amount of paid to "rent" money for a period of time.

Go to **Cram101.com** for the Practice Tests for this Chapter.

Vendor	A person who sells property to a vendee is a vendor. The words vendor and vendee are more commonly applied to the seller and purchaser of real estate, and the words seller and buyer are more commonly applied to the seller and purchaser of personal property.
Transaction cost	A transaction cost is a cost incurred in making an economic exchange. For example, most people, when buying or selling a stock, must pay a commission to their broker; that commission is a transaction cost of doing the stock deal.
Users	Users refer to people in the organization who actually use the product or service purchased by the buying center.
Purchasing power	The amount of goods that money will buy, usually measured by the CPI is referred to as purchasing power.
Leverage	Leverage is using given resources in such a way that the potential positive or negative outcome is magnified. In finance, this generally refers to borrowing.
Committee	A long-lasting, sometimes permanent team in the organization structure created to deal with tasks that recur regularly is the committee.
Accounts payable	A written record of all vendors to whom the business firm owes money is referred to as accounts payable.
Transactions cost	Any cost associated with bringing buyers and sellers together is referred to as transactions cost.

Journal	Book of original entry, in which transactions are recorded in a general ledger system, is referred to as a journal.
Inventory	Tangible property held for sale in the normal course of business or used in producing goods or services for sale is an inventory.
Expense	In accounting, an expense represents an event in which an asset is used up or a liability is incurred. In terms of the accounting equation, expenses reduce owners' equity.
Supply	Supply is the aggregate amount of any material good that can be called into being at a certain price point; it comprises one half of the equation of supply and demand. In classical economic theory, a curve representing supply is one of the factors that produce price.
Profit	Profit refers to the return to the resource entrepreneurial ability; total revenue minus total cost.
Bar code	Bar code refers to a printed code that makes use of lines of various widths to encode data about products.
Logistics	Those activities that focus on getting the right amount of the right products to the right place at the right time at the lowest possible cost is referred to as logistics.
Ford	Ford is an American company that manufactures and sells automobiles worldwide. Ford introduced methods for large-scale manufacturing of cars, and large-scale management of an industrial workforce, especially elaborately engineered manufacturing sequences typified by the moving assembly lines.
Distribution	Distribution in economics, the manner in which total output and income is distributed among individuals or factors.
Dealer	People who link buyers with sellers by buying and selling securities at stated prices are referred to as a dealer.
Warehouse	Warehouse refers to a location, often decentralized, that a firm uses to store, consolidate, age, or mix stock; house product-recall programs; or ease tax burdens.
Nike	Because Nike creates goods for a wide range of sports, they have competition from every sports and sports fashion brand there is. Nike has no direct competitors because there is no single brand which can compete directly with their range of sports and non-sports oriented gear, except for Reebok.
DaimlerChrysler	In 2002, the merged company, DaimlerChrysler, appeared to run two independent product lines, with few signs of corporate integration. In 2003, however, it was alleged by the Detroit News that the "merger of equals" was, in fact, a takeover.
Contract	A contract is a "promise" or an "agreement" that is enforced or recognized by the law. In the civil law, a contract is considered to be part of the general law of obligations.
Revenue	Revenue is a U.S. business term for the amount of money that a company receives from its activities, mostly from sales of products and/or services to customers.
Information technology	Information technology refers to technology that helps companies change business by allowing them to use new methods.
Technology	The body of knowledge and techniques that can be used to combine economic resources to produce goods and services is called technology.
Analyst	Analyst refers to a person or tool with a primary function of information analysis, generally with a more limited, practical and short term set of goals than a researcher.
In transit	A state in which goods are in the possession of a bailee or carrier and not in the hands of the buyer, seller, lessee, or lessor is referred to as in transit.

Outbound	Communications originating inside an organization and destined for customers, prospects, or other people outside the organization are called outbound.
Operation	A standardized method or technique that is performed repetitively, often on different materials resulting in different finished goods is called an operation.
Competitive advantage	A business is said to have a competitive advantage when its unique strengths, often based on cost, quality, time, and innovation, offer consumers a greater percieved value and there by diffetiating it from its competitors.
Supplier evaluation	Supplier evaluation refers to a tool used by many firms to differentiate and discriminate among suppliers. A supplier evaluation often involves report cards where potential suppliers are rated based on different criteria such as quality, technical capability, or ability to meet schedule demands.
Evaluation	The consumer's appraisal of the product or brand on important attributes is called evaluation.
Buyer	A buyer refers to a role in the buying center with formal authority and responsibility to select the supplier and negotiate the terms of the contract.
Service	Service refers to a "non tangible product" that is not embodied in a physical good and that typically effects some change in another product, person, or institution. Contrasts with good.
Production	The creation of finished goods and services using the factors of production: land, labor, capital, entrepreneurship, and knowledge.
Manufacturing	Production of goods primarily by the application of labor and capital to raw materials and other intermediate inputs, in contrast to agriculture, mining, forestry, fishing, and services a manufacturing.
Industry	A group of firms that produce identical or similar products is an industry. It is also used specifically to refer to an area of economic production focused on manufacturing which involves large amounts of capital investment before any profit can be realized, also called "heavy industry".
Purchasing	Purchasing refers to the function in a firm that searches for quality material resources, finds the best suppliers, and negotiates the best price for goods and services.
Deregulation	The lessening or complete removal of government regulations on an industry, especially concerning the price that firms are allowed to charge and leaving price to be determined by market forces a deregulation.
Management	Management characterizes the process of leading and directing all or part of an organization, often a business, through the deployment and manipulation of resources. Early twentieth-century management writer Mary Parker Follett defined management as "the art of getting things done through people."
Supply chain management	Supply chain management deals with the planning and execution issues involved in managing a supply chain. Supply chain management spans all movement and storage of raw materials, work-in-process inventory, and finished goods from point-of-origin to point-of-consumption.
Supply chain	Supply chain refers to the flow of goods, services, and information from the initial sources of materials and services to the delivery of products to consumers.
Margin	A deposit by a buyer in stocks with a seller or a stockbroker, as security to cover fluctuations in the market in reference to stocks that the buyer has purchased but for which he has not paid is a margin. Commodities are also traded on margin.
Profit margin	Profit margin is a measure of profitability. It is calculated using a formula and written as

	a percentage or a number. Profit margin = Net income before tax and interest / Revenue.
Regulation	Regulation refers to restrictions state and federal laws place on business with regard to the conduct of its activities.
Economic regulation	Economic regulation refers to see industrial regulation and social regulation.
Freight in	Freight in refers to a part of the cost of inventory. It is the transportation cost of the goods purchased.
Tariff	A tax imposed by a nation on an imported good is called a tariff.
Discount	The difference between the face value of a bond and its selling price, when a bond is sold for less than its face value it's referred to as a discount.
Negotiation	Negotiation is the process whereby interested parties resolve disputes, agree upon courses of action, bargain for individual or collective advantage, and/or attempt to craft outcomes which serve their mutual interests.
Controlling	A management function that involves determining whether or not an organization is progressing toward its goals and objectives, and taking corrective action if it is not is called controlling.
Common carrier	One who undertakes, for hire or reward, to transport the goods of such of the public as choose to employ him is a common carrier.
Firm	An organization that employs resources to produce a good or service for profit and owns and operates one or more plants is referred to as a firm.
Raw material	Raw material refers to a good that has not been transformed by production; a primary product.
Intermodal transportation	Intermodal transportation is the use of more than one mode of transportation to move goods or products.
Points	Loan origination fees that may be deductible as interest by a buyer of property. A seller of property who pays points reduces the selling price by the amount of the points paid for the buyer.
Interest	In finance and economics, interest is the price paid by a borrower for the use of a lender's money. In other words, interest is the amount of paid to "rent" money for a period of time.
Cost structure	The relative proportion of an organization's fixed, variable, and mixed costs is referred to as cost structure.
Total cost	The sum of fixed cost and variable cost is referred to as total cost.
Domestic	From or in one's own country. A domestic producer is one that produces inside the home country. A domestic price is the price inside the home country. Opposite of 'foreign' or 'world.'.
Gross domestic product	Gross domestic product refers to the total value of new goods and services produced in a given year within the borders of a country, regardless of by whom.
Competitiveness	Competitiveness usually refers to characteristics that permit a firm to compete effectively with other firms due to low cost or superior technology, perhaps internationally.
Free On Board	Free On Board is an Incoterm. It means that the seller pays for transportation of the goods to the port of shipment, plus loading costs. The buyer pays freight, insurance, unloading costs and transportation from the port of destination to his factory. The passing of risks occurs when the goods pass the ship's rail at the port of shipment.
Performance	The process by which someone evaluates an employee's work behaviors by measurement and

measurement	comparison with previously established standards, documents the results, and communicates the results to the employee is called performance measurement.
Commodity	Could refer to any good, but in trade a commodity is usually a raw material or primary product that enters into international trade, such as metals or basic agricultural products.
Tender	An unconditional offer of payment, consisting in the actual production in money or legal tender of a sum not less than the amount due.
Unit cost	Unit cost refers to cost computed by dividing some amount of total costs by the related number of units. Also called average cost.
Option	A contract that gives the purchaser the option to buy or sell the underlying financial instrument at a specified price, called the exercise price or strike price, within a specific period of time.
Broker	In commerce, a broker is a party that mediates between a buyer and a seller. A broker who also acts as a seller or as a buyer becomes a principal party to the deal.
Agent	A person who makes economic decisions for another economic actor. A hired manager operates as an agent for a firm's owner.
Customs	Customs is an authority or agency in a country responsible for collecting customs duties and for controlling the flow of people, animals and goods (including personal effects and hazardous items) in and out of the country.
Intermediaries	Intermediaries specialize in information either to bring together two parties to a transaction or to buy in order to sell again.
Variable	A variable is something measured by a number; it is used to analyze what happens to other things when the size of that number changes.
Operational planning	The process of setting work standards and schedules necessary to implement the tactical objectives is operational planning.
Authority	Authority in agency law, refers to an agent's ability to affect his principal's legal relations with third parties. Also used to refer to an actor's legal power or ability to do something. In addition, sometimes used to refer to a statute, case, or other legal source that justifies a particular result.
Market	A market is, as defined in economics, a social arrangement that allows buyers and sellers to discover information and carry out a voluntary exchange of goods or services.
Principal	In agency law, one under whose direction an agent acts and for whose benefit that agent acts is a principal.
Labor	People's physical and mental talents and efforts that are used to help produce goods and services are called labor.
Variable cost	The portion of a firm or industry's cost that changes with output, in contrast to fixed cost is referred to as variable cost.
Compliance	A type of influence process where a receiver accepts the position advocated by a source to obtain favorable outcomes or to avoid punishment is the compliance.
Fixed cost	The cost that a firm bears if it does not produce at all and that is independent of its output. The presence of a fixed cost tends to imply increasing returns to scale. Contrasts with variable cost.
Total variable Cost	The total of all costs that vary with output in the short run is called total variable cost.

Go to **Cram101.com** for the Practice Tests for this Chapter.

Merger	Merger refers to the combination of two firms into a single firm.
Consolidation	The combination of two or more firms, generally of equal size and market power, to form an entirely new entity is a consolidation.
Users	Users refer to people in the organization who actually use the product or service purchased by the buying center.
Distribution center	Designed to facilitate the timely movement of goods and represent a very important part of a supply chain is a distribution center.
International trade	The export of goods and services from a country and the import of goods and services into a country is referred to as the international trade.
Level of service	The degree of service provided to the customer by self, limited, and full-service retailers is referred to as the level of service.
Asset	An item of property, such as land, capital, money, a share in ownership, or a claim on others for future payment, such as a bond or a bank deposit is an asset.
Drawback	Drawback refers to rebate of import duties when the imported good is re-exported or used as input to the production of an exported good.
Exempt	Employees who are not covered by the Fair Labor Standards Act are exempt. Exempt employees are not eligible for overtime pay.
Frequency	Frequency refers to the speed of the up and down movements of a fluctuating economic variable; that is, the number of times per unit of time that the variable completes a cycle of up and down movement.
Economy	The income, expenditures, and resources that affect the cost of running a business and household are called an economy.
Economies of scale	In economics, returns to scale and economies of scale are related terms that describe what happens as the scale of production increases. They are different terms and not to be used interchangeably.
Gain	In finance, gain is a profit or an increase in value of an investment such as a stock or bond. Gain is calculated by fair market value or the proceeds from the sale of the investment minus the sum of the purchase price and all costs associated with it.
Allocate	Allocate refers to the assignment of income for various tax purposes. A multistate corporation's nonbusiness income usually is distributed to the state where the nonbusiness assets are located; it is not apportioned with the rest of the entity's income.
Electronic Data Systems	Electronic Data Systems is a global information technology consulting company that defined the outsourcing business when it was established in 1962 by Ross Perot.
Marketing	Promoting and selling products or services to customers, or prospective customers, is referred to as marketing.
Positioning	The art and science of fitting the product or service to one or more segments of the market in such a way as to set it meaningfully apart from competition is called positioning.
Complexity	The technical sophistication of the product and hence the amount of understanding required to use it is referred to as complexity. It is the opposite of simplicity.
Information system	An information system is a system whether automated or manual, that comprises people, machines, and/or methods organized to collect, process, transmit, and disseminate data that represent user information.
Electronic data	Electronic data interchange refers to the direct exchange between organizations of data via a

interchange	computer-to-computer interface.
Business unit	The lowest level of the company which contains the set of functions that carry a product through its life span from concept through manufacture, distribution, sales and service is a business unit.
Personnel	A collective term for all of the employees of an organization. Personnel is also commonly used to refer to the personnel management function or the organizational unit responsible for administering personnel programs.
Leverage	Leverage is using given resources in such a way that the potential positive or negative outcome is magnified. In finance, this generally refers to borrowing.
Automation	Automation allows machines to do work previously accomplished by people.
Committee	A long-lasting, sometimes permanent team in the organization structure created to deal with tasks that recur regularly is the committee.
Wall Street Journal	Dow Jones & Company was founded in 1882 by reporters Charles Dow, Edward Jones and Charles Bergstresser. Jones converted the small Customers' Afternoon Letter into The Wall Street Journal, first published in 1889, and began delivery of the Dow Jones News Service via telegraph. The Journal featured the Jones 'Average', the first of several indexes of stock and bond prices on the New York Stock Exchange.
Continuous improvement	The constant effort to eliminate waste, reduce response time, simplify the design of both products and processes, and improve quality and customer service is referred to as continuous improvement.
Bid	A bid price is a price offered by a buyer when he/she buys a good. In the context of stock trading on a stock exchange, the bid price is the highest price a buyer of a stock is willing to pay for a share of that given stock.
Publicity	Publicity refers to any information about an individual, product, or organization that's distributed to the public through the media and that's not paid for or controlled by the seller.
Brand	A name, symbol, or design that identifies the goods or services of one seller or group of sellers and distinguishes them from the goods and services of competitors is a brand.
Managing director	Managing director is the term used for the chief executive of many limited companies in the United Kingdom, Commonwealth and some other English speaking countries. The title reflects their role as both a member of the Board of Directors but also as the senior manager.
Appeal	Appeal refers to the act of asking an appellate court to overturn a decision after the trial court's final judgment has been entered.
Trend	Trend refers to the long-term movement of an economic variable, such as its average rate of increase or decrease over enough years to encompass several business cycles.
Collaboration	Collaboration occurs when the interaction between groups is very important to goal attainment and the goals are compatible. Wherein people work together —applying both to the work of individuals as well as larger collectives and societies.
Organizational structure	Organizational structure is the way in which the interrelated groups of an organization are constructed. From a managerial point of view the main concerns are ensuring effective communication and coordination.
Outsourcing	Outsourcing refers to a production activity that was previously done inside a firm or plant that is now conducted outside that firm or plant.
John Deere	John Deere (February 7, 1804 - May 17, 1886) was an American blacksmith and manufacturer who

Go to **Cram101.com** for the Practice Tests for this Chapter.

founded one of the largest agricultural and construction equipment manufacturers in the world.

Logistics Management	Logistics management refers to the practice of organizing the cost-effective flow of raw materials, in-process inventory, finished goods, and related information from point of origin to point of consumption to satisfy customer requirements.
Compaq	Compaq was founded in February 1982 by Rod Canion, Jim Harris and Bill Murto, three senior managers from semiconductor manufacturer Texas Instruments. Each invested $1,000 to form the company. Their first venture capital came from Ben Rosen and Sevin-Rosen partners. It is often told that the architecture of the original PC was first sketched out on a placemat by the founders while dining in the Houston restaurant, House of Pies.
Capital	Capital generally refers to financial wealth, especially that used to start or maintain a business. In classical economics, capital is one of four factors of production, the others being land and labor and entrepreneurship.
Inventory turns	In business management, inventory turns measures the number of times capital invested in goods to be sold turns over in a year.
Capital asset	In accounting, a capital asset is an asset that is recorded as property that creates more property, e.g. a factory that creates shoes, or a forest that yields a quantity of wood.
Integration	Economic integration refers to reducing barriers among countries to transactions and to movements of goods, capital, and labor, including harmonization of laws, regulations, and standards. Integrated markets theoretically function as a unified market.
Restructuring	Restructuring is the corporate management term for the act of partially dismantling and reorganizing a company for the purpose of making it more efficient and therefore more profitable.
Customer service	The ability of logistics management to satisfy users in terms of time, dependability, communication, and convenience is called the customer service.
Investment	Investment refers to spending for the production and accumulation of capital and additions to inventories. In a financial sense, buying an asset with the expectation of making a return.
Operating margin	In business, operating margin is the ratio of operating income divided by net sales.
Administrative support	Support services such as personnel, budget, purchasing, data processing which support or facilitate the service programs of the agency are types of administrative support. Also means work assisting an administrator through office management, clerical supervision, data collection and reporting, workflow/project tracking.
Consultant	A professional that provides expert advice in a particular field or area in which customers occassionaly require this type of knowledge is a consultant.
Vendor	A person who sells property to a vendee is a vendor. The words vendor and vendee are more commonly applied to the seller and purchaser of real estate, and the words seller and buyer are more commonly applied to the seller and purchaser of personal property.
Airborne Express	Airborne Express was an express delivery company and cargo airline. Headquartered in Seattle, Washington, its hub was at Wilmington, Ohio. It was founded as the Airborne Flower Traffic Association of California in 1946 to fly flowers to the state of Hawaii and was merged into DHL in 2003.
Management team	A management team is directly responsible for managing the day-to-day operations (and profitability) of a company.
Strategic partnership	Strategic partnership refers to an association between two firms by which they agree to work together to achieve a strategic goal. This is often associated with long-term supplier-

	customer relationships.
Partnership	In the common law, a partnership is a type of business entity in which partners share with each other the profits or losses of the business undertaking in which they have all invested.
Strategic planning	The process of determining the major goals of the organization and the policies and strategies for obtaining and using resources to achieve those goals is called strategic planning.
Profit center	Responsibility center where the manager is accountable for revenues and costs is referred to as a profit center.
Fund	Independent accounting entity with a self-balancing set of accounts segregated for the purposes of carrying on specific activities is referred to as a fund.
Electronic funds transfer	A disbursement system that uses wire, telephone, telegraph, or computer to transfer cash from one location to another is referred to as electronic funds transfer.
Leadership	Management merely consists of leadership applied to business situations; or in other words: management forms a sub-set of the broader process of leadership.
Contribution	In business organization law, the cash or property contributed to a business by its owners is referred to as contribution.
Strategic alliance	Strategic alliance refers to a long-term partnership between two or more companies established to help each company build competitive market advantages.
Consumption	In Keynesian economics consumption refers to personal consumption expenditure, i.e., the purchase of currently produced goods and services out of income, out of savings (net worth), or from borrowed funds. It refers to that part of disposable income that does not go to saving.

Go to **Cram101.com** for the Practice Tests for this Chapter.

Commerce	Commerce is the exchange of something of value between two entities. It is the central mechanism from which capitalism is derived.
Purchasing	Purchasing refers to the function in a firm that searches for quality material resources, finds the best suppliers, and negotiates the best price for goods and services.
Management	Management characterizes the process of leading and directing all or part of an organization, often a business, through the deployment and manipulation of resources. Early twentieth-century management writer Mary Parker Follett defined management as "the art of getting things done through people."
Warehouse	Warehouse refers to a location, often decentralized, that a firm uses to store, consolidate, age, or mix stock; house product-recall programs; or ease tax burdens.
Trend	Trend refers to the long-term movement of an economic variable, such as its average rate of increase or decrease over enough years to encompass several business cycles.
Ford	Ford is an American company that manufactures and sells automobiles worldwide. Ford introduced methods for large-scale manufacturing of cars, and large-scale management of an industrial workforce, especially elaborately engineered manufacturing sequences typified by the moving assembly lines.
Journal	Book of original entry, in which transactions are recorded in a general ledger system, is referred to as a journal.
Supply	Supply is the aggregate amount of any material good that can be called into being at a certain price point; it comprises one half of the equation of supply and demand. In classical economic theory, a curve representing supply is one of the factors that produce price.
Materials management	Materials management refers to the activity that controls the transmission of physical materials through the value chain, from procurement through production and into distribution.
Electronic commerce	Electronic commerce or e-commerce, refers to any activity that uses some form of electronic communication in the inventory, exchange, advertisement, distribution, and payment of goods and services.
Ford Motor Company	Ford Motor Company introduced methods for large-scale manufacturing of cars, and large-scale management of an industrial workforce, especially elaborately engineered manufacturing sequences typified by the moving assembly lines. Henry Ford's combination of highly efficient factories, highly paid workers, and low prices revolutionized manufacturing and came to be known around the world as Fordism by 1914.
Information system	An information system is a system whether automated or manual, that comprises people, machines, and/or methods organized to collect, process, transmit, and disseminate data that represent user information.
Data warehouse	A Data warehouse is a repository of integrated information, available for queries and analysis. Data and information are extracted from heterogeneous sources as they are generated.
Enterprise resource planning systems	Integrated information systems that capture all a company's information in a single database are called enterprise resource planning systems.
Enterprise resource planning system	Enterprise resource planning system refers to a system that integrates financial, planning, and control systems into a single architecture.
Enterprise	Computer-based production and operations system that links multiple firms into one integrated

Go to **Cram101.com** for the Practice Tests for this Chapter.

resource planning	production unit is enterprise resource planning.
Electronic data interchange	Electronic data interchange refers to the direct exchange between organizations of data via a computer-to-computer interface.
Deregulation	The lessening or complete removal of government regulations on an industry, especially concerning the price that firms are allowed to charge and leaving price to be determined by market forces a deregulation.
Supply chain	Supply chain refers to the flow of goods, services, and information from the initial sources of materials and services to the delivery of products to consumers.
Integration	Economic integration refers to reducing barriers among countries to transactions and to movements of goods, capital, and labor, including harmonization of laws, regulations, and standards. Integrated markets theoretically function as a unified market.
Enterprise	Enterprise refers to another name for a business organization. Other similar terms are business firm, sometimes simply business, sometimes simply firm, as well as company, and entity.
Operation	A standardized method or technique that is performed repetitively, often on different materials resulting in different finished goods is called an operation.
Competitor	Other organizations in the same industry or type of business that provide a good or service to the same set of customers is referred to as a competitor.
Industry	A group of firms that produce identical or similar products is an industry. It is also used specifically to refer to an area of economic production focused on manufacturing which involves large amounts of capital investment before any profit can be realized, also called "heavy industry".
Technology	The body of knowledge and techniques that can be used to combine economic resources to produce goods and services is called technology.
Product line	A group of products that are physically similar or are intended for a similar market are called the product line.
Inventory	Tangible property held for sale in the normal course of business or used in producing goods or services for sale is an inventory.
Option	A contract that gives the purchaser the option to buy or sell the underlying financial instrument at a specified price, called the exercise price or strike price, within a specific period of time.
Configuration	An organization's shape, which reflects the division of labor and the means of coordinating the divided tasks is configuration.
Production	The creation of finished goods and services using the factors of production: land, labor, capital, entrepreneurship, and knowledge.
Dealer	People who link buyers with sellers by buying and selling securities at stated prices are referred to as a dealer.
Production line	A production line is a set of sequential operations established in a factory whereby materials are put through a refining process to produce an end-product that is suitable for onward consumption; or components are assembled to make a finished article.
Manufacturing	Production of goods primarily by the application of labor and capital to raw materials and other intermediate inputs, in contrast to agriculture, mining, forestry, fishing, and services a manufacturing.

Go to **Cram101.com** for the Practice Tests for this Chapter.

Supply chain management	Supply chain management deals with the planning and execution issues involved in managing a supply chain. Supply chain management spans all movement and storage of raw materials, work-in-process inventory, and finished goods from point-of-origin to point-of-consumption.
Process reengineering	Process reengineering refers to the total rethinking and redesign of organizational process to improve performance and innovation; involves analyzing, streamlining, and reconfiguring actions and tasks to achieve work goals.
Business process	Business process refers to the individual activities of an enterprise. Processes can be viewed at a high level, for example, 'marketing,' or at the level of detailed subprocesses, for example, 'customer retention.'.
Reengineering	The fundamental rethinking and redesign of business processes to achieve improvements in critical measures of performance, such as cost, quality, service, speed, and customer satisfaction is referred to as reengineering.
Business Week	Business Week is a business magazine published by McGraw-Hill. It was first published in 1929 under the direction of Malcolm Muir, who was serving as president of the McGraw-Hill Publishing company at the time. It is considered to be the standard both in industry and among students.
Restructuring	Restructuring is the corporate management term for the act of partially dismantling and reorganizing a company for the purpose of making it more efficient and therefore more profitable.
Productivity	Productivity refers to the total output of goods and services in a given period of time divided by work hours.
Economy	The income, expenditures, and resources that affect the cost of running a business and household are called an economy.
New economy	New economy, this term was used in the late 1990's to suggest that globalization and/or innovations in information technology had changed the way that the world economy works.
Competitive advantage	A business is said to have a competitive advantage when its unique strengths, often based on cost, quality, time, and innovation, offer consumers a greater percieved value and there by diffetiating it from its competitors.
Market	A market is, as defined in economics, a social arrangement that allows buyers and sellers to discover information and carry out a voluntary exchange of goods or services.
Globalization	The increasing world-wide integration of markets for goods, services and capital that attracted special attention in the late 1990s is called globalization.
Leverage	Leverage is using given resources in such a way that the potential positive or negative outcome is magnified. In finance, this generally refers to borrowing.
Logistics	Those activities that focus on getting the right amount of the right products to the right place at the right time at the lowest possible cost is referred to as logistics.
Standardization	Standardization, in the context related to technologies and industries, is the process of establishing a technical standard among competing entities in a market, where this will bring benefits without hurting competition.
Business unit	The lowest level of the company which contains the set of functions that carry a product through its life span from concept through manufacture, distribution, sales and service is a business unit.
Enabling	Enabling refers to giving workers the education and tools they need to assume their new decision-making powers.

Users	Users refer to people in the organization who actually use the product or service purchased by the buying center.
Reorganization	Reorganization occurs, among other instances, when one corporation acquires another in a merger or acquisition, a single corporation divides into two or more entities, or a corporation makes a substantial change in its capital structure.
Accounting	A system that collects and processes financial information about an organization and reports that information to decision makers is referred to as accounting.
Cost management	The approaches and activities of managers in short-run and long-run planning and control decisions that increase value for customers and lower costs of products and services are called cost management.
Allocation of resources	Allocation of resources refers to the society's decisions on how to divide up its scarce input resources among the different outputs produced in the economy, and among the different firms or other organizations that produce those outputs.
Corporation	A legal entity chartered by a state or the Federal government that is distinct and separate from the individuals who own it is a corporation. This separation gives the corporation unique powers which other legal entities lack.
Discount	The difference between the face value of a bond and its selling price, when a bond is sold for less than its face value it's referred to as a discount.
Buyer	A buyer refers to a role in the buying center with formal authority and responsibility to select the supplier and negotiate the terms of the contract.
Distribution center	Designed to facilitate the timely movement of goods and represent a very important part of a supply chain is a distribution center.
Distribution	Distribution in economics, the manner in which total output and income is distributed among individuals or factors.
Revenue	Revenue is a U.S. business term for the amount of money that a company receives from its activities, mostly from sales of products and/or services to customers.
Transaction processing	Computations and calculations used to review and document HRM decisions and practices is transaction processing.
Wall Street Journal	Dow Jones & Company was founded in 1882 by reporters Charles Dow, Edward Jones and Charles Bergstresser. Jones converted the small Customers' Afternoon Letter into The Wall Street Journal, first published in 1889, and began delivery of the Dow Jones News Service via telegraph. The Journal featured the Jones 'Average', the first of several indexes of stock and bond prices on the New York Stock Exchange.
Service	Service refers to a "non tangible product" that is not embodied in a physical good and that typically effects some change in another product, person, or institution. Contrasts with good.
Purchase order	A form on which items or services needed by a business firm are specified and then communicated to the vendor is a purchase order.
Material requirements planning	A dependent demand inventory planning and control system that schedules the precise amount of all materials required to support the production of desired end products is referred to as material requirements planning.
Consultant	A professional that provides expert advice in a particular field or area in which customers occassionaly require this type of knowledge is a consultant.
Functional	Functional organization is a method of organization in which chapters and sections of a

336

organization	manual correspond to business functions, not specific departments or work groups.
Vendor	A person who sells property to a vendee is a vendor. The words vendor and vendee are more commonly applied to the seller and purchaser of real estate, and the words seller and buyer are more commonly applied to the seller and purchaser of personal property.
Net income	Net income is equal to the income that a firm has after subtracting costs and expenses from the total revenue. Expenses will typically include tax expense.
Mistake	In contract law a mistake is incorrect understanding by one or more parties to a contract and may be used as grounds to invalidate the agreement. Common law has identified three different types of mistake in contract: unilateral mistake, mutual mistake, and common mistake.
Market share	That fraction of an industry's output accounted for by an individual firm or group of firms is called market share.
Gain	In finance, gain is a profit or an increase in value of an investment such as a stock or bond. Gain is calculated by fair market value or the proceeds from the sale of the investment minus the sum of the purchase price and all costs associated with it.
End user	End user refers to the ultimate user of a product or service.
Promotion	Promotion refers to all the techniques sellers use to motivate people to buy products or services. An attempt by marketers to inform people about products and to persuade them to participate in an exchange.
Yield	The interest rate that equates a future value or an annuity to a given present value is a yield.
Coupon	In finance, a coupon is "attached" to a bond, either physically (as with old bonds) or electronically. Each coupon represents a predetermined payment promized to the bond-holder in return for his or her loan of money to the bond-issuer. .
Sales promotion	Sales promotion refers to the promotional tool that stimulates consumer purchasing and dealer interest by means of short-term activities.
Firm	An organization that employs resources to produce a good or service for profit and owns and operates one or more plants is referred to as a firm.
Bill of material	A bill of material is a list of all the materials needed to manufacture a product or product component.
Inventory management	The planning, coordinating, and controlling activities related to the flow of inventory into, through, and out of an organization is referred to as inventory management.
Inventory turns	In business management, inventory turns measures the number of times capital invested in goods to be sold turns over in a year.
Contribution	In business organization law, the cash or property contributed to a business by its owners is referred to as contribution.
Assignment	A transfer of property or some right or interest is referred to as assignment.
Performance measurement	The process by which someone evaluates an employee's work behaviors by measurement and comparison with previously established standards, documents the results, and communicates the results to the employee is called performance measurement.
Negotiation	Negotiation is the process whereby interested parties resolve disputes, agree upon courses of action, bargain for individual or collective advantage, and/or attempt to craft outcomes which serve their mutual interests.
Procurement	Procurement is the acquisition of goods or services at the best possible total cost of

Go to **Cram101.com** for the Practice Tests for this Chapter.

ownership, in the right quantity, at the right time, in the right place for the direct benefit or use of the governments, corporations, or individuals generally via, but not limited to a contract.

Levy	Levy refers to imposing and collecting a tax or tariff.
Keiretsu	Keiretsu is a set of companies with interlocking business relationships and shareholdings. It is a type of business group.
Parent company	Parent company refers to the entity that has a controlling influence over another company. It may have its own operations, or it may have been set up solely for the purpose of owning the Subject Company.
Profit	Profit refers to the return to the resource entrepreneurial ability; total revenue minus total cost.
Frequency	Frequency refers to the speed of the up and down movements of a fluctuating economic variable; that is, the number of times per unit of time that the variable completes a cycle of up and down movement.
Exchange	The trade of things of value between buyer and seller so that each is better off after the trade is called the exchange.
American National Standards Institute	The American National Standards Institute or ANSI is a nonprofit organization that oversees the development of standards for products, services, processes and systems in the United States. The organization also coordinates U.S. standards with international standards so that American products can be used worldwide.
Accounts payable	A written record of all vendors to whom the business firm owes money is referred to as accounts payable.
Audit	An examination of the financial reports to ensure that they represent what they claim and conform with generally accepted accounting principles is referred to as audit.
Invoice	The itemized bill for a transaction, stating the nature of the transaction and its cost. In international trade, the invoice price is often the preferred basis for levying an ad valorem tariff.
Credit	Credit refers to a recording as positive in the balance of payments, any transaction that gives rise to a payment into the country, such as an export, the sale of an asset, or borrowing from abroad.
Accounts receivable	Accounts receivable is one of a series of accounting transactions dealing with the billing of customers which owe money to a person, company or organization for goods and services that have been provided to the customer. This is typically done in a one person organization by writing an invoice and mailing or delivering it to each customer.
Investment	Investment refers to spending for the production and accumulation of capital and additions to inventories. In a financial sense, buying an asset with the expectation of making a return.
Diffusion	Diffusion is the process by which a new idea or new product is accepted by the market. The rate of diffusion is the speed that the new idea spreads from one consumer to the next.
Protocol	Protocol refers to a statement that, before product development begins, identifies a well-defined target market; specific customers' needs, wants, and preferences; and what the product will be and do.
Property	Assets defined in the broadest legal sense. Property includes the unrealized receivables of a cash basis taxpayer, but not services rendered.
Collaboration	Collaboration occurs when the interaction between groups is very important to goal attainment

Go to **Cram101.com** for the Practice Tests for this Chapter.

and the goals are compatible. Wherein people work together —applying both to the work of individuals as well as larger collectives and societies.

Domestic	From or in one's own country. A domestic producer is one that produces inside the home country. A domestic price is the price inside the home country. Opposite of 'foreign' or 'world.'.
Gross domestic product	Gross domestic product refers to the total value of new goods and services produced in a given year within the borders of a country, regardless of by whom.
Business model	A business model is the instrument by which a business intends to generate revenue and profits. It is a summary of how a company means to serve its employees and customers, and involves both strategy (what an business intends to do) as well as an implementation.
Bid	A bid price is a price offered by a buyer when he/she buys a good. In the context of stock trading on a stock exchange, the bid price is the highest price a buyer of a stock is willing to pay for a share of that given stock.
EBay	eBay manages an online auction and shopping website, where people buy and sell goods and services worldwide.
Auction	A preexisting business model that operates successfully on the Internet by announcing an item for sale and permitting multiple purchasers to bid on them under specified rules and condition is an auction.
Consumer to consumer	Consumer to consumer electronic commerce involves the electronically-facilitated transactions between consumers through some third party. A common example is the online auction, in which a consumer posts an item for sale and other consumers bid to purchase it; the third party generally charges a flat fee or commission.
Oracle	In 2004, sales at Oracle grew at a rate of 14.5% to $6.2 billion, giving it 41.3% and the top share of the relational-database market. Their main competitors in the database arena are IBM DB2 and Microsoft SQL Server, and to a lesser extent Sybase, Teradata, Informix, and MySQL. In the applications arena, their main competitor is SAP.
Core	A core is the set of feasible allocations in an economy that cannot be improved upon by subset of the set of the economy's consumers (a coalition). In construction, when the force in an element is within a certain center section, the core, the element will only be under compression.
Markup	Markup is a term used in marketing to indicate how much the price of a product is above the cost of producing and distributing the product.
Foundation	A Foundation is a type of philanthropic organization set up by either individuals or institutions as a legal entity (either as a corporation or trust) with the purpose of distributing grants to support causes in line with the goals of the foundation.
Browser	A program that allows a user to connect to the World Wide Web by simply typing in a URL is a browser.
Yahoo	Yahoo is an American computer services company. It operates an Internet portal, the Yahoo Directory and a host of other services including the popular Yahoo Mail. Yahoo is the most visited website on the Internet today with more than 400 million unique users. The global network of Yahoo! websites received 3.4 billion page views per day on average as of October 2005.
Interest	In finance and economics, interest is the price paid by a borrower for the use of a lender's money. In other words, interest is the amount of paid to "rent" money for a period of time.
Advertising	Advertising refers to paid, nonpersonal communication through various media by organizations

Go to **Cram101.com** for the Practice Tests for this Chapter.

and individuals who are in some way identified in the advertising message.

Extranet	An extension of the Internet that connects suppliers, customers, and other organizations via secure websites is an extranet.
Intranet	Intranet refers to a companywide network, closed to public access, that uses Internet-type technology. A set of communications links within one company that travel over the Internet but are closed to public access.
Channel	Channel, in communications (sometimes called communications channel), refers to the medium used to convey information from a sender (or transmitter) to a receiver.
Aggregation	Aggregation refers to the combining of two or more things into a single category. Data on international trade necessarily aggregate goods and services into manageable groups.
Banner ad	A banner ad is a form of advertising on the World Wide Web. This form of online advertising entails embedding an advertisement into a web page.
Contract	A contract is a "promise" or an "agreement" that is enforced or recognized by the law. In the civil law, a contract is considered to be part of the general law of obligations.
Trade show	A type of exhibition or forum where manufacturers can display their products to current as well as prospective buyers is referred to as trade show.
Marketing	Promoting and selling products or services to customers, or prospective customers, is referred to as marketing.
Expense	In accounting, an expense represents an event in which an asset is used up or a liability is incurred. In terms of the accounting equation, expenses reduce owners' equity.
Security	Security refers to a claim on the borrower future income that is sold by the borrower to the lender. A security is a type of transferable interest representing financial value.
Intermediaries	Intermediaries specialize in information either to bring together two parties to a transaction or to buy in order to sell again.
Expedia	Founded as a division of Microsoft in 1996, Expedia was spun off in 1999, and was purchased by USA Networks in 2001 (USA changed its name to InterActiveCorp in 2003). IAC spun off its travel group of businesses under the Expedia name in August 2005.
Disintermedi-tion	A reduction in the flow of funds into the banking system that causes the amount financial intermediation to decline is referred to as disintermediation.
Reintermediation	Reintermediation can be defined as the reintroduction of an intermediary between end users (consumers) and a producer.
Travelocity	According to Sabre Holdings, Travelocity is the sixth-largest travel agency in the United States. In addition to its primary US consumer site, Travelocity operates a full-service business agency, Travelocity Business, and comparable websites in Canada, Germany, France, the Scandinavian countries, and the United Kingdom, and is a partner in Asian travel hubs Tabini and Zuji.
Personalization	The consumer-initiated practice of generating content on a marketer's website that is custom tailored to an individual's specific needs and preferences is called personalization.
Stock	In financial terminology, stock is the capital raized by a corporation, through the issuance and sale of shares.
In transit	A state in which goods are in the possession of a bailee or carrier and not in the hands of the buyer, seller, lessee, or lessor is referred to as in transit.
Intervention	Intervention refers to an activity in which a government buys or sells its currency in the

Go to **Cram101.com** for the Practice Tests for this Chapter.

	foreign exchange market in order to affect its currency's exchange rate.
Business cycle	Business cycle refers to the pattern followed by macroeconommic variables, such as GDP and unemployment that rise and fall irregularly over time, relative to trend.
Loyalty	Marketers tend to define customer loyalty as making repeat purchases. Some argue that it should be defined attitudinally as a strongly positive feeling about the brand.
Information technology	Information technology refers to technology that helps companies change business by allowing them to use new methods.
Customer loyalty	Marketers tend to define customer loyalty as making repeat purchases. Some argue that it should be defined attitudinally as a strongly positive feeling about the brand.
Raw material	Raw material refers to a good that has not been transformed by production; a primary product.
Customer service	The ability of logistics management to satisfy users in terms of time, dependability, communication, and convenience is called the customer service.
Appeal	Appeal refers to the act of asking an appellate court to overturn a decision after the trial court's final judgment has been entered.
Transaction cost	A transaction cost is a cost incurred in making an economic exchange. For example, most people, when buying or selling a stock, must pay a commission to their broker; that commission is a transaction cost of doing the stock deal.
Inputs	The inputs used by a firm or an economy are the labor, raw materials, electricity and other resources it uses to produce its outputs.
Commodity	Could refer to any good, but in trade a commodity is usually a raw material or primary product that enters into international trade, such as metals or basic agricultural products.
Spot transaction	The predominant type of exchange rate transaction, involving the immediate exchange of bank deposits denominated in different currencies is a spot transaction.
Licensing	Licensing is a form of strategic alliance which involves the sale of a right to use certain proprietary knowledge (so called intellectual property) in a defined way.
Ariba	Ariba is a software and information technology services company, headquartered in Sunnyvale, California, USA. The focus of their products and services is cost savings in procurement via electronic commerce, also known as spend management.
Hosting	Internet hosting service is a service that runs Internet servers, allowing organizations and individuals to serve content on the Internet.
Open market	In economics, the open market is the term used to refer to the environment in which bonds are bought and sold.
Asset	An item of property, such as land, capital, money, a share in ownership, or a claim on others for future payment, such as a bond or a bank deposit is an asset.
Extension	Extension refers to an out-of-court settlement in which creditors agree to allow the firm more time to meet its financial obligations. A new repayment schedule will be developed, subject to the acceptance of creditors.
Data processing	Data processing refers to a name for business technology in the 1970s; included technology that supported an existing business and was primarily used to improve the flow of financial information.
Management information system	A computer-based system that provides information and support for effective managerial decision makin is referred to as a management information system.

Electronic data processing	Electronic data processing can refer to the use of automated methods to process commercial data. Typically, this uses relatively simple, repetitive activities to process large volumes of similar information.
Budget	Budget refers to an account, usually for a year, of the planned expenditures and the expected receipts of an entity. For a government, the receipts are tax revenues.
Quantity discount	A quantity discount is a price reduction given for a large order.
Cost structure	The relative proportion of an organization's fixed, variable, and mixed costs is referred to as cost structure.
Exchange rate	Exchange rate refers to the price at which one country's currency trades for another, typically on the exchange market.
Variable	A variable is something measured by a number; it is used to analyze what happens to other things when the size of that number changes.
Evaluation	The consumer's appraisal of the product or brand on important attributes is called evaluation.
Product life cycle	Product life cycle refers to a series of phases in a product's sales and cash flows over time; these phases, in order of occurrence, are introductory, growth, maturity, and decline.
Cost curve	A cost curve is a graph of the costs of production as a function of total quantity produced. In a free market economy, productively efficient firms use these curves to find the optimal point of production, where they make the most profits.
Aid	Assistance provided by countries and by international institutions such as the World Bank to developing countries in the form of monetary grants, loans at low interest rates, in kind, or a combination of these is called aid. Aid can also refer to assistance of any type rendered to benefit some group or individual.
Total cost	The sum of fixed cost and variable cost is referred to as total cost.
Project management	Project management is the discipline of organizing and managing resources in such a way that these resources deliver all the work required to complete a project within defined scope, time, and cost constraints.
Project manager	Project manager refers to a manager responsible for a temporary work project that involves the participation of other people from various functions and levels of the organization.
Personnel	A collective term for all of the employees of an organization. Personnel is also commonly used to refer to the personnel management function or the organizational unit responsible for administering personnel programs.
Trust	An arrangement in which shareholders of independent firms agree to give up their stock in exchange for trust certificates that entitle them to a share of the trust's common profits.
Compaq	Compaq was founded in February 1982 by Rod Canion, Jim Harris and Bill Murto, three senior managers from semiconductor manufacturer Texas Instruments. Each invested $1,000 to form the company. Their first venture capital came from Ben Rosen and Sevin-Rosen partners. It is often told that the architecture of the original PC was first sketched out on a placemat by the founders while dining in the Houston restaurant, House of Pies.
Volatility	Volatility refers to the extent to which an economic variable, such as a price or an exchange rate, moves up and down over time.
Dell Computer	Dell Computer, formerly PC's Limited, was founded on the principle that by selling personal computer systems directly to customers, PC's Limited could best understand their needs and

provide the most effective computing solutions to meet those needs.

Return on Assets	The Return on Assets percentage shows how profitable a company's assets are in generating revenue.
Customer satisfaction	Customer satisfaction is a business term which is used to capture the idea of measuring how satisfied an enterprise's customers are with the organization's efforts in a marketplace.
British Petroleum	British Petroleum, is a British energy company with headquarters in London, one of four vertically integrated private sector oil, natural gas, and petrol (gasoline) "supermajors" in the world, along with Royal Dutch Shell, ExxonMobil and Total.
Innovation	Innovation refers to the first commercially successful introduction of a new product, the use of a new method of production, or the creation of a new form of business organization.
Process innovation	The development and use of new or improved production or distribution methods is called process innovation. It is an approach in business process reengineering by which radical changes are made through innovations.
Balance	In banking and accountancy, the outstanding balance is the amount of money owned, (or due), that remains in a deposit account (or a loan account) at a given date, after all past remittances, payments and withdrawal have been accounted for. It can be positive (then, in the balance sheet of a firm, it is an asset) or negative (a liability).
Harvard Business Review	Harvard Business Review is a research-based magazine written for business practitioners, it claims a high ranking business readership and enjoys the reverence of academics, executives, and management consultants. It has been the frequent publishing home for well known scholars and management thinkers.
Outsourcing	Outsourcing refers to a production activity that was previously done inside a firm or plant that is now conducted outside that firm or plant.

Industry	A group of firms that produce identical or similar products is an industry. It is also used specifically to refer to an area of economic production focused on manufacturing which involves large amounts of capital investment before any profit can be realized, also called "heavy industry".
Safeway	On April 18, 2005, Safeway began a 100 million dollar brand re-positioning campaign labeled "Ingredients for life". This was done in an attempt to differentiate itself from its competitors, and to increase brand involvement. Steve Burd described it as "branding the shopping experience".
Kroger	As well as stocking a variety of national brand products, Kroger also employs one of the largest networks of private label manufacturing in the country. Forty-two plants (either wholly owned or used with operating agreements) in seventeen states create about half of the nearly eight thousand private label products. A three-tiered marketing strategy divides the brand names for shoppers' simplicity and understanding.
Service	Service refers to a "non tangible product" that is not embodied in a physical good and that typically effects some change in another product, person, or institution. Contrasts with good.
Customer service	The ability of logistics management to satisfy users in terms of time, dependability, communication, and convenience is called the customer service.
Electronic data interchange	Electronic data interchange refers to the direct exchange between organizations of data via a computer-to-computer interface.
Marketing	Promoting and selling products or services to customers, or prospective customers, is referred to as marketing.
Distribution center	Designed to facilitate the timely movement of goods and represent a very important part of a supply chain is a distribution center.
Distribution	Distribution in economics, the manner in which total output and income is distributed among individuals or factors.
Complexity	The technical sophistication of the product and hence the amount of understanding required to use it is referred to as complexity. It is the opposite of simplicity.
Manufacturing	Production of goods primarily by the application of labor and capital to raw materials and other intermediate inputs, in contrast to agriculture, mining, forestry, fishing, and services a manufacturing.
Inventory	Tangible property held for sale in the normal course of business or used in producing goods or services for sale is an inventory.
Supply	Supply is the aggregate amount of any material good that can be called into being at a certain price point; it comprises one half of the equation of supply and demand. In classical economic theory, a curve representing supply is one of the factors that produce price.
Purchasing	Purchasing refers to the function in a firm that searches for quality material resources, finds the best suppliers, and negotiates the best price for goods and services.
Performance measurement	The process by which someone evaluates an employee's work behaviors by measurement and comparison with previously established standards, documents the results, and communicates the results to the employee is called performance measurement.
Supply chain	Supply chain refers to the flow of goods, services, and information from the initial sources of materials and services to the delivery of products to consumers.
Evaluation	The consumer's appraisal of the product or brand on important attributes is called evaluation.

Go to **Cram101.com** for the Practice Tests for this Chapter.

353

Firm	An organization that employs resources to produce a good or service for profit and owns and operates one or more plants is referred to as a firm.
Management	Management characterizes the process of leading and directing all or part of an organization, often a business, through the deployment and manipulation of resources. Early twentieth-century management writer Mary Parker Follett defined management as "the art of getting things done through people."
Performance improvement	Performance improvement is the concept of measuring the output of a particular process or procedure then modifying the process or procedure in order to increase the output, increase efficiency, or increase the effectiveness of the process or procedure.
Performance feedback	The process of providing employees with information regarding their performance effectiveness is referred to as performance feedback.
Buyer	A buyer refers to a role in the buying center with formal authority and responsibility to select the supplier and negotiate the terms of the contract.
Instrument	Instrument refers to an economic variable that is controlled by policy makers and can be used to influence other variables, called targets. Examples are monetary and fiscal policies used to achieve external and internal balance.
Operation	A standardized method or technique that is performed repetitively, often on different materials resulting in different finished goods is called an operation.
Purchase order	A form on which items or services needed by a business firm are specified and then communicated to the vendor is a purchase order.
Contract	A contract is a "promise" or an "agreement" that is enforced or recognized by the law. In the civil law, a contract is considered to be part of the general law of obligations.
Commodity	Could refer to any good, but in trade a commodity is usually a raw material or primary product that enters into international trade, such as metals or basic agricultural products.
Supply chain management	Supply chain management deals with the planning and execution issues involved in managing a supply chain. Supply chain management spans all movement and storage of raw materials, work-in-process inventory, and finished goods from point-of-origin to point-of-consumption.
Market	A market is, as defined in economics, a social arrangement that allows buyers and sellers to discover information and carry out a voluntary exchange of goods or services.
Target price	Target price refers to estimated price for a product or service that potential customers will
Variance	Variance refers to a measure of how much an economic or statistical variable varies across values or observations. Its calculation is the same as that of the covariance, being the covariance of the variable with itself.
Price variance	The difference between the actual price and the budgeted price multiplied by the actual quantity of input. Also called input-price variance or rate variance.
Budget	Budget refers to an account, usually for a year, of the planned expenditures and the expected receipts of an entity. For a government, the receipts are tax revenues.
Chrysler	The Chrysler Corporation was an American automobile manufacturer that existed independently from 1925–1998. The company was formed by Walter Percy Chrysler on June 6, 1925, with the remaining assets of Maxwell Motor Company.
Rebate	Rebate refers to a sales promotion in which money is returned to the consumer based on proof of purchase.
Margin	A deposit by a buyer in stocks with a seller or a stockbroker, as security to cover fluctuations in the market in reference to stocks that the buyer has purchased but for which

he has not paid is a margin. Commodities are also traded on margin.

Manufacturing costs	Costs incurred in a manufacturing process, which consist of direct material, direct labor, and manufacturing overhead are referred to as manufacturing costs.
Profit	Profit refers to the return to the resource entrepreneurial ability; total revenue minus total cost.
Trend	Trend refers to the long-term movement of an economic variable, such as its average rate of increase or decrease over enough years to encompass several business cycles.
Technology	The body of knowledge and techniques that can be used to combine economic resources to produce goods and services is called technology.
Business Week	Business Week is a business magazine published by McGraw-Hill. It was first published in 1929 under the direction of Malcolm Muir, who was serving as president of the McGraw-Hill Publishing company at the time. It is considered to be the standard both in industry and among students.
Index number	An index number expresses the cost of a market basket of goods relative to its cost in some 'base' period, which is simply the year or years used as a basis of comparison.
Business unit	The lowest level of the company which contains the set of functions that carry a product through its life span from concept through manufacture, distribution, sales and service is a business unit.
Consolidation	The combination of two or more firms, generally of equal size and market power, to form an entirely new entity is a consolidation.
Raw material	Raw material refers to a good that has not been transformed by production; a primary product.
Target pricing	Manufacturer deliberately adjusting the composition and features of a product to achieve the target price to consumers is referred to as target pricing.
Tangible	Having a physical existence is referred to as the tangible. Personal property other than real estate, such as cars, boats, stocks, or other assets.
Assignment	A transfer of property or some right or interest is referred to as assignment.
Open purchase order	Open purchase order refers to a copy of the purchase order sent to the accounts payable department and reviewed prior to payment for the goods ordered. It is intended to eliminate small repetitive requests for expendable supplies, material or services by allowing multiple pickups and billings on one order.
Points	Loan origination fees that may be deductible as interest by a buyer of property. A seller of property who pays points reduces the selling price by the amount of the points paid for the buyer.
Interest	In finance and economics, interest is the price paid by a borrower for the use of a lender's money. In other words, interest is the amount of paid to "rent" money for a period of time.
Gain	In finance, gain is a profit or an increase in value of an investment such as a stock or bond. Gain is calculated by fair market value or the proceeds from the sale of the investment minus the sum of the purchase price and all costs associated with it.
Expense	In accounting, an expense represents an event in which an asset is used up or a liability is incurred. In terms of the accounting equation, expenses reduce owners' equity.
Administration	Administration refers to the management and direction of the affairs of governments and institutions; a collective term for all policymaking officials of a government; the execution and implementation of public policy.

Fiscal year	A fiscal year is a 12-month period used for calculating annual ("yearly") financial reports in businesses and other organizations. In many jurisdictions, regulatory laws regarding accounting require such reports once per twelve months, but do not require that the twelve months constitute a calendar year (i.e. January to December).
Negotiation	Negotiation is the process whereby interested parties resolve disputes, agree upon courses of action, bargain for individual or collective advantage, and/or attempt to craft outcomes which serve their mutual interests.
Allocate	Allocate refers to the assignment of income for various tax purposes. A multistate corporation's nonbusiness income usually is distributed to the state where the nonbusiness assets are located; it is not apportioned with the rest of the entity's income.
Production	The creation of finished goods and services using the factors of production: land, labor, capital, entrepreneurship, and knowledge.
Production function	Production function refers to a function that specifies the output in an industry for all combinations of inputs.
Internal customer	An individuals or unit within the firm that receives services from other entities within the organization is an internal customer.
Level of service	The degree of service provided to the customer by self, limited, and full-service retailers is referred to as the level of service.
Users	Users refer to people in the organization who actually use the product or service purchased by the buying center.
Total cost	The sum of fixed cost and variable cost is referred to as total cost.
Investment	Investment refers to spending for the production and accumulation of capital and additions to inventories. In a financial sense, buying an asset with the expectation of making a return.
Inventory investment	Spending by firms on additional holdings of raw materials, parts, and finished goods is called inventory investment.
In transit	A state in which goods are in the possession of a bailee or carrier and not in the hands of the buyer, seller, lessee, or lessor is referred to as in transit.
Warehouse	Warehouse refers to a location, often decentralized, that a firm uses to store, consolidate, age, or mix stock; house product-recall programs; or ease tax burdens.
Revenue	Revenue is a U.S. business term for the amount of money that a company receives from its activities, mostly from sales of products and/or services to customers.
Velocity	Velocity refers to the number of times per year that the average dollar in the money supply is spent for final goods and services; nominal GDP divided by the money supply.
Capital	Capital generally refers to financial wealth, especially that used to start or maintain a business. In classical economics, capital is one of four factors of production, the others being land and labor and entrepreneurship.
Working capital	The dollar difference between total current assets and total current liabilities is called working capital.
Stock	In financial terminology, stock is the capital raized by a corporation, through the issuance and sale of shares.
Safety stock	Safety stock is additional inventory planned to buffer against the variability in supply and demand plans, that could otherwise result in inventory shortages.
Warranty	An obligation of a company to replace defective goods or correct any deficiencies in

Go to **Cram101.com** for the Practice Tests for this Chapter.

	performance or quality of a product is called a warranty.
Total supply	Total supply refers to the supply schedule or the supply curve of all sellers of a good or service.
Administrative support	Support services such as personnel, budget, purchasing, data processing which support or facilitate the service programs of the agency are types of administrative support. Also means work assisting an administrator through office management, clerical supervision, data collection and reporting, workflow/project tracking.
Personnel	A collective term for all of the employees of an organization. Personnel is also commonly used to refer to the personnel management function or the organizational unit responsible for administering personnel programs.
Policy	Similar to a script in that a policy can be a less than completely rational decision-making method. Involves the use of a pre-existing set of decision steps for any problem that presents itself.
Public policy	Decision making by government. Governments are constantly concerned about what they should or should not do. And whatever they do or do not do is public policy. public program All those activities designed to implement a public policy; often this calls for the creation of organizations, public agencies, and bureaus.
Leadership	Management merely consists of leadership applied to business situations; or in other words: management forms a sub-set of the broader process of leadership.
Specific performance	A contract remedy whereby the defendant is ordered to perform according to the terms of his contract is referred to as specific performance.
Assessment	Collecting information and providing feedback to employees about their behavior, communication style, or skills is an assessment.
Action plan	Action plan refers to a written document that includes the steps the trainee and manager will take to ensure that training transfers to the job.
Performance target	A task established for an employee that provides the comparative basis for performance appraisal is a performance target.
External analysis	External analysis refers to the phase of the promotional planning process that focuses on factors such as the characteristics of an organization's customers, market segments, positioning strategies, competitors, and marketing environment.
Competitor	Other organizations in the same industry or type of business that provide a good or service to the same set of customers is referred to as a competitor.
Frequency	Frequency refers to the speed of the up and down movements of a fluctuating economic variable; that is, the number of times per unit of time that the variable completes a cycle of up and down movement.
Trial	An examination before a competent tribunal, according to the law of the land, of the facts or law put in issue in a cause, for the purpose of determining such issue is a trial. When the court hears and determines any issue of fact or law for the purpose of determining the rights of the parties, it may be considered a trial.
Benchmarking	The continuous process of comparing the levels of performance in producing products and services and executing activities against the best levels of performance is benchmarking.
Cooperative	A business owned and controlled by the people who use it, producers, consumers, or workers with similar needs who pool their resources for mutual gain is called cooperative.
Performance	A type of benchmarking that allows initiator firms to compare themselves against benchmark

benchmarking	firms on performance issues such as cost structures, various types of productivity performance, speed of concept to market, and quality measures is called performance benchmarking.
Market share	That fraction of an industry's output accounted for by an individual firm or group of firms is called market share.
Market leader	The market leader is dominant in its industry. It has substantial market share and often extensive distribution arrangements with retailers. It typically is the industry leader in developing innovative new business models and new products (although not always).
Strategic benchmarking	Strategic benchmarking refers to a type of benchmarking that involves observing how others compete. This type of benchmarking typically involves target firms that have been identified as 'world class'.
Controlling	A management function that involves determining whether or not an organization is progressing toward its goals and objectives, and taking corrective action if it is not is called controlling.
Business plan	A detailed written statement that describes the nature of the business, the target market, the advantages the business will have in relation to competition, and the resources and qualifications of the owner is referred to as a business plan.
Critical success factor	Critical Success Factor is a business term for an element which is necessary for an organization or project to achieve its mission.
Success factor	The term success factor refers to the characteristics necessary for high performance; knowledge, skills, abilities, behaviors.
Competitive Strategy	An outline of how a business intends to compete with other firms in the same industry is called competitive strategy.
Not invented here	Not Invented Here (NIH) is a pejorative term used to describe a persistent corporate or institutional culture that either intentionally or unintentionally avoids using previously performed research or knowledge because the research and developed knowledge was not originally executed in-house.
Journal	Book of original entry, in which transactions are recorded in a general ledger system, is referred to as a journal.
Consultant	A professional that provides expert advice in a particular field or area in which customers occassionaly require this type of knowledge is a consultant.
Focus group	A small group of people who meet under the direction of a discussion leader to communicate their opinions about an organization, its products, or other given issues is a focus group.
Integration	Economic integration refers to reducing barriers among countries to transactions and to movements of goods, capital, and labor, including harmonization of laws, regulations, and standards. Integrated markets theoretically function as a unified market.
Maturity	Maturity refers to the final payment date of a loan or other financial instrument, after which point no further interest or principal need be paid.
Best practice	Best practice is a management idea which asserts that there is a technique, method, process, activity, incentive or reward that is more effective at delivering a particular outcome than any other technique, method, process, etc.
Productivity	Productivity refers to the total output of goods and services in a given period of time divided by work hours.
Punitive	Damages designed to punish flagrant wrongdoers and to deter them and others from engaging in

	similar conduct in the future are called punitive.
Consumer good	Products and services that are ultimately consumed rather than used in the production of another good are a consumer good.
Continuous improvement	The constant effort to eliminate waste, reduce response time, simplify the design of both products and processes, and improve quality and customer service is referred to as continuous improvement.
Comprehensive	A comprehensive refers to a layout accurate in size, color, scheme, and other necessary details to show how a final ad will look. For presentation only, never for reproduction.
Senior management	Senior management is generally a team of individuals at the highest level of organizational management who have the day-to-day responsibilities of managing a corporation.
Supplier evaluation	Supplier evaluation refers to a tool used by many firms to differentiate and discriminate among suppliers. A supplier evaluation often involves report cards where potential suppliers are rated based on different criteria such as quality, technical capability, or ability to meet schedule demands.
Corporate goal	A strategic performance target that the entire organization must reach to pursue its vision is a corporate goal.

Go to **Cram101.com** for the Practice Tests for this Chapter.

Purchasing	Purchasing refers to the function in a firm that searches for quality material resources, finds the best suppliers, and negotiates the best price for goods and services.
Evaluation	The consumer's appraisal of the product or brand on important attributes is called evaluation.
Management	Management characterizes the process of leading and directing all or part of an organization, often a business, through the deployment and manipulation of resources. Early twentieth-century management writer Mary Parker Follett defined management as "the art of getting things done through people."
Journal	Book of original entry, in which transactions are recorded in a general ledger system, is referred to as a journal.
Materials management	Materials management refers to the activity that controls the transmission of physical materials through the value chain, from procurement through production and into distribution.
Harvard Business Review	Harvard Business Review is a research-based magazine written for business practitioners, it claims a high ranking business readership and enjoys the reverence of academics, executives, and management consultants. It has been the frequent publishing home for well known scholars and management thinkers.
Performance measurement	The process by which someone evaluates an employee's work behaviors by measurement and comparison with previously established standards, documents the results, and communicates the results to the employee is called performance measurement.
Supply	Supply is the aggregate amount of any material good that can be called into being at a certain price point; it comprises one half of the equation of supply and demand. In classical economic theory, a curve representing supply is one of the factors that produce price.
Balanced scorecard	A framework for implementing strategy by translating an organization's mission and strategy into a set of performance measures is called balanced scorecard.
Supply chain management	Supply chain management deals with the planning and execution issues involved in managing a supply chain. Supply chain management spans all movement and storage of raw materials, work-in-process inventory, and finished goods from point-of-origin to point-of-consumption.
Supply chain	Supply chain refers to the flow of goods, services, and information from the initial sources of materials and services to the delivery of products to consumers.
Industry	A group of firms that produce identical or similar products is an industry. It is also used specifically to refer to an area of economic production focused on manufacturing which involves large amounts of capital investment before any profit can be realized, also called "heavy industry".
Logistics	Those activities that focus on getting the right amount of the right products to the right place at the right time at the lowest possible cost is referred to as logistics.
Trend	Trend refers to the long-term movement of an economic variable, such as its average rate of increase or decrease over enough years to encompass several business cycles.
Performance improvement	Performance improvement is the concept of measuring the output of a particular process or procedure then modifying the process or procedure in order to increase the output, increase efficiency, or increase the effectiveness of the process or procedure.
Management accounting	Management accounting measures and reports financial and nonfinancial information that helps managers make decisions to fulfill the goals of an organization. It focuses on internal reporting.
Competitive advantage	A business is said to have a competitive advantage when its unique strengths, often based on cost, quality, time, and innovation, offer consumers a greater percieved value and there by

differtiating it from its competitors.

Information system	An information system is a system whether automated or manual, that comprises people, machines, and/or methods organized to collect, process, transmit, and disseminate data that represent user information.
Business strategy	Business strategy, which refers to the aggregated operational strategies of single business firm or that of an SBU in a diversified corporation refers to the way in which a firm competes in its chosen arenas.
Human resources	Human resources refers to the individuals within the firm, and to the portion of the firm's organization that deals with hiring, firing, training, and other personnel issues.
General Motors	General Motors is the world's largest automaker. Founded in 1908, today it employs about 327,000 people around the world. With global headquarters in Detroit, it manufactures its cars and trucks in 33 countries.
American Management Association	American Management Association International is the world's largest membership-based management development and executive training organization. Their products include instructor led seminars, workshops, conferences, customized corporate programs, online learning, books, newsletters, research surveys and reports.
Best practice	Best practice is a management idea which asserts that there is a technique, method, process, activity, incentive or reward that is more effective at delivering a particular outcome than any other technique, method, process, etc.
Benchmarking	The continuous process of comparing the levels of performance in producing products and services and executing activities against the best levels of performance is benchmarking.
Accounting	A system that collects and processes financial information about an organization and reports that information to decision makers is referred to as accounting.
Niche	In industry, a niche is a situation or an activity perfectly suited to a person. A niche can imply a working position or an area suited to a person who occupies it. Basically, a job where a person is able to succeed and thrive.
Controlling	A management function that involves determining whether or not an organization is progressing toward its goals and objectives, and taking corrective action if it is not is called controlling.
Personnel	A collective term for all of the employees of an organization. Personnel is also commonly used to refer to the personnel management function or the organizational unit responsible for administering personnel programs.
Specialist	A specialist is a trader who makes a market in one or several stocks and holds the limit order book for those stocks.
Time management	Time Management refers to tools or techniques for planning and scheduling time, usually with the aim to increase the effectiveness and/or efficiency of personal and corporate time use.
Cost management	The approaches and activities of managers in short-run and long-run planning and control decisions that increase value for customers and lower costs of products and services are called cost management.
Partnership	In the common law, a partnership is a type of business entity in which partners share with each other the profits or losses of the business undertaking in which they have all invested.
Integration	Economic integration refers to reducing barriers among countries to transactions and to movements of goods, capital, and labor, including harmonization of laws, regulations, and standards. Integrated markets theoretically function as a unified market.

Go to **Cram101.com** for the Practice Tests for this Chapter.

Contribution	In business organization law, the cash or property contributed to a business by its owners is referred to as contribution.
Continuous improvement	The constant effort to eliminate waste, reduce response time, simplify the design of both products and processes, and improve quality and customer service is referred to as continuous improvement.
Driving force	The key external pressure that will shape the future for an organization is a driving force. The driving force in an industry are the main underlying causes of changing industry and competitive conditions.
Market	A market is, as defined in economics, a social arrangement that allows buyers and sellers to discover information and carry out a voluntary exchange of goods or services.
Competitive market	A market in which no buyer or seller has market power is called a competitive market.
Firm	An organization that employs resources to produce a good or service for profit and owns and operates one or more plants is referred to as a firm.
Respondent	Respondent refers to a term often used to describe the party charged in an administrative proceeding. The party adverse to the appellant in a case appealed to a higher court.
Gain	In finance, gain is a profit or an increase in value of an investment such as a stock or bond. Gain is calculated by fair market value or the proceeds from the sale of the investment minus the sum of the purchase price and all costs associated with it.
Planning horizon	The length of time it takes to conceive, develop, and complete a project and to recover the cost of the project on a discounted cash flow basis is referred to as planning horizon.
Scope	Scope of a project is the sum total of all projects products and their requirements or features.
Manufacturing cycle time	The total amount of production time required per unit is manufacturing cycle time.
Manufacturing	Production of goods primarily by the application of labor and capital to raw materials and other intermediate inputs, in contrast to agriculture, mining, forestry, fishing, and services a manufacturing.
Product development	In business and engineering, new product development is the complete process of bringing a new product to market. There are two parallel aspects to this process : one involves product engineering ; the other marketing analysis. Marketers see new product development as the first stage in product life cycle management, engineers as part of Product Lifecycle Management.
Product development teams	Combinations of work teams and problem-solving teams that create new designs for products or services that will satisfy customer needs are product development teams.
Prototyping	An iterative approach to design in which a series of mock-ups or models are developed until the customer and the designer come to agreement as to the final design is called prototyping.
Technology	The body of knowledge and techniques that can be used to combine economic resources to produce goods and services is called technology.
Business unit	The lowest level of the company which contains the set of functions that carry a product through its life span from concept through manufacture, distribution, sales and service is a business unit.
Marketing	Promoting and selling products or services to customers, or prospective customers, is

371

	referred to as marketing.
Procurement	Procurement is the acquisition of goods or services at the best possible total cost of ownership, in the right quantity, at the right time, in the right place for the direct benefit or use of the governments, corporations, or individuals generally via, but not limited to a contract.
Board of directors	The group of individuals elected by the stockholders of a corporation to oversee its operations is a board of directors.
Committee	A long-lasting, sometimes permanent team in the organization structure created to deal with tasks that recur regularly is the committee.
Interest	In finance and economics, interest is the price paid by a borrower for the use of a lender's money. In other words, interest is the amount of paid to "rent" money for a period of time.
Core	A core is the set of feasible allocations in an economy that cannot be improved upon by subset of the set of the economy's consumers (a coalition). In construction, when the force in an element is within a certain center section, the core, the element will only be under compression.
Core competency	A company's core competency are things that a firm can (alsosns) do well and that meet the following three conditions. 1. It provides customer benefits, 2. It is hard for competitors to imitate, and 3. it can be leveraged widely to many products and market. A core competency can take various forms, including technical/subject matter knowhow, a reliable process, and/or close relationships with customers and suppliers. It may also include product development or culture such as employee dedication. Modern business theories suggest that most activities that are not part of a company's core competency should be outsourced.
Outsourcing	Outsourcing refers to a production activity that was previously done inside a firm or plant that is now conducted outside that firm or plant.
Organizational structure	Organizational structure is the way in which the interrelated groups of an organization are constructed. From a managerial point of view the main concerns are ensuring effective communication and coordination.
Commodity	Could refer to any good, but in trade a commodity is usually a raw material or primary product that enters into international trade, such as metals or basic agricultural products.
New product development	New product development is the complete process of bringing a new product to market. There are two parallel aspects to this process : one involves product engineering ; the other marketing analysis.
Supplier evaluation	Supplier evaluation refers to a tool used by many firms to differentiate and discriminate among suppliers. A supplier evaluation often involves report cards where potential suppliers are rated based on different criteria such as quality, technical capability, or ability to meet schedule demands.
Sourcing decisions	Whether a firm should make or buy component parts are sourcing decisions.
Assignment	A transfer of property or some right or interest is referred to as assignment.
Functional manager	A manager who is responsible for a department that performs a single functional task and has employees with similar training and skills is referred to as a functional manager.
Users	Users refer to people in the organization who actually use the product or service purchased by the buying center.
Gap	In December of 1995, Gap became the first major North American retailer to accept independent monitoring of the working conditions in a contract factory producing its garments. Gap is the

Go to **Cram101.com** for the Practice Tests for this Chapter.

largest specialty retailer in the United States.

Credit	Credit refers to a recording as positive in the balance of payments, any transaction that gives rise to a payment into the country, such as an export, the sale of an asset, or borrowing from abroad.
Information technology	Information technology refers to technology that helps companies change business by allowing them to use new methods.
Production	The creation of finished goods and services using the factors of production: land, labor, capital, entrepreneurship, and knowledge.
Control system	A control system is a device or set of devices that manage the behavior of other devices. Some devices or systems are not controllable. A control system is an interconnection of components connected or related in such a manner as to command, direct, or regulate itself or another system.
Inventory	Tangible property held for sale in the normal course of business or used in producing goods or services for sale is an inventory.
Buyer	A buyer refers to a role in the buying center with formal authority and responsibility to select the supplier and negotiate the terms of the contract.
Operation	A standardized method or technique that is performed repetitively, often on different materials resulting in different finished goods is called an operation.
Administrator	Administrator refers to the personal representative appointed by a probate court to settle the estate of a deceased person who died.
Teamwork	That which occurs when group members work together in ways that utilize their skills well to accomplish a purpose is called teamwork.
Warehouse	Warehouse refers to a location, often decentralized, that a firm uses to store, consolidate, age, or mix stock; house product-recall programs; or ease tax burdens.
Operations management	A specialized area in management that converts or transforms resources into goods and services is operations management.
Fund	Independent accounting entity with a self-balancing set of accounts segregated for the purposes of carrying on specific activities is referred to as a fund.
Service	Service refers to a "non tangible product" that is not embodied in a physical good and that typically effects some change in another product, person, or institution. Contrasts with good.
Customer service	The ability of logistics management to satisfy users in terms of time, dependability, communication, and convenience is called the customer service.
Distribution	Distribution in economics, the manner in which total output and income is distributed among individuals or factors.
Consortia	B2B marketplaces sponsored by a group of otherwise competitive enterprises in a specific industry like automobile manufacturing or airline operations are called a consortia.
Performance requirement	Performance requirement refers to a requirement that an importer or exporter achieve some level of performance, in terms of exporting, domestic content, etc., in order to obtain an import or export license.
Revenue	Revenue is a U.S. business term for the amount of money that a company receives from its activities, mostly from sales of products and/or services to customers.
Assessment	Collecting information and providing feedback to employees about their behavior,

Go to **Cram101.com** for the Practice Tests for this Chapter.

	communication style, or skills is an assessment.
Total cost	The sum of fixed cost and variable cost is referred to as total cost.
Contract	A contract is a "promise" or an "agreement" that is enforced or recognized by the law. In the civil law, a contract is considered to be part of the general law of obligations.
Capital	Capital generally refers to financial wealth, especially that used to start or maintain a business. In classical economics, capital is one of four factors of production, the others being land and labor and entrepreneurship.
Working capital	The dollar difference between total current assets and total current liabilities is called working capital.
Consolidation	The combination of two or more firms, generally of equal size and market power, to form an entirely new entity is a consolidation.
Competitor	Other organizations in the same industry or type of business that provide a good or service to the same set of customers is referred to as a competitor.
Competitive bidding	A situation where two or more companies submit bids for a product, service, or project to a potential buyer is competitive bidding.
Accumulation	The acquisition of an increasing quantity of something. The accumulation of factors, especially capital, is a primary mechanism for economic growth.
Trust	An arrangement in which shareholders of independent firms agree to give up their stock in exchange for trust certificates that entitle them to a share of the trust's common profits.
Investment	Investment refers to spending for the production and accumulation of capital and additions to inventories. In a financial sense, buying an asset with the expectation of making a return.
Vertical integration	Vertical integration refers to production of different stages of processing of a product within the same firm.
Strategic planning	The process of determining the major goals of the organization and the policies and strategies for obtaining and using resources to achieve those goals is called strategic planning.
Leverage	Leverage is using given resources in such a way that the potential positive or negative outcome is magnified. In finance, this generally refers to borrowing.
Business philosophy	A business philosophy is any of a range of approaches to accounting, marketing, public relations, operations, training, labor relations, executive time management, investment, and/or corporate governance claimed to improve business performance in some measurable or otherwise provable way.
Return on investment	Return on investment refers to the return a businessperson gets on the money he and other owners invest in the firm; for example, a business that earned $100 on a $1,000 investment would have a ROI of 10 percent: 100 divided by 1000.
Insourcing	Insourcing refers to process of producing goods or providing services within the organization rather than purchasing those same goods or services from outside vendors.
Asset	An item of property, such as land, capital, money, a share in ownership, or a claim on others for future payment, such as a bond or a bank deposit is an asset.
Human capital	Human capital refers to the stock of knowledge and skill, embodied in an individual as a result of education, training, and experience that makes them more productive. The stock of knowledge and skill embodied in the population of an economy.
Fixed asset	Fixed asset, also known as property, plant, and equipment (PP&E), is a term used in

	accountancy for assets and property which cannot easily be converted into cash. This can be compared with current assets such as cash or bank accounts, which are described as liquid assets. In most cases, only tangible assets are referred to as fixed.
Fixed cost	The cost that a firm bears if it does not produce at all and that is independent of its output. The presence of a fixed cost tends to imply increasing returns to scale. Contrasts with variable cost.
Principal	In agency law, one under whose direction an agent acts and for whose benefit that agent acts is a principal.
Volatility	Volatility refers to the extent to which an economic variable, such as a price or an exchange rate, moves up and down over time.
Commodity markets	Commodity markets are markets where raw or primary products are exchanged. These raw commodities are traded on regulated exchanges, in which they are bought and sold in standardized Contracts.
Speculation	The purchase or sale of an asset in hopes that its price will rise or fall respectively, in order to make a profit is called speculation.
Collaboration	Collaboration occurs when the interaction between groups is very important to goal attainment and the goals are compatible. Wherein people work together —applying both to the work of individuals as well as larger collectives and societies.
Pact	Pact refers to a set of principles endorsed by 21 of the largest U.S. ad agencies aimed at improving the research used in preparing and testing ads, providing a better creative product for clients, and controlling the cost of TV commercials.
Wall Street Journal	Dow Jones & Company was founded in 1882 by reporters Charles Dow, Edward Jones and Charles Bergstresser. Jones converted the small Customers' Afternoon Letter into The Wall Street Journal, first published in 1889, and began delivery of the Dow Jones News Service via telegraph. The Journal featured the Jones 'Average', the first of several indexes of stock and bond prices on the New York Stock Exchange.
Market share	That fraction of an industry's output accounted for by an individual firm or group of firms is called market share.
Recruitment	Recruitment refers to the set of activities used to obtain a sufficient number of the right people at the right time; its purpose is to select those who best meet the needs of the organization.
Cessna	Cessna, located in Wichita, Kansas, is a manufacturer of general aviation aircraft, from small two-seat, single-engine aircraft to business jets. The company traces its history to June 1911, when Clyde Cessna, a farmer in Rago, Kansas, built a wood-and-fabric plane and became the first person to build and fly an aircraft between the Mississippi River and the Rocky Mountains.
Shares	Shares refer to an equity security, representing a shareholder's ownership of a corporation. Shares are one of a finite number of equal portions in the capital of a company, entitling the owner to a proportion of distributed, non-reinvested profits known as dividends and to a portion of the value of the company in case of liquidation.

Printed in the United Kingdom
by Lightning Source UK Ltd.
123268UK00001B/32/A